BILATERALISM, MULTILATERALISM AND CANADA IN U.S. TRADE POLICY

Already published in the International Trade Series:

Fixing Farm Trade
Policy Options for the United States
Robert L. Paarlberg (1988)

THE COUNCIL ON FOREIGN RELATIONS SERIES
ON INTERNATIONAL TRADE

C. MICHAEL AHO, EDITOR

BILATERALISM, MULTILATERALISM AND CANADA IN U.S. TRADE POLICY

WILLIAM DIEBOLD, JR., EDITOR

BALLINGER PUBLISHING COMPANY
A Subsidiary of Harper & Row, Publishers, Inc.

International Standard Book Number: 0-88730-287-4

Library of Congress Catalog Card Number: 88-6229

Printed in the United States of America

Library of Congress Cataloging-in-Publication Data

Bilateralism, multilateralism and Canada in U.S. trade policy.

  (The Council on Foreign Relations series on international trade)
  Includes index.
  1. United States — Commercial policy. 2. United States — Commerce —
Canada. 3. Canada — Commerce — United States. 4. International Trade.
I. Diebold, William.
HF1455.B54   1988   382'.0973'071   88-6229
ISBN 0-88730-287-4

89 90 91 HC 6 5 4 3 2

Contents

Foreword

C. MICHAEL AHO

On January 2, 1988 the United States and Canada signed a historic agreement which would create a free trade area between the world's largest trading partners. The two countries have flirted with the idea of some type of special trading arrangement for more than a century. But on almost every occasion, discussions have stopped short of formal negotiations because one side or the other—usually Canada—has backed out.

But this time both countries saw the negotiations to their conclusion. Although the agreement needs to be implemented in both countries, the mere fact that it was negotiated will have a profound effect upon the world trading system.

What was different this time? How will this agreement affect the world trading system now and in the future? Does this agreement represent a turning point in U.S. trade policy? What would happen if the agreement failed to be implemented? All of these issues are addressed in this book. A glance at the chapter titles indicates the breadth of the coverage: *The History and the Issues, Why Canada Acted, What GATT Says (Or Does Not Say), What is at Stake?, A Mexican View, The New Bilateralism*? Bill Diebold has done a splendid job in identifying the issues and in identifying keen observers from different points of view.

What was different this time? Bill Diebold in his opening and closing chapters and Gilbert Winham both look into this question. The negotiation of a bilateral agreement with Canada (and earlier with Israel) came amid a period of widespread uncertainty over the future course of U.S. trade policy. The willingness to pursue bilateral negotiations was just one way in which U.S. trade policy fundamentally changed under the Reagan administration. Unprecedented deficits and unprecedented private sector complaints spawned unprecedented administrative and unprecedented legislative action on trade. In September 1985 after almost five years of neglect of trade issues, the U.S. administration declared that the high dollar was not a sign of strength, but the source of trade problems; self-initiated over a dozen unfairness complaints (under Section 301) against other countries; and set the bilateral negotiations with Canada in motion. Since then sanctions have been applied against Japan, and, according to Treasury Secretary Baker, this administration all told has provided more import relief than any of its predecessors in the past fifty years. Meanwhile, Congress was threatening to pass restrictive trade measures, and it was the congressional threat that was among the primary factors motivating Canada in its push for a free trade agreement.

For its part, the Reagan administration deserves credit for successfully negotiating the pact with Canada, but it did come perilously close to failure. Frustrated with progress on the multilateral front, the United States in effect backed into the bilateral with Canada. Throughout most of the negotiations the administration appeared not to appreciate the significance of the bilateral talks. Consultations with Congress and the private sector were spotty and the administration did not take sufficient steps to mobilize allies in the legislature. In the closing weeks, Treasury Secretary Baker was brought in to provide political impetus and to close the deal, yet when the Canadian delegation left Washington with just two days to go before the deadline; it looked as if it all had come to naught. But after receiving calls from congressional supporters of a pact (Democrats at that) Secretary Baker made a late night call to Canada where the Mulroney cabinet was meeting to decide how to handle the public relations of a failure. He persuaded them to put the talks back on track.

The bilateral talks also coincided with the launching of the Uruguay Round of multilateral trade negotiations under the auspices of the General Agreement on Tariffs and Trade (GATT). The simultaneity of the bilateral and multilateral negotiations means that, on the one hand a successful bilateral could be a catalyst for the multilateral, but on the other hand, the bilateral is constrained by the multilateral. Some observers are concerned that this agreement is a step towards a breakdown and a fragmentation of the trading system. How will this pact blend into the multilateral process? What are the implications? Bill Diebold, in his closing chapter, and Andreas Lowenfeld both examine the relationship between the bilateral pact and the multilateral process.

Without a doubt, these negotiations have provided a valuable learning experience for both countries. Most of the issues being negotiated in Geneva are the same as those negotiated in the bilateral. You learn to negotiate by negotiating, and both countries learned a great deal. You learn the pitfalls, the problems, the stumbling blocks as you go through the negotiating process. And when tentative deals are brought back to show to the domestic constituencies that must be coopted, they also learn in the process. In this manner the tradeoffs are explored; the political sentiments are assessed, and political leaders are forced to confront tough choices.

For years the U.S. Congress had been talking about the need for greater discipline in subsidies, and for rules covering services, investment, and intellectual property, but no one ever asked the U.S. Congress to do anything or to "give anything" in exchange for greater discipline or new rules. The tradeoffs were largely unexplored, but during the final weeks of the negotiation the U.S. Congress became more aware of them as they were consulted more frequently. The U.S. private sector also learned a great deal in the process. They learned that services contains heterogeneous sectors and about the pitfalls and stumbling blocks in some of those sectors like shipping. Services is not just a collection of sectors in which the United States has a competitive advantage. Now both countries' negotiators can take these lessons to the negotiations in Geneva.

These bilateral talks did result in pioneering, path-breaking agreements that could serve as a catalyst for the Uruguay Round. Canada and the United States have gone further and faster in services and investment than they could reasonably expect to achieve in the multilateral talks, and if these agreements are tabled in Geneva that could accelerate that process. But they did not do as much as they might have. Murray Smith in his chapter lays out what might have been accomplished.

The pact could have a valuable demonstration effect on the U.S. Congress where the perception is that the U.S. government has always sold itself out in international trade negotiations. The Congress is looking for a way to solve problems, but they believe problems cannot be solved through international negotiations because they lack credibility—they never yield anything substantial. But just maybe, this U.S.–Canadian pact has provided some solutions, and something substantial has been achieved. The way we will know that is if the private sector in the United States (and in Canada) comes forward and vocally proclaims, "This is what we have always wanted. This is something concrete." The U.S. private sector will be the ultimate judge of the agreement. If they believe the agreement is a good one and they speak up and tell their elected representatives, it will have a salutory effect on the trade policy process in the United States, and it will improve the prospects for the Uruguay Round.

Trade policymaking is a delicate balancing act, even in the best of times. It always pays for the import-competing interests to complain and to ask for government help and protection. Under normal circumstances, a countervailing force of exporters and those interests with a stake in open markets can be mobilized to tell the other side of the story. But the last seven years have been anything but normal in the

United States. U.S. exports in 1986 were less than in 1980. When exports are flat or declining legislators cannot count on hearing from that countervailing force to balance against the complaining interests. Congress has been hearing only one side of the story. So if the private sector speaks up and begins to tell the other side of the story, trade policymaking in the United States will be improved and the Uruguay Round will have more credibility.

As Jonathan Aronson and I argued in *Trade Talks: America Better Listen!*, the Uruguay Round would be different, more difficult and probably last longer than any of the seven rounds that preceded it. It could take ten years, but the U.S. Congress will not wait that long for results. Here again, a successful implementation of the U.S.–Canadian trade agreement could enhance the prospects for the Uruguay Round. To the extent that the agreements in these new areas break new ground, they could help to shorten the duration of the round and bring it to a successful conclusion before the U.S. Congress loses its patience.

The outlook for implementation is uncertain. The Canadian electorate is split over the issue of the trade agreement, and Canadian Prime Minister Mulroney is lagging badly in the polls. The leader of the two opposition parties in Canada have promised to tear up the agreement if elected. The next election in Canada will likely be fought in large measure over the agreement. In the United States, the administration—in conjunction with the private sector—needs to initiate a broad-scale educational effort on Capitol Hill as to the benefits of an agreement, otherwise it could fail to be implemented. If that happened, it could mark an unfortunate turning point in U.S. trade policy.

Failure would send a very bad signal to the rest of the world, and the Uruguay Round would suffer a setback. If the United States and Canada cannot reach an agreement in the new areas, how much can be expected in a multilateral forum where the common denominator is much lower?

The Reagan administration would have sacrificed its only opportunity to demonstrate the benefits of a liberalizing strategy to a restive Congress. Without a bilateral or a credible multilateral option, Congress will be more likely to act unilaterally. Whether the pact is implemented or not, the history of U.S. and Canadian trade policy will have been altered by these negotiations. The status quo that existed before the talks will no longer prevail. The consequences of failure are reviewed by Murray Smith and by Bill Diebold in his closing chapter.

And what of the future? Bill Diebold raises the policy issues associated with such a bilateral accord. How durable will the agreement be? An agreement such as this creates a whole host of legal, political, and institutional questions. Ideally, you want an agreement that is strong enough to hold together over time, and yet flexible enough to evolve with changing circumstances.

This is not an ideal agreement by any stretch of the imagination. The failure to develop a common set of rules to govern subsidies and to reach an agreement on intellectual property protection are two of the more obvious drawbacks. But it is a good agreement, and we should not allow the best to be the enemy of the good. Our task is to make the good better. But how will the deficiencies be filled in? Apart from the provision for five to seven years negotiation on subsidy rules, it is unclear how the other provisions will be expanded or clarified.

What about third countries and the treatment of outsiders? What if the United States should wish to enter into another bilateral agreement? The problem with bilateral agreements is that when a second bilateral agreement is entered into it tends to undermine the expectations engendered by the first. President Reagan in his 1988 State of the Union address spoke of including Mexico in a North American accord. Mexico is clearly the most significant third country, and Gerardo Bueno in his chapter examines the pact from a Mexican perspective. Certainly if the United States and Mexico entered into a substantive bilateral pact (and let me hasten to add, neither Mexico or the United States would be so inclined for years to come) including automobile trade, Canada would be affected. What is Canada's say in future bilateral agreements the United States may enter into or vice versa? Do we jointly decide, and how do we jointly decide?

Can third countries accede to the agreement in general or to a part of the agreement? Again, who decides, and how do they decide? The negotiations pointed out the tension that exists between generalizability and uniqueness. Where the United States was the demandeur on services, investment and intellectual property, it hoped that any agreements could be generalized by extending them to cover other countries. But where Canada was the demandeur on contingent protection and dispute settlement, the United States preferred that the agreement stress the uniqueness of the bilateral relationship. The probability that the U.S. Congress will accept changes in U.S. trade laws and procedures is greater if those changes uniquely apply to Canada. The U.S. Congress is wary of setting a precedent that other countries may request during the multilateral talks. Whether there is a similar reluctance on Canada's part in the new areas of services and investment is unknown to me, but it would make sense.

How will progress or lack thereof in the Uruguay Round affect the agreement? Both countries were constrained by these multilateral negotiations. For example, the United States did not want to go too far on agriculture. Its major complaints are against the European Community. If the United States and Canada were fundamentally to change their farm programs as part of the bilateral agreement, then they both would have fewer bargaining chips and less leverage in the Uruguay Round.

But what happens if contentious issues like agriculture do not get resolved in the Uruguay Round? Perhaps what we need is a sequential negotiating process by which Canada and the United States agree to recontract after the multilateral talks are completed in order to improve the bilateral agreement. That would enhance durability.

Finally, a question often posed by Canadian friends, will the United States hold up its side of the bargain? Yes, if the completed agreement is the result of an active, vocal private sector "selling" it to Congress, explaining that this agreement is in their commercial interest. Upon completion of the agreement, they are going to respond to its provisions by investing, planning their sourcing and operations, and redirecting resources. Although the private sector is not homogeneous, those parts that change their behavior will have a vested interest in the pact's integrity. If someone proposes abrogating or undermining the pact, they will mobilize in opposition and that will increase the likelihood that the United States will stick to its side of the bargain.

This book is coming out at a most opportune time. Now that the detailed text of the agreement has been released and the implementation process has begun in both countries, the time has come to begin focusing on the policy issues associated with such a significant bilateral agreement. Given the complexity of the issues and the lack of precedent, it is fair to say that many of the issues raised in this book have not yet received adequate attention. It is also fair to say both countries will be grappling with these issues for years to come.

Bilateralism, Multilateralism and Canada in U.S. Trade Policy is the second in a series of books on trade issues that will be produced by the Council on Foreign Relations' International Trade Project. The first, *Fixing Farm Trade,* was released during the fall of 1987. Future volumes will focus upon international corporate alliances, the developing countries in the trading system, the U.S. domestic politics of trade, trade problems in high-technology industries, and the future of U.S. trade policy, among others. A follow-up book on the implementation of the U.S.–Canada agreement will also be done. In all, the Project will produce 10–12 monographs over the next two years. These monographs will be based upon a series of Council study groups.

On behalf of the Council, I would like to thank the Ford Foundation for its generous funding of this study and General Motors and the Rockefeller Foundation for their generous funding of the International Trade Project. I would personally like to thank William Eberle who so ably chaired the study group, and the members of the Project's Steering Committee (see Appendix) chaired so ably by Edmund T. Pratt, Jr. I would also like to thank Peter Tarnoff, president of the Council, and William Gleysteen, director of studies, for their unwavering support.

Allow me to conclude on a personal note. Bill Diebold was my predecessor at the Council. As Thomas Jefferson said upon being appointed to serve as envoy to France after Benjamin Franklin, "I succeed him; no one could replace him." I owe Bill an enormous debt of gratitude for the counsel and comments he has given to me over the past several years. I was pleased that we could prevail upon him to call upon his vast knowledge and experience accumulated over the past half century in order to produce this book. For those of you that know him, you will understand my wife Amy's remark after enjoying a dinner with Bill and Ruth (and Amy normally disdains dinner with economists), "They don't make them like that anymore!" For those of you that don't know him, you will find Bill's extraordinary perspective in his introductory and closing chapters. Bill's skill, attention and thoughtful comments were also evident to the other authors in this volume who expressed their pleasure for having the opportunity to work with him. I feel the same way and with luck we can prevail upon him again soon.

C. Michael Aho is Director of the International Trade Project and Director of Economic Studies at the Council on Foreign Relations.

Preface

This is an odd book in several ways. It deals with a fundamental aspect of American foreign trade policy but devotes most of its space to a single set of negotiations (with, to be sure, the country's largest trading partner). In spite of this focus, the book does not deal with the details of the Canadian-American free trade agreement that resulted from these negotiations. Much attention is given to the aims and objectives of the Canadian government, but the book is basically a study of American policy and the international trading system. Although the features of the free trade agreement provide central themes, our work was almost entirely completed before the agreement was arrived at. As we go to press it is still unknown whether the agreement will be adopted.

This odd combination of features did not seriously impede us as we carried out the study, but it might be useful for readers to bear in mind the timing of the analysis and the writing. The study group at the Council on Foreign Relations met five times between December 1986 and June 1987. First drafts of all the chapters in this book were discussed at those sessions. In the next few months the authors revised their manuscripts. The first four chapters were ready for press before the beginning of October when the two governments published a summary of the *Elements of the Agreement*. Chapter 5 was revised to take account of that document but only the final chapter was able to deal with it in any detail and then, at the last minute, had to be altered again to take account of the text of the agreement itself. For reasons set out in the early part of Chapter 6, the analysis in the earlier chapters remains vital to an understanding of the subjects with which this book deals. Naturally, the passage of time has left some traces but readers should not be put off by this. As the epilogues added to several chapters at the end of 1987 show, no author had to make any major changes in his thinking when he learned the outcome of the negotiations.

As editor and part author of the book, I know I speak for the other authors as well when I acknowledge the indispensable help of the study group members named in Appendix II. A mixture of Canadians, Americans and one Mexican, of scholars, businessmen, lawyers, and officials of both governments, the group provided stimulating, critical discussions of a wide range of issues and brought forth many ideas that have found their way into this book. We owe particular debt to the chairman, William D. Eberle, who not only brought to bear his great experience as a trade negotiator and his exceptional connections with current activities, but also guided the discussions so that they both moved along through a sometimes overloaded agenda and focused attention on the issues that most needed to be thrashed out. The group was not asked to come to any conclusions and has no responsibility for the views expressed in this book. Neither do the authors have a collective view; each writes altogether individually. As will be apparent, there are differences among them on a number of points, and between me and them as well, but there seemed no need to pursue these points in detail.

A second Council group of special value to me was concerned with deepening American understanding of the broader ramifications in Canada of the idea of "free trade" with the United States. The discussion leaders included Robert Bourassa, David Crane, Donald Macdonald, Bob Rae, and Mitchell Sharp. As chairman of those off-the-record sessions I am particularly grateful to Janice Murray, the group director, for her hard and able work in putting the meetings together and helping to ask the right questions.

At a late stage in this study, Murray Smith, one of the authors, organized a seminar at the Institute for Research on Public Policy in Ottawa at which Michael Aho and I were able to pose some of the questions with which we were concerned. The group was an exceptionally able and experienced one and the members were frank in what they said in ways that were most helpful to me in particular. We are grateful to them and to Murray Smith for organizing the meeting.

Many more conferences and people contributed to this book. The period from 1985 through 1987—and this will clearly be true in 1988 as well—was marked by a profusion of Canadian-American conferences (of which there is no shortage in an average year either). The authors, and other members of the study group, attended a large number of these, meeting one another in many venues. The sessions and the organizations responsible are far too numerous to mention, even though all these meetings contributed in one way or another to this book. So have the many written pages that have come out of these sessions or were otherwise produced by the organizations behind them. Quite a few of these have been written by the authors of this volume or other members of the study group, but only a few are acknowledged in the notes.

I and the other authors have a great debt to a large number of people who have taken the time to talk with us about the issues dealt with in the book and related questions or have criticized our writings. I had several particularly fruitful visits to Canada in connection with this work. But it is impossible to name names and do justice, not least in my own case, since, as passages in Chapter 1 show, some of my debts go back to my earliest endeavors to study United States foreign trade policy rather a long time ago.

As always, however, a few exceptions have to be made. Gardner Patterson was good enough to read a late version of Chapter 1 and give me valuable comments on key issues. Joseph Greenwald made a number of important points about two drafts of the last chapter which have brought better balance and focus. The officials of both countries who helped are best left anonymous, especially when their guidance has not been followed, but it would be churlish not to thank Robert Johnstone, the consul general of Canada in New York, not only for help with Canadian materials and contacts but especially for discussing with me many issues with which he usually had a firsthand familiarity from his work in Ottawa when the first trade talks began. Michael Aho and I are also grateful to Robert MacDougall, the Canadian consul, for making sure that we saw all the Canadian documents it was proper for us to see in a timely fashion.

Finally as editor, author, and alumnus of the staff of the Council on Foreign Relations, I have to thank the present staff there. As I know firsthand what is involved in running a study group and producing a book with multiple authors, I insisted from the beginning that they do all this work. I am particularly grateful to my successor at the Council, C. Michael Aho, for entrusting me with this study which enabled me to pursue some longstanding interests and for full support on all aspects of the project. Suzanne Hooper was indispensable in organizing our activities, keeping the show on the road and editing the manuscript. Stephanie Hoelscher played a key part in the project and wrote very good summaries of the discussions of our off-the-record meetings.

My wife, Ruth, has been indulgent as always about what must sometimes have seemed an extravagant amount of time put into this volume. By occasionally demanding explanations of issues or people, she has helped me clarify either my thinking or my expression, or both. And she is getting to know quite a lot about Canada and the Americans who concern themselves with that country.

The structure of the book is quite simple. The first chapter provides an historical account of the issues in American trade policy and the evolution of the international trading system that are central to the themes of this book and poses basic questions to be discussed. In Chapter 2, Gilbert Winham of Dalhousie University, analyzes Canadian aims and the decision to propose a free trade area. Then, Andreas

Lowenfeld of the New York University law school describes the GATT requirements for a free trade area and explores some of the uncertain areas that are crucial to the Canadian-American agreement. In Chapter 4, Murray Smith of the Institute for Research on Public Policy in Ottawa (who was at the C.D. Howe Institute in Toronto during most of the study) suggests a number of ways in which some central problems could be dealt with, thus establishing a benchmark against which to measure the actual agreement. In the process, he puts the decisions the United States and Canada must make in a broad setting. Then, Gerardo Bueno of El Colegio de Mexico, who had quietly sat through a number of the group's discussions and asked some pertinent questions, provides *A Mexican View* that comprises not only a concise analysis of Mexican interests in the Canadian-American agreement but also some interesting suggestions about what might be done in the future. In the final chapter I say something about the terms of the agreement, return to basic questions, and, in the light of the analysis provided by my colleagues, set out some personal conclusions and recommendations for policy.

January 1988   *William Diebold, Jr.*

1

The History and the Issues

WILLIAM DIEBOLD, JR.

BILATERALISM VERSUS MULTILATERALISM: the dichotomy is familiar. It suggests a clear choice; one so fundamental that either word is taken to characterize a country's whole trade policy. And in American thinking and policy for several generations now, great moral freight has been attached to the words. The issue has been regarded as almost Manichean. On the one side are the children of light, and on the other the forces of darkness—and we have had no doubt which is which.

However, the issues are not really that simple. The bilateral agreements which the United States began negotiating in the 1930s produced a major expansion of the area of multilateral, largely non-discriminatory, trade even before there was a General Agreement on Tariffs and Trade (GATT). And, a multilateral agreement negotiated under GATT has spawned innumerable bilateral agreements which restrict trade in textiles and clothing, and create much discrimination.

At a minimum, a distinction seems called for between formal and substantive bilateralism or multilateralism. But that is far from the end of the matter. The bilateral agreements of Cordell Hull were basically different from those of Hjalmar Schacht. Major multilateral negotiations usually comprise many sets of bilateral negotiations. Substantive bilateralism can reduce trade barriers through bargains in which partner countries treat one another better than they treat others. A country following multilateral principles can treat all with perfect equality by reducing no trade barriers at all. For groups of countries, such as the European Community (EC) and the Sterling Area before it, multi-

1

lateralism among themselves was obtained by discriminating against outsiders.

To blur the simple dichotomy or to deny a monopoly of wisdom and virtue to either bilateralism or multilateralism is not to be either agnostic or indifferent about the alternatives. The balance between the two elements, the content of each, and the *kind* of bilateralism or multilateralism that is involved are fundamental characteristics of national trade policies and international arrangements. Cumulatively, these factors and the dynamic relationship between bilateral and multilateral elements shape the way the world trading system works.

As the EC and Sterling Area examples indicate, "bilateral" and "multilateral" do not exhaust the possibilities. There is no established generic term that covers customs unions, free trade areas, regional agreements or other arrangements between more than two countries. They may be called "plurilateral," with the understanding that even when quite large groups take part they do not include as many countries as GATT.[1] In principle, at least, GATT is open to any country that will take on its obligations and is accepted by the members. It is thus potentially as universal or "global" an organization as the United Nations, but the weight and character of its obligations make for significant differences. Similarly, plurilateral agreements and their effects differ greatly depending upon their provisions, who is in them, and on what terms (if any) they are open to others. By this definition, the EC and a variety of free trade areas and regional agreements are plurilateral. It is difficult to generalize about such entities, so plurilateral arrangements will be considered in this chapter only when specific questions or possibilities arise.

Clearly one cannot make much sense of bilateralism and multilateralism in trade policy, either analytically or prescriptively, without discussing nondiscrimination, reciprocity, and the reduction of trade barriers (or the lack of it). Choices between bilateral and multilateral trade practices are often shaped (or dictated) by the convertibility of currencies, the availability of credit, and other financial and monetary conditions. As these issues are not likely to determine Canadian-American trade relations for some time to come, little will be said about them in this book.[2] "Unilateralism," as engaged in by either Canada or the United States, is a rather different matter from the question of bilateralism or multilateralism in their trading arrangements, and will make its appearance here in due course.

How is one to cope with so many variables? One could produce a matrix to bring out similarities and differences, a model to focus on determining factors, or a taxonomy with attendant prose to ring the changes on combinations and permutations. Instead, this chapter provides a broad (and incomplete) historical narrative that sets out some of the elements of bilateralism and multilateralism in past American trade policy. Given the nature of that policy for the last fifty years and more, this entails saying something about the international trading system as a whole. The result should be a realistic view not only of the mix (or mixes) of bilateral and multilateral elements in international trade relations, but also of how the blend may be changing as time passes. We can then state in some reasonable form the issues that Canada and the United States must deal with as they face not only one another and the international trading system, but also their internal problems, whether one calls them economic or political.

The Twenties

In February 1923 President Harding approved the use of the unconditional most-favored-nation (MFN) clause in American commercial treaties. That action reversed the American insistence on the conditional form of the clause that had begun with the first commercial treaty with France in 1778. The United States then signed an unconditional MFN treaty with Brazil in October 1923. In the next ten years about two dozen such treaties were signed, and by the beginning of 1933 there were only 48 conditional MFN agreements left in the world, out of a total of 625.[3] The results of this reversal in American policy, however, were not those which one of the principal champions of the reform had hoped for.

Professor Frank W. Taussig of Harvard, the historian of the American tariff, was appointed by President Wilson as the first chairman of the Tariff Commission when it was created in 1916. Work began almost immediately on a *Report on Reciprocity and Commercial Treaties* that appeared at the beginning of 1919. On the basis of this very substantial historical study (which gave a good deal of attention to Canada), the members of the Commission concluded that "a policy of special arrangements, such as the United States has followed in recent decades, leads to troublesome complications. Whether as regards our reciprocity treaties or as regards our interpretation of the most-favored-nation clause, the separate and individual treatment of each case tends to create misunderstanding and friction with countries which, though supposed to be not concerned, yet are in reality much concerned."[4]

Part of the trouble was that no matter how a given MFN clause was written, the United States tended to interpret it as conditional and European countries as unconditional. Even if conditionality was clear, there were opportunities for dispute over what was an equivalent concession when a country claimed its MFN rights to a tariff reduction made to a third party. To make matters worse, changing the American tariff required action by Congress so it was hard—and often imposs- ible—to give other countries anything. The efforts to work out reciproc- ity treaties in the last part of the nineteenth century did not amount to very much. The one negotiated with Canada in 1911 had fallen through when the government in Ottawa fell. The American legislation that would have reduced duties was still on the books.

Instead of continuing its past practices, said the Tariff Commission, the United States should adopt "a clear and simple policy . . . of equal- ity of treatment. . . . Equality of treatment should mean that the United States treat all countries on the same terms, and in return require equal treatment from every other country." There might be exceptions, such as had been allowed in the past, when there were "special political ties and political responsibilities" (as in the case of the United States and Hawaii and Cuba) or "where one country has a long frontier line in common with another" (such as Spain and Portugal, and Canada and the United States).

When the United States granted another country MFN, did that mean tariffs would fall? Or should duties be raised against goods from a country that did not get MFN, because it discriminated against the United States? The authors of the Report preferred a conciliatory mode as opposed to a retaliatory one, but supposed it unlikely that many duties could be cut much below the level to which they had been reduced at the beginning of the Wilson administration in 1913. So they concluded that, in the short run, the method of "additional duties" was to be preferred, but that in the long run, depending in part on what the peace settlement brought, it might be possible to go the other way. In any case, as flexibility would be needed, it was necessary to delegate power to the president to levy the additional duties, subject to criteria laid down by Congress.

Writing in 1918, in a time of war but with peace at hand, the Tariff Commission said (in a passage written by Taussig) that in shaping American trade policy, an important difference from the past was that "The United States has become committed to far-reaching participa- tion in world politics. The American Government can no longer shape its commercial negotiations solely with reference to the results of each particular arrangement. It must consider the world at large and shape its commercial policy in conformity with the political and humanitarian principles which govern its general attitude in the international sphere." The aim of insisting on equal treatment was not to put the

United States in an especially advantageous position. "The United States should ask no special favors and grant no special favors. It should exercise its powers and should impose its penalties, not for the purpose of securing discrimination in its favor, but to prevent discrimination to its disadvantage."

The Commission said its recommendations were compatible with either conditional or unconditional forms of the MFN clause, and stated no conclusion as to which was preferable. Perhaps this was a result of uncertainty about what the postwar world would look like, or a tactic to leave the administration free in the peace negotiations, but it probably simply reflected a disagreement among the commissioners. One, William Culbertson, later published the memorandum he wrote at the time. In it, he expressed a certain exasperation with the fact that after studying the subject "more carefully probably than any other organization . . . in the end we make no recommendations." He believed that unconditional MFN "certainly follows as a logical conclusion upon the advocacy of a policy of equality of treatment." As a Republican he later, in the Harding administration, actively urged on Secretary of State Hughes and Secretary of Commerce Hoover the shift to the policy of unconditional MFN that they adopted. A decade later Culbertson was a strong advocate of the Trade Agreements Act.[5]

In an article published in 1924, Jacob Viner, who, I believe, had been on the staff of the Tariff Commission when the 1919 Report was drafted, stated his own conclusions in no uncertain terms:

> The most-favored-nation clause in American commercial treaties, as conditionally interpreted and applied by the United States, has probably been the cause in the last century of more diplomatic controversy, more variations in construction, more international ill-feeling, more conflict between international obligations and municipal law and between judicial interpretation and executive practice, more confusion and uncertainty of operation, than have developed under all the unconditional most-favored-nation pledges of all other countries combined.[6]

Part of the trouble in the nineteenth century, and again after World War I, was that American tariffs were going up. In 1933 Taussig registered disillusionment with the reform that he had done so much to bring about. Although under conditional MFN "endless bickerings resulted and no happy results were attained," the adoption of unconditional MFN had not done much to improve the situation. It was fine in principle, "but as applied by us in practice, it can bring about no good result."[7] He acknowledged that it was his Tariff Commission that had concluded that the best way to persuade countries to provide equal treatment was to threaten them with higher tariffs, but that was with the tariff of 1913 in mind. By the time Harding had adopted the policy, the Fordney-McCumber Act had established record heights and then Hawley-Smoot had gone even further. Who could imagine adding another 50 percent to prohibitive rates? "We have already done practically all the damage [a penalty] could inflict." After all, "what is expected to lie underneath the most-favored-nation arrangements is that *there shall be some favor.*" In reality, "this equality of treatment, so far as our side is concerned, in fact is an equality not of favorable treatment, but of equally bad treatment all around."

Part of the damage, Taussig said, was to Canadian-American relations:

> Most significant and most regrettable of this is our unfriendly commercial relations with the Dominion of Canada, our nearest neighbor, our best customer, the country that should be our warmest friend and indeed remains, I fully believe, at heart strongly attached to us, notwithstanding the harsh and even boorish manner in which we have so long dealt with her. We have not only failed to attract Canada, but have alienated her; let us hope, not irrevocably.

"What now should be done?" asked Taussig. "My conclusion is that the whole present policy should be scrapped; that this pretense of a general most-favored-nation system should be given up; and that the next practicable step is to make separate arrangements for reciprocal reductions of duty." Such a policy might well involve some unfortunate "bargaining and bickering," but in the end it might widen the area of MFN treatment. One could not expect quick results.

In retrospect, it is not altogether clear just what Taussig had in mind. Would duties be reduced only on goods coming from countries that reciprocated? Did he now see the two-column tariff he had rather disliked in the past as a necessity? Was he calling for conditional MFN or abandoning MFN entirely? Or did he want to use reciprocal bargaining for selective tariff reductions that would be generalized?[8] Taussig had long ago pointed out that reciprocal concessions to a major supplier were similar to a general tariff reduction and tended to bring matching arrangements with other suppliers.[9] Was that the positive side of the arrangement? He did say that the executive branch would have to be given the power to reduce duties by a certain percentage in the course of negotiations. This turned out to be a key point for ideas about trade that were in circulation in Washington in the spring of 1933.

The Hull Trade Agreements

The New Deal was an experimental, eclectic movement, not an ideological one. Franklin Roosevelt was not elected on a program that spelled out many of the measures that were eventually adopted during his first years in office. It could have been taken for granted that a Democratic administration would make at least a gesture toward tariff reduction since it was the traditional party position, but there was ample reason to doubt that much would be done at a time when massive unemployment and collapsed demand dominated the domestic economy. As true New Deal measures emerged—the Agricultural Adjustment Act (AAA), the National Recovery Act (NRA) in industry, the Bituminous Coal Mining Act—they did not foreshadow any movement toward trade liberalization and even provided for new controls on imports. The first international test of the new administration was the London Economic Conference of 1933 which had been in preparation for several years. As the discussions proceeded, the instruction came from Washington to reject proposals for international agreements on monetary matters in order to leave the new administration as free as possible to reflate the economy and devalue the dollar.

When it came to trade policy, however, the key figure was Cordell Hull with his lifelong devotion to a classical form of trade barrier reduction and with his responsibilities, as secretary of state, for peace, which he thought was closely connected with trade. Hull carried weight in the Democratic party as he had served in both houses of Congress and as national chairman. Roosevelt needed support in the conservative wing of his own party and in the South. It is beyond the scope of this chapter to trace out all the politics, or to debate whether Hull's connection between trade and peace was naive but motivating, or to spell out the dissonances between the trade policies and other New Deal measures. It is necessary, however, to recall that three of the themes of this chapter—bilateralism, reciprocity, and MFN—were vital components of the program that began in 1934 and turned around American trade policy for the first time, on a sustained basis, since the beginning of the Republic.

So far as Hull was concerned, the trade changes could have started in 1933, but Roosevelt had a different set of priorities and more than enough measures to put before Congress. Hull would have liked to propose a major trade initiative at the London Economic Conference, but the voices that carried the day in the White House stressed monetary independence. Perhaps that was just as well, since Hull's experience at the conference helped force him to concentrate on the method of trade reform. In the past he had proposed multilateral action on trade and probably had that in mind for London, but that meeting seems to have done much to persuade him "that public opinion in no country, especially our own, would at that time support a multilateral undertaking."[10] The key talks apparently took place after it became clear that the United States was not going to accept proposals for international action on money. To do anything about trade would require hard bargaining, not another conference. As it turned out, this was also a key factor in selling his program in the United States as well.

Reciprocal bilateral bargaining seemed a logical step and, practically speaking, the only real choice if anything were to be done to reduce foreign or American tariffs. It appealed to the tradition of "the Yankee trader" as Percy Bidwell and others pointed out. It also stressed the value of trade agreements as a way to expand American exports (which had fallen more than those of most trading countries). That expectation helped make Henry Wallace, the secretary of agriculture, Hull's main ally in the cabinet. However, it would be a mistake to forget that both Hull and Wallace (and many other people who supported the trade agreements program) were also convinced that American tariffs should be reduced for the good of the country as well as for world trade.

Unconditional MFN was something else again. It looked to many people like a formula for giving something away and weakening American bargaining power. One struck a balanced bargain with one country, and then "gave away" the same tariff reduction to others. In contrast, conditional MFN seemed to be a logical way to insist on reciprocal concessions that would guarantee American access to specific foreign markets for exports. George Peek, special adviser to the president on foreign trade, had a plan to use conditional MFN and barter to dispose of agricultural surpluses. Hull and his supporters argued that the United States had more to gain from unconditional MFN, and they won the fight.

Their basic argument was, quite simply, that a country "gave away" nothing by granting MFN; it got in return the tariff reductions that other countries made to one another. In that way discrimination against the United States was reduced, and the amount of world trade that was open to multilateral competition would continue to grow. To be sure there were legitimate concerns about losing bargaining power. To meet them two techniques were adopted. Usually a tariff would only be lowered in dealings with the country that was the principal supplier of the commodity in question. Sometimes the classification of goods in the tariff schedules would be altered (usually by introducing new subdivisions) in order to permit the tariff to be reduced on products of a certain price, quality or character and not others (either because they came mainly from a different country or because of domestic resistance). Similar methods had long been used by other countries and if pushed too far, they could limit the value of trade barrier reductions and diminish equality of treatment. However, in American practice in the 1930s these practices looked, by and large, like fairly reasonable compromises with the practicalities of bargaining and coping with domestic pressures. In 1938 one-third of American imports of products on which there had been concessions came from countries other than those to which the concessions had been made.[11]

A more troublesome problem was how to apply MFN to quotas, exchange controls and state trading. Several formulas were devised, often based on shares of trade during some earlier "representative period." Both practically and intellectually the formulas were not satisfactory, but they secured some *quid pro quo* for the reduction of American tariffs and were generally seen at the time as better than nothing. They did not offer much promise of general trade liberalization and in fact foreshadowed a set of problems that are still with us.

There is little doubt that the American initiative achieved two important objectives. It limited foreign discrimination against American imports, and it reduced American tariffs. An experienced official, looking back, came to the conclusion that, "Measured solely by the statistical results, these bilateral agreements taken together went further toward correcting the excesses of the Smoot-Hawley Tariff than did even the most far-reaching of the subsequent multilateral negotiations until the Kennedy Round."[12] The American record was, however, exceptional; in the rest of the world, there was a considerable increase in trade restriction and discrimination during the 1930s. Bilateral agreements flourished in which governments not only exchanged exclusive privileges, but often sought to balance trade. The motives varied and combined: export promotion; the conservation of foreign exchange; coping with inconvertible currencies; controlling imports; and supporting political aims. There was also exploitation of weaker countries, as in the German agreements in southeastern Europe. It was this period more than any other that gave bilateralism such a bad name among trade liberalizers and made multilateralism an almost unchallenged objective of later plans for reconstructing world trade.

The Trade Agreements Act permitted the president to withhold MFN treatment from any country that discriminated unduly against American exports. This provision was invoked only against Germany and, temporarily, Australia. That others were discriminating is clear, but the whole approach of the Hull program was to find ways, however incomplete, to reduce the amount of restriction and discrimination in the world. Although Nazi bilateralism was blatant, there is little doubt that political elements entered into the American decision. Similar considerations may explain why no effort was made to reach an agreement with Japan, and why much tariff reclassification was directed against imports from that country.[13]

Agreements were made with most of the other major trading partners. The one with Canada (effective at the beginning of 1936) was the most important for several years. Canada was the United States' largest supplier and second largest market (after Britain). There was a special American interest in the Canadian agreement because it was in part an attack on Imperial Preference. Then when an agreement was reached with the United Kingdom at the end of 1938, a supplementary agreement was made with Canada including some American concessions intended, in part, to compensate Canada for British concessions on American wheat and lumber. Other Commonwealth countries were involved and, from an American point of view, it was possible to imagine that at least a few steps had been taken toward checking the world's movement toward restriction, discrimination and bilateralism.[14]

American proponents of these bilateral trade agreements believed all along that they would improve the general conditions of world trade. By the late 1930s American commentators often spoke in these terms. But if there was to be any reshaping of the world trading system, the British were central. They, however, were concerned primarily with other matters. In agreeing to negotiate bilaterally with the Americans, the British may have believed that they had a good opportunity to make an economically favorable bargain because of the importance Washington was thought to attach to having an agreement with London. Some British clearly saw political advantages to reaching an agreement with the United States at a time when international relations were growing more troubled. There was certainly little evidence that the British had any intention of moving away from either Imperial Preference or the extensive bilateral arrangements they had made even while adhering to nominal MFN principles. (Argentina's sterling earnings had to be spent in the United Kingdom; a number of countries had to promise to buy substantial quantities of British coal; Danish ham and bacon destined for the British market had to be cured with British salt and wrapped in burlap made in the United Kingdom.) An American economist, writing in 1939, may have been a bit harsh, but was not far off the mark when he said:

> If the British concept of most-favored-nation relations can be compressed into a single statement, it would be that they are willing to grant equality

of treatment in the British market for something more, in some cases a great deal more, in return as regards their exports. . . . In other cases the principle has been completely set aside by the negotiation of bilateral payments and clearing agreements. . . . A real conflict exists between the commercial policy systems of the United States and Great Britain. . . . It appears as though America may, therefore, have to struggle alone in the endeavor to promote the principles underlying its trade policy. The odds are heavy against succeeding, but the stakes are high.[15]

Before that prediction could be tested, both countries had to concentrate on greater issues. By the time the shape of the world trading system was again their common concern, their positions had altered in important ways, and so had some of their thinking. But quite a few of the basic issues were dismayingly familiar.

The GATT World

We have heard often enough that GATT was the Trade Agreements Program writ large. And so it was in many ways: an emphasis on reducing trade barriers by bargaining; a basic commitment to unconditional MFN and to rules which minimized discrimination in other forms of trade controls as well as tariffs; and reciprocity, in the fundamental sense that when a country took on obligations it received the advantages (and rights) that resulted from the obligations of others. The big difference from the Trade Agreements Program was that GATT was multilateralism incarnate. This meant many things. For instance, it stressed the broadest aspects of reciprocity: what one gained was not just what the immediate bargaining partner conceded, but benefits from the system as a whole. Multilateralism also permitted countries to choose those commitments (outside the basic ones) which they found advantageous and which did not subject them—in principle at least— to the one-sided bargains prevalent in a world where there are no rules and where market power, in all its different senses, can be freely used by those who have it. This broadening was not seen to be in conflict with the objectives of the Hull program, but rather as an improvement on it made possible by the difference between the conditions of 1944 and those of 1934.

However natural it may seem for the GATT approach to have come out of prewar American policy, it was not inevitable. Wars have usually brought an increase in American barriers against imports, if only because there are new industries to protect. (This time there were some special, and not badly handled, arrangements for such things as the artificial rubber industry and the greatly expanded aluminum capacity.) It would not have been hard to imagine an American effort to improve the conditions of world trade that took the form of an international agreement on principles, the application of which was up to each country or to be worked out in later detailed negotiations. Perhaps enough people who counted were familiar with the record of the League of Nations in dealing with trade matters to avoid that. Certainly the major emphasis in all fields of economic policy was on working out fairly concrete arrangements with stated obligations and rights, as in the case of trade.

It would also not have been out of the question to think in terms of an agreement that would come into effect once conditions were more or less normal. (It had been argued that the International Monetary Fund [IMF] could not work properly in the period right after the war, and in many respects that proved correct.) There was a clear risk that such an arrangement would never come into effect. "We must act before the vested interests get their vests on," Will Clayton once said. Part of the realism that went with the idealism of the GATT system was that countries in balance-of-payments difficulties could reduce tariffs but still control imports until their positions improved. At the same time, their exports could increase as a result of the reduced tariffs in countries with healthier balances of payments. As a result, there was, in the years before European currencies became convertible, a kind of lopsided reciprocity between the two sides of the Atlantic.

The path to the multilateral trade agency—and the IMF, and the World Bank and other multilateral bodies—was not strictly multilateral. It was an article of faith in wartime Washington that the postwar organization of the international economic system depended on understandings between the United States and the United Kingdom. By and large, the British shared this view and tried to take advantage of the American conviction. Their own divisions of opinion suppressed a trade equivalent of Keynes's monetary plan and made the United States not only the initiator but also the *demandeur* in trade. The story of Article VII of the Lend-Lease agreements, the American Trade Proposals and their acceptance as part of the British loan agreement does not need to be retold to emphasize that the origins of GATT had as strong a bilateral element as did the Bretton Woods agreements, although both benefitted from major Canadian contributions as well.

There was no question that GATT had to be multilateral. Otherwise it could not include any substantial amount of world trade (even in the days when Britain and France were still the centers of empires). Even more important, the whole concept of a postwar international economic system that was supposed to avoid "the errors of last time" was based on cooperation among sovereign states. No country would engage in lasting cooperation unless its interests were served. The British and Americans had had to compromise to agree on the new measures in the first place. They could not sensibly ignore the interests of other countries, or the arrangements would come apart once other countries got strong enough. And if they did not get strong enough, the effort to set up an improved international economic system would have failed.[16] Nevertheless, the successful operation of the multilateral system depended on some bilateral, or plurilateral, agreements at key moments.

Britain did not prove to be quite the partner the Americans had originally hoped for, but then came Europe, and now also Japan. None of these "partnerships" has been altogether satisfactory, but they have all been important in keeping GATT, and the multilateral system generally, in operation. There are dramatic stories of how Eric Wyndham White, the director general of GATT, managed the Kennedy Round by bringing the key negotiators together at the right moments. Summits are credited with reaffirming the major countries' political commitments to the success of the Tokyo Round, and the issuing of instructions to national bureaucracies that brought it to an end. In his major study Gilbert Winham tells of a number of instances in which agreements between two or three major trading countries shaped the whole course of those multilateral trade negotiations which occupied so much of the seventies. He concludes that "much of the Tokyo Round consisted of an interaction between two preponderant parties at the negotiation: the European Community and the United States."[17]

Another dimension of multilateralism is reflected in the report of a meeting of the Economic and Financial Group of the Council on Foreign Relations War and Peace Studies in the spring of 1944. The group was asked to comment on a plan drafted by a group of experts in Washington which called for "a multilateral attack on the [trade] problem without, however, wholly rejecting the utilization of bilateral negotiations. But, said Mr. Viner, the latter would, so to speak, be multilaterally planned bilateral agreements. They would be negotiated for the purpose of promoting the multilateral ends advocated by the memorandum." An exchange followed as to the risks of this approach, including, on the one hand, the need to be sure that multilateral negotiations came to a firm conclusion and, on the other, to prevent the bilateral preoccupations of the negotiating countries from becoming predominant. Perhaps the four or five most important countries could reach an agreement, with "other countries then being admitted to participation on the understanding that no important reservations would be permitted." Britain, Canada and the United States would be the logical starting group but it would be wise to add "other non-Anglo-Saxon countries at the outset." There would also have to be some incentive for other countries to join in these arrangements. To keep them from getting benefits without undertaking any obligations, Mr. Viner suggested that it might be wise to cancel the signatories' MFN obligations to those that did not sign on.[18]

This is the first time that one of the basic issues about plurilateral agreements (using that term in its wider sense) has entered into our discussion. It came up in a quite explicit form in the negotiation of GATT and the Charter of the International Trade Organization (ITO). No one quarrelled with the idea that signatories had to pledge MFN to one another. Naturally the new agreement did not oblige them to treat other countries the same way. But should they even be allowed to? The American drafters thought not. After all, there had to be some inducement to join. Moreover, enforcement of the GATT rules was to be largely in the form of withdrawing GATT benefits from violators; doing that could leave outsiders who received MFN treatment relatively better off. Therefore, the Americans proposed that after approximately one year, countries should no longer extend tariff concessions made within GATT to outsiders unless the organization agreed.[19] The Czechs balked at this, claiming that they would not dare treat the USSR that way. Various compromises were worked out, but in the end the relevant provisions of the ITO Charter were weak and eventually were not carried over into GATT, which is still silent on the subject. There have never, so far as I am aware, been any significant controversies centering on these issues.

What would the world trading system look like today if GATT members had been refused permission to provide outsiders with MFN treatment? At a minimum, a certain number of key trading countries would have had two-column tariffs. Would more countries have stayed out of GATT—or joined it sooner?[20] What would have happened to the Generalized System of Preferences (GSP)? Would the United Nations Trade and Development Organization (UNCTAD) have achieved the goal of some of its founders? Would the near-fetishism with which the USSR regards MFN have brought it into GATT long ago?

Another and earlier speculation on departures from MFN within GATT makes interesting reading today. Writing before 1950, Jacob Viner recalled that "the fear of retaliation, or counter-measures of some sort, has always been the most effective of all barriers to official discrimination." Looking at some provisions of the ITO Charter (which were mostly carried over into GATT) he noted "an impressive list of types of preferential tariff arrangements" that escaped MFN rules. They might make the future of plurilateral agreements quite different from their past.

> When the Charter approves departures from the most-favored-nation principle, the significance of this approval does not lie merely in that it gives the odor of sanctity to practices which, whether widely followed or not, were hitherto not in good repute, although its significance even on this score is by no means negligible. What is of greater significance is that when the Charter gives its approval to a departure from the most-favored-nation treatment, it at the same time assures to the countries that take advantage of it that they will not in consequence have to pay any price for their exercise of the privilege in the form of the loss of any claims they may have, legal or otherwise, to the receipt of most-favored-nation treatment from other countries. The provisions of the Charter with respect to customs unions, free-trade areas, and new regional arrangements, *taken by themselves,* do constitute what is on paper at least an appreciable removal of preexisting barriers to official discrimination in trade barriers, and it is significant that many of these provisions are written in terms of hearty encouragement rather than of regrettable departure from an ideal made necessary by special circumstances or by the less-than-universal acceptance of the ideal. It should be conceded, however, that much can be said in support of the preferability of a code, even if imperfect, enforced by international sanction to an even better code enforced only by the sanctions of the possibility of unilateral national retaliation.[21]

Evolution

A major reason why GATT puts so much emphasis on MFN is that equal treatment is the engine of substantive multilateralism (so long as barriers are being reduced); the discrimination MFN was supposed to prevent took many forms, but in the 1930s, as has been pointed out, a particularly troublesome one was bilateralism in the sense of the exchange of exclusive privileges or the insistence on certain conditions of bilateral trade—which might be balance or barter. When GATT came into being, the forces for bilateralism were at least as strong, and maybe more so. Immediately after the war there was widespread acceptance of the clear and forceful demonstration by Howard Ellis that "no device portends more restriction of international trade in the post-war setting than bilateral trade arrangements."[22] However, it was also true, as Gardner Patterson and Judd Polk pointed out, that when countries were in severe balance-of-payments difficulties, bilateral agreements made it possible for them to carry on some trade that would not have taken place otherwise.[23] Ragnar Frisch showed that in some circumstances trade could be maximized by discrimination.[24] Charles Kindleberger added his voice with the thought that "instinct seems to suggest that there is room for a position between the idealistic attempt to re-establish a bygone multilateralism and the cynicism which would suggest that bilateralism is the inescapable road of the future. This middle course is discrimination to enlarge trade."[25] It was easy to see how such arguments might be abused to excuse discriminatory practices, but unless GATT could cope with this set of real problems it would have to defer its operation to a very uncertain future.

A realistic way out was sought by adding to the fine print of an already complex agreement and permitting discrimination in import restrictions (mostly quotas and exchange controls) by countries in balance-of-payments difficulties. Surveillance and constant pressure by and through GATT and the IMF—which worked together quite closely in those days—played an important part in limiting the abuse of these provisions and in pushing countries to reduce the discrimination as their payments positions improved and then to get rid of it altogether. (However, the largest single factor was probably the advantage one or the other country saw in escaping from the restraints of bilateral agreements into the wider choice and freer movement that the multilateral arrangements permitted.) When bilateral agreements in Europe gave way to Europe-wide arrangements for trade and payments that still discriminated against outside countries, something like the same process—but with less help from GATT and the Fund—limited the duration of the new arrangements.[26] Thus we have an instance of a complex dynamic in which bilateral bargains (even quite restrictive ones) merge into regional agreements (discriminating against outsiders) that presently open into multilateral undertakings.

Another source of discrimination was more enduring: regional integration, primarily in Western Europe. From the mid-1950s until today major questions about the functioning of the international trading system have revolved around the changing arrangements made among changing numbers of countries, their impact on outside countries, and their compatibility with the rather general provisions of GATT concerning customs unions and free trade areas. An extension of the theme has concerned relations between European countries and those in the developing world where the idea of geographical grouping has been confounded with the evolution of ex-colonial preferences and the use of preferential access as an aid to development. The textile arrangements operate largely through bilateral agreements. Developing countries often worked out preferential arrangements among themselves. To the inherent ambiguity of widening the area of tariff-free trade within a group, while inescapably sharpening the difference between internal trade and that with outside countries, has been added the question of the conduct of the new units—primarily the European Community—as negotiating and bargaining entities.

This is not the place to discuss these issues at length or to go into other departures from MFN within the GATT system in its first twenty years. It is enough to take the thumbnail sketch of history drawn by Gardner Patterson in his excellent analysis of the subject published in 1966. "Had this study been written a decade ago the conclusion would have been that discrimination was declining, not increasing, and that there had been a resurgence of support at the policy level for unconditional most-favored-nation treatment." But the decade had brought changes and it had to be said that "Twenty years after World War II discrimination according to source was a widely used and in most policy-formulating circles a thoroughly respectable policy instrument. Unconditional most-favored-nation treatment was under attack from all sides."[27]

Patterson thought the Kennedy Round, which was going on at the time, might mitigate the effects of discrimination. Only a few years later, however, an American who had been deeply involved in the multilateral negotiations had very much in mind the amount of discrimination permitted by the GATT rules on regional and other preferences when he asked if "the Kennedy Round may emerge in the perspective of history as the twilight of the GATT."[28]

The Tokyo Round introduced a new kind of discrimination among GATT countries. The codes on subsidies and other matters are said to apply only to those countries that sign them, but the basic GATT commitment to equal treatment limits the extent to which code privileges can be confined to signatories. Had there been more vigorous use of the codes in recent years, we would understand this situation more clearly. How much incentive to sign the codes is lost? Do signatories feel a loss of reciprocity? A related question is whether, if two (or more) signatories agree on how they would apply the code (say to certain subsidies), they would have to give the same treatment to other signatories that did not accept the same obligations? (As this question could rise out of a Canadian-American agreement, it is taken up later in this book.)

Some people call the code arrangements "conditional MFN." This does not seem wise, given the historical meaning of that term. A key feature of conditional MFN was that when country A made a concession to country B as part of a bargain, country C—if entitled to conditional MFN from country A—had to make an equivalent or compensatory concession. The exact nature of that concession and whether it was truly equivalent was itself a matter for negotiation (and country A could be extremely disagreeable if it so desired). This was a major source of dissatisfaction with conditional MFN in the first place. As Richard Snyder remarked, "The conditional clause does not grant equality, but the *opportunity to purchase equality*."[29] In the case of the codes, membership is open to any country that accepts common rules which are, presumably, all written down, and that is quite a different matter. To be sure, there might be arguments over just how the rules apply to a new member (such as whether certain practices amount to subsidies), and over the special treatment of developing countries (provided for but not spelled out in codes). The emphasis, however, is quite different. A closer equivalent is the stipulation in the government procurement code of which entities' purchases are to be covered. In any of these cases, there is the question of whether the emphasis is on inducing countries to sign up or on excluding anyone whose views might make it more difficult to manage an efficient operation.

The idea that there can be progress in trade liberalization if a few countries are permitted to make bargains among themselves that are initially exclusive is not limited to the codes or customs unions and free trade areas. A group largely made up of experienced former American trade officials, headed by John Leddy, made a detailed proposal for major steps that leading trading countries might take to liberalize trade among themselves. Other countries could join those nations when they were ready to take on the same obligations.[30] This was what Viner would have called a plurilateral agreement. Some years later, in *The New Multilateralism*, Miriam Camps and I said that while an increased use of "selective" and "differentiated" agreements might be important in increasing cooperation, it would also be necessary to make better provision than in the past for the protection of the interests of outside countries.[31] In a similar vein, the "seven wisemen" brought together by Arthur Dunkel, the director general of GATT, urged that even when they were not hurt directly, countries should make formal complaints "if a bilateral arrangement impairs the objectives of the General Agreement."[32] On the basis of his long experience with GATT negotiations, Gardner Patterson has pointed out to me that although major trading countries often can take into account the interests of others while they are working out an agreement, it is much harder for them to change the terms of a bargain once it has been struck, for to do so can easily upset the delicate balance of the bargain. A familiar question that raises similar issues is whether the GATT provisions about customs unions and free trade areas should be much more detailed than they now are, with additional criteria to be met. The need seems particularly clear when one realizes that the European Community, for example, does not establish the same kinds of internal requirements for its members' use of some nontariff barriers as it does for tariffs, and cannot speak with a single voice about many of them to the rest of the world. As issues become more complex, it is harder to apply predetermined formulas to them, and it may become necessary to make greater use of procedures that grant waivers of normal rules of equal treatment when particular combinations of circumstances warrant.

It is obvious that ideas of this sort are highly relevant to the problems of relating a Canadian-American agreement to the multilateral trading system. Unfortunately, there has been little experience with testing such ideas in practice. That is, at least in part, because the troubles that Gardner Patterson saw besetting the liberal trading system and the idea of equal treatment in the mid-1960s have become considerably greater.

Deterioration

The gloomy process is too familiar to need much exposition. The seventies, with their stagflation and oil shocks, have given way to the eighties, with their recessions and slow growth, financial instability, maladjusted exchange rates and debt crises. In both decades the pressure for new trade barriers has been strong in many parts of the world. Bilateralism has increased, whether the aim was to obtain a secure supply of oil in the seventies or to find a market for capital goods and construction services in the eighties.

A substantial volume of world trade escapes the basic GATT rules: agriculture; textiles and clothing; steel; automobiles; ships; and a number of products which are subject to so-called voluntary export restraints and orderly marketing agreements. Japanese goods, which have set world export records, are also singled out by many countries for limitations that have no sanction in GATT. Developing countries are given tariff preferences on numerous products but are subject to sharp restrictions on others and often on the volume of sales at preferential rates.

Although a major effort was made to deal with nontariff barriers and trade distorting practices in the Tokyo Round, the resulting codes are having only modest effects. It is far from clear whether the GATT methods, which worked so well for tariffs and the direct trade controls of the postwar period, are going to make a major impact on what are now seen as among the most important impediments to the efficient movement of goods, investment and services. If this is the case, we cannot speak with any confidence of having a workable system of cooperation in matters of international trade.

The troubles run deep. In *The New Multilateralism*, Miriam Camps and I explained why and made some suggestions for improving matters. We said that the international trading system could be kept from further erosion only if it could be changed in major ways. It is hard to believe that this is likely to be done in the foreseeable future.[33] The fact that a new round of multilateral trade negotiations has been started is certainly encouraging, but it would be foolish to take progress (much less success) for granted. At a minimum one must bear in mind: 1) how long it took to get assent for even the simple commitment to negotiate; 2) how many opportunities there are for anyone to delay or block progress; and 3) how many reasons one or another of the key governments, including the United Sates, might find to drag its heels at some time in the next few years.

The best case for a more positive assessment rests on either widespread fear of the consequences of outright trade war (which would spread to other economic relations), or a heightened appreciation of the costs of the continued deterioration of the cooperative trading system. Some aspects of the increasing internationalization of business and the limits it puts on governmental policies can help matters. So might some aspects of the rapid, but not fully understood, progress toward the internationalization of the American economy. In the meantime, in very unfavorable conditions, Canada and the United States must carry on trade policies, in relation to one another and to the rest of the world. Among the many troublesome pressures, some push the United States away from its previous strong support of nondiscrimination and toward a degree of substantive bilateralism.

These forces are more numerous and pervasive than is generally realized. Some stem from the heavy imbalance in American foreign trade that has lasted for a number of years and the related strains of structural adjustment in the U.S. economy (whether change is resisted or takes place). The pressure to limit imports can be greater if they come from some countries and not others (or, at least, more difficult for the U.S. government to withstand). The drive to increase exports may be directed at all markets, but some are more responsive than others, and that affects American attitudes. As a result, the trade deficit comes to be looked at in segments; the focus is on large "unfavorable" balances—using the traditional term—with countries that simultaneously provide the most troublesome competition in the American market and import less than might be expected from the United States. The idea that all countries should be treated equally fades as some are seen to be quite unlike others.

The most overt and specific departures from MFN are in many ways the least important. The Cuban preferences that were once the special exception for the United States are long since gone, as are those for the Philippines. The long-standing denial of MFN to most communist countries is a matter of foreign policy and domestic politics. The special arrangement for some Caribbean countries has only minor effects. The so-called free trade area with Israel is economically more important, but can hardly be taken as an indicator of a major change in American trade policy. A speech by Secretary of State Shultz suggesting that the United States would like to negotiate free trade areas with a number of countries stands rather alone among most U.S. government statements on trade policy and appears to have had no significant follow-through (with the possible exception of Canada, to which we shall come later).[34] The Generalized System of Preferences is a major departure from equal treatment, but one that is undertaken by most industrial countries (though with some differences). As the United States, unilaterally and by negotiation, alters its GSP system with regard to products, the amounts that can enter free of duty, and the eligibility of countries, there are factors at play that will have elements of discrimination and bilateralism. That is equally true of measures that look primarily like protective steps, such as orderly marketing agreements, export restraints urged on foreign countries and American import controls of the sort applied to steel.

What may be of greatest long-run importance in the matter of discrimination and bilateralism in American trade practice is both the central position that nontariff barriers have assumed in international trade negotiations and the American emphasis on "fair trade" and the domestic laws intended to bring it about. The effort to protect intellectual property, an increasingly important trade issue, often leads the U.S. government to put pressure on individual foreign countries whose practices it objects to rather than trusting to the slower efforts to reach international agreements.[35] A similar process is at work in dealing with foreign practices that hamper American service industries. Closely related are the efforts to deal with specific segments of trade, such as the numerous and complex negotiations with Japan over high-technology industries. Sometimes these all come together, as when the United States and Japan negotiate the opening of government contracts to American firms in communications, market shares in semiconductors, and whether certain Japanese practices amount to subsidies that will be countervailed against and others not.

In dealing with other countries as well, Americans are tempted to play tit-for-tat with regulations and nontariff barriers and, since equal access can be difficult to judge, there is a tendency to suppose it does not exist unless trade is nearly in balance. U.S. fair trade actions often end up with arrangements specifying the volume or price of imports from individual foreign countries and these may differ considerably from one nation to another. Private business arrangements can have their own forms of discrimination and bilateralism when, for instance, American firms agree to produce certain things in certain countries (and sometimes to export them) for the sake of sales or permission to invest. Countertrade takes many forms, some akin to barter and most with some bilateral elements.

Coloring all these factors is a concern with reciprocity. Perhaps Richard Snyder went too far when he said "Reciprocity is substantive bilateralism,"[36] but it is certainly true that there is a push in that direction. This was apparent in 1934 when it had to be demonstrated that to exchange pledges of unconditional MFN was as much reciprocity as to fall back on barter. In the 1980s the focus of reciprocity is either on major segments of unbalanced trade, or on the specifics of how other countries treat the United States through nontariff barriers. The American approach is colored by the view that the American market is the most open in the world, which leads to the conviction that there is no true reciprocity between the United States and most of the rest of the world, and especially its allies among the other industrial nations. In economic relations a special version of this attitude is the belief that in many foreign countries the government, directly and through its help to business, creates extensive unfair competition that American companies cannot be expected to deal with by themselves. The primary response comes through U.S. fair trade laws. In part these are a substitute for effective international codes on subsidies and other matters. The result is the imposition of a unilateral American definition of what is unfair, instead of the application of an international standard and the use of a multilateral mechanism in settling disputes. The outcome is often not reciprocity in any meaningful sense, but rather a restriction on trade accepted by the other country as less damaging than further unilateral American action.

The sense of unfairness and lack of reciprocity goes beyond trade, however. Ever since the late 1960s many Americans have felt that other countries—particularly Western Europe and Japan—were not contributing as much to international security and political stability as was the

United States. This was reflected in the measures taken by Connally and Nixon in 1971, and has not been far below the surface ever since. It reappears in different forms quite frequently. It affects trade and other economic measures of the sort mentioned above. It increases the pressure on American officials and politicians to appear tough and aggressive in pursuit of American interests (which are usually rather narrowly conceived). The demand for reciprocity from others pushes aside concern for what sound like abstract, old-fashioned, nice nelly-isms such as "equal treatment." The argument from economic self-interest—that equal treatment encourages the most efficient use of resources—carries little weight when people believe that world trade and production are already distorted by government interventions and the abuse of market power by private and public bodies.

All this does not add up to the conclusion that the United States has "gone bilateral" in its foreign trade policy (or practice). There are elements of such a development. In addition to those cited (whose full impact is hard to judge without much closer study than I know of), there is the formal bilateralism which is inescapable when going after problems that exist in some countries and not others. To get satisfaction for American interests inevitably becomes the first objective; to reconcile it with strict regard for rules of equal treatment is almost bound to be a secondary concern. If another country, perhaps a weaker one, discriminates in favour of the United States to create what Americans consider fair or equal conditions, the United States is not likely to complain (in spite of what the Tariff Commission said in 1919 about not asking special favors or "securing discrimination in its favor").

In principle, though, the United States still stands strongly for nondiscrimination. It is neither surprising nor fatal that more emphasis should be put on the treatment of American products in foreign markets than on how the United States treats foreign activities. Challenges from abroad about equal treatment have to be met if they cannot be turned away with *tu quoque*. Almost certainly, the traditional American support for equal treatment is not as firmly based as it used to be. It could once be said with confidence that such a policy served the national interest because American industry could take care of itself and in fact could thrive in fair competition. This is still said—but is it believed?

A more encouraging line of inquiry is whether in the pursuit of national economic interests—which are increasingly understood to be worldwide—the United States might not be led to a reappraisal of the value of equal treatment and its complex relationship with multilateralism. Are there perhaps some kinds of bilateral agreements that will do more to reduce trade barriers and minimize disputes more effectively than multilateral agreements are likely to, at least for the time being? This has become an interesting—and very real—question in Canadian-American relations, as the following chapters will show.

Canada and the United States

The deterioration of the multilateral trading system played a part in bringing about the Canadian-American bilateral negotiations for a free trade area (or something like it). The idea was not a new one. There were reciprocal arrangements in the nineteenth century that were eventually dropped as both countries moved toward the higher tariff protection which they associated with their economic development. In 1911 a reciprocal agreement was reached, but it never came into effect because the Canadian government fell, and largely on that issue. Canada's participation in the Ottawa Agreements of 1932 which strengthened Imperial Preference gave the United States a natural target—to reduce the discrimination that put American exports at a disadvantage in Canada compared with goods coming from Britain. A step in that direction was achieved in the trade agreements of 1936 and 1938. The war brought many kinds of cooperation between Canada and the United States. There were those in both countries who saw the Hyde Park Agreement of 1941 as "a calculated step towards economic integration," but Canadian officials pulled back their prime minister when he leaned too far in that direction. They saw it as "a functional agreement," and did not read as much into it as Mackenzie King, who told the House of Commons that Canada and the United States were "laying the foundations of a new world order."[37] Just after the war it was King who put an end to the negotiations in which Canadian and American officials had worked out an all-but-complete plan for free trade between the two countries.

There are some interesting might-have-beens in this experience. If the 1911 agreement had succeeded, would the Tariff Commission have taken a different view of equal treatment in its 1919 Report? Would the rest of the world have accepted the Canadian-American agreement as an unquestionable exception to most-favored-nation treatment because, as Americans argued, "It is impossible for any country . . . which is not contiguous to the United States, to duplicate the conditions of economic relationship with the United States that are offered by Canada?"[38] And in the late forties, what difference would it have made if the United States and Canada had announced the formation of a free trade area before GATT, or the ITO Charter, was put into final form? Alternatively, what mix of bilateralism, plurilateralism and multilateralism might have developed within the GATT framework if a Canadian-American agreement had been the first test of Article XXIV?

The GATT world, with its emphasis on reducing trade barriers and working out cooperative, multilateral relations among sovereign countries, seemed most attractive to Canada. As its relations with Britain and the United States changed, it was looking for opportunities to make its independent place in the world. Heavily dependent on international trade and finance, not well-positioned for regional integration since its neighbor was so much larger, Canada was a natural supporter (and one of the architects) of GATT. The General Agreement offered Canada some elbow room and provided rules and procedures which went at least some distance toward limiting the use strong countries might make of their power. These were real advantages for a country that saw itself as an emerging middle power next door to a superpower with an economy ten times as large.

Canada benefitted considerably from the opening of world trade that took place with GATT's help. It was granted certain accommodations: it was the only major country to have a flexible exchange rate for many years; its tariffs, even after the Kennedy Round, were somewhat higher than those of most industrial countries. The creation of the Common Market in Europe bothered many Canadians; Britain's entry caused more worry than material damage. The multilateral system allowed Canada to develop useful economic relations with many parts of the world (it carried on trade with China while the United States had no relations with that country).

Still, the American place in the Canadian economy grew. Some of this came from the growth of American direct investment in Canada in all fields. The provinces and private firms borrowed heavily in New York, individual Canadians invested there as well. The American demand for Canadian raw materials grew. As Canadians became wealthier, they imported more from the United States. Trade barriers were reduced in a variety of ways: through negotiations in successive GATT rounds between the two countries, and as the result of the working of MFN; by bilateral agreements on automobiles and defense production; and some through unilateral action in both countries. Most of the trade between the two countries became free of tariffs; much of the rest moved at low rates of duty. A significant amount of trade was among closely affiliated enterprises, usually American owned.

To some it appeared as though there was almost a *de facto* Canadian-American free trade area. However, there was also another side to the story. The largest formal action to remove tariffs on a segment of trade between the two countries—the Automotive Pact of 1965—was not the result of a drive to free trade; it was a consequence of an effort to avoid a serious dispute over subsidized exports of Canadian automobiles to the United States. As tariffs fell away, other practices were seen as creating other kinds of trade distortion, whether they were intended to or not. What Canadians considered a subsidy to encourage regional development looked to Americans like a subsidization of tire exports to the United States. An American tax measure which was designed to cope with similar European practices was successfully challenged by Canada in GATT.

The close economic relations between the two countries created political and psychological problems, and often generated friction. In the 1960s, when the Kennedy administration's measures to improve the balance of payments threatened to damage Canada, arrangements were made to exempt that country. Such "exceptionalism" made some Canadians uneasy since it underscored their country's dependence on the United States, but the material advantages carried the day, at least as far as the Canadian government was concerned. In 1971 the harsh monetary and trade measures of the Nixon administration initially included no exceptions for Canada, and indeed Secretary of the Treasury Connally produced a so-called "laundry list" of demands on the Canadians. Later, Ottawa's regulation of investment and its measures to foster Canadian ownership and control in energy and publishing brought complaints from Americans. Disputes piled up during the difficult 1970s and while they were kept more or less under control, they had to be dealt with *ad hoc* as there was no general understanding—beyond GATT obligations—regarding the U.S.–Canada economic relationship. In spite of it all, the processes of integration continued, adding to the denseness and complexity of economic ties between the two countries.

All through the sixties and seventies many Canadians weighed the pros and cons of establishing closer trade relations with the United States, usually through some form of "free trade area." There was little comparable activity in the United States, except for the work of Sperry Lea under the auspices of the binational Canadian-American Committee; he produced not only studies, but a draft agreement. In Canada, the Private Planning Association sponsored a multivolume study; the Economic Council put out a major report; a committee of the Senate held hearings over several years and made three reports; and a number of individual scholars wrote books and articles. Almost all of these efforts came to the conclusion that there were economic advantages to Canada of more open and lasting trading arrangements with the

United States. Some stressed the need to reorganize much of the Canadian economy in order to meet new standards of international competitiveness, which would require regular access to a larger market. Others emphasized the danger that American import restrictions would hurt Canada, even if they were not directed primarily at that country. Rodney Grey, a former trade official, made incisive analyses of American "contingent protection"—mostly through the fair trade laws—and showed how it would bear especially heavily on Canada.[39] All this work stirred attention, but led to no action by the government. The basic pattern was the same as it had been in earlier years: some Canadians became persuaded of the advantages of negotiating a free trade arrangement with the United States, and then other Canadians rejected the idea on the grounds that it would result in American dominance, Canadian economic decline and, perhaps, the political and cultural absorption of the nation.

It was not until 1983 that a Canadian government proposed a serious discussion of the subject with the United States. The American government had, through all of this, quite sensibly stood still and waited. Any American initiative was bound to stir fears and incite the opposition of those Canadians who believed the national interest required resistance to any tightening of the already close—they would say overly close—ties with the United States. The Trudeau government proposed in 1983 the exploration of measures to free trade in certain industries, or sectors. Naturally, the Americans added some others. The piecemeal approach made it difficult to strike balanced bargains and to generate broad support, but it also had the advantage of permitting progress where agreement could be reached even if other sectors could not be touched. Before the possibilities could be tested, a Canadian election brought into office a party that seemed to have closer ties with business than the former Liberal government. This seemed likely to further the negotiations because it appeared that much of Canadian business had come to favor something like a free trade area. Nevertheless, it took the Mulroney government some time to decide what to do. Then, in 1985, it said it wanted to work toward a comprehensive understanding. Terminology varied, as to free, or freer, or enhanced trade, but negotiations began in 1986.[40]

These are the negotiations which were going on as the study group at the Council on Foreign Relations discussed the issues dealt with in this book. Inevitably, a number of key problems confronting the Canadian and American negotiators found their way into the discussion and into the pages that follow. We do not try, however, to analyze most of them or judge the merits of particular proposals and rejections. Our focus is on the relationship between this set of bilateral negotiations and its possible results for both the future trade policies of the two countries and the multilateral trading system, which Canada and the United States have both done so much to build and which has deteriorated drastically in recent years. This introductory chapter concludes by posing in broad terms some of the basic policy questions that are then explored and discussed from various points of view in the four chapters that follow. The answers, such as they are, may be found in the traditional place, in the back of the book, in the final chapter.

Alternative Approaches and Key Questions

In their public statements, the two governments—and most of the supporters of the free trade area idea as well—have spoken as if there were almost no question that a successful negotiation would produce an arrangement compatible with Article XXIV of GATT (concerning free trade areas and customs unions). They have, indeed, acted as if there were nothing much to think about. This might be taken as a cynical view reflecting the belief that "anything is GATTable," because either the terms of the General Agreement have been stretched so far that they exercise no restraint, or the objections of other countries can be ignored or overcome. In either event there would still be serious questions about the effect of the bilateral agreement on the multilateral system.

At the other extreme, the "no problem" attitude can hardly mean that Canada and the United States will be so heedful of the niceties of multilateral standards that they will leave troublesome problems between them to fester, simply because solutions that are otherwise acceptable would offend the international rules. The rules are, after all, not that rigid and GATT does provide for the possibility of a waiver of the rules when cases warrant. A waiver was requested and granted to the United States in connection with the 1965 Automotive Pact (Canada did not need one because of the form of its undertakings). But to ask for a waiver rather than claim that an agreement fits the provisions of Article XXIV raises still further questions.

Most likely, when the two governments pass lightly over the GATT issues it is because they want to deal with first things first, that is, to discover what they can agree about. Whether this is a wise course or not we need not judge, any more than we shall argue in this book about the merits of most of the issues on the negotiating agenda. For our purposes, it is enough to hold that it cannot be taken for granted that there are no issues worth discussing regarding the relationship of the bilateral agreement to the multilateral system. If this chapter has shown anything, it is that the relationship between bilateral and multilateral elements in the trading system is not simple, or clear-cut, or inalterable.

With the multilateral trading system in its current state of deterioration—and with other major partners, like the EC and Japan, presenting problems that do nothing to stop the erosion—one could easily justify Canada and the United States going about the business of working out a new bilateral relationship while leaving the consequences for the international trading system to be tended to later. There are certainly people in both countries who hold this view, those in the United States being more vocal. However, there is really not much to be said for such an approach unless one has determined that American (and Canadian) trade policy should pursue very different objectives from those of the past. There is a case for that view, but it poses troublesome issues and calls for lines of inquiry that do not start with the Canadian-American relationship (at least for the United States).

At the opposite extreme is the view that Canada and the United States could arrive at a bilateral understanding that would actually strengthen the multilateral system. At first glance this may sound hopelessly idealistic but, as it turns out, a number of well-informed people take the possibility quite seriously. It gets a good deal of attention in the chapters that follow. No one suggests that the only reason the two countries should work out a bilateral agreement is to strengthen the multilateral system, but if that can be accomplished while also solving—or at least mitigating—bilateral problems, new dimensions are added to familiar arguments.

There are, then, two groups of questions that must be asked about any bilateral agreement. First, there are those concerning its compatibility with the multilateral system or the costs versus advantages of certain kinds of incompatibility. Second, there are the intriguing questions of whether there are ways of improving the multilateral system through bilateral action. Each set of questions must be applied to at least three different parts of a potential agreement.

The questions about compatibility with Article XXIV of GATT concern the amount of trade that is covered, the durability and timing of the agreement and, what is of special importance for the Canadian-American relationship, which sectors can safely be omitted, such as agriculture and the so-called "cultural industries." There is more to GATT, though, than Article XXIV. Clearly a dispute-settlement arrangement is crucial to the bilateral agreement; the term probably conceals the breadth of issues that may have to be taken up through it.

How will it relate to the dispute-settlement procedure of GATT, which is both one of the most controversial and important parts of that agreement and one which is likely to be focus of attention in the Uruguay Round? Will Canada or the United States be giving up any of their GATT rights by accepting a bilateral dispute-settlement agreement?

Of crucial importance to the bilateral agreement, and unclear in relation to Article XXIV, are matters concerning subsidies, government procurement and other nontariff barriers, and fair trade generally. The equal treatment commitments of GATT have not been dissolved by the creation of codes in some of these fields; but where matters stand and how Article XXIV applies is far from certain. If the bilateral agreement goes well beyond the subsidies code in defining acceptable and unacceptable practices, for example, can this remain a bilateral matter or will other GATT signatories have rights to the same treatment? If so, will either Canada or the United States be unwilling to agree to an otherwise acceptable bilateral bargain?

Then there are the new areas: agreements on services; intellectual property; and the touchy matter of investment, even if only trade-related investment matters are taken up. These are fields in which GATT has few or no rules, therefore (it is assumed, but may not be so) there are few Article XXIV issues. One wonders, though, whether good lawyers might not be able to find ways to apply the unconditional MFN pledge. Even if not, one must question whether it makes any sense to think of arrangements in these new fields simply in bilateral terms. Both Canada and the United States have such problems with other countries and they are partly covered by the GATT codes. So what should be done bilaterally, and what multilaterally? Could Canadian-American arrangements become models for other countries? Could the bilateral agreements be opened to other countries later on when they are ready to go as far as the pioneers?

Similar questions can be asked about agreements on nontariff barriers and fair trade. Would the bilateral arrangements be seen as expanding the GATT codes so that others could join in? Bilateral agreements would not simply be models; they would give other countries an incentive to get the same benefits (as might be true of tariffs as well). Should that happen, a new set of questions arises. Do the terms of the agreement apply easily to the new applicant, or are we faced with the traditional problem of conditional MFN? Will the two original partners be happy to extend to a third country the same treatment they laboriously worked out between themselves? What happens if one is willing and the other not? What if the third country is only interested in one bilateral agreement, say the one on subsidies? Would the two original partners be willing to consider that agreement in isolation, especially if it was acceptable in the first place only as part of the overall package? Might it turn out that for Canada and the United States, or for one of them, the real advantage of the bilateral agreement is the preferred position gained in the partner's market compared to the position of Europe, Japan, or some other supplier?

These last questions open the door to another issue that has been rather glibly spoken of, but rarely analyzed. To be truly liberalizing, it has been said, a bilateral agreement should be open-ended so that other countries can accede to it on the same terms. But what do "the same terms" mean if there are important differences among the countries' economic practices? All the questions about what was acceptable bilaterally and perhaps not more widely reappear here. Who will decide what is a fair *quid pro quo*? The views of the two original parties may be quite different; one may have a much stronger interest than the other in closer relations with the third country. The greater weight of the larger original party is going to be obvious to Canadians if not to Americans. Which of the many possible third partners is most, or least, acceptable—Mexico, Japan or the European Community, for instance?

One cannot answer these questions without a view of what the long-run American trade policy should be. Does a bilateral agreement with Canada push the United States toward the bilateralism that began to show itself in the early 1980s? Can something so special be a precedent? Does any movement in that direction help break down the already weakened case for the classical multilateral, unconditional MFN formula?

Another set of questions concerns Canada. These the book does not take up in any detail, as it is basically a study of American trade policy; but some of the questions are inescapable. As this is written, no one knows whether the agreement reached in October 1987 will be accepted by the two countries. It could be turned down, in the classic pattern, by Canadians who are against the whole idea. Or this time the United States might be, in one way or another, the naysayer. In either case, what would follow in bilateral or multilateral relations?

There are also less clean-cut issues. For Canada to have broached the possibility of a bilateral agreement was a most important act. Not all Canadians support it and many of those that do have reservations on certain points. The persistence of division among Canadians after an agreement was negotiated would affect its operation and, ultimately, its meaning. Of special importance for this book is the question of whether the Canadian decision to seek the agreement was a reversal of the traditional preference for multilateral arrangements that was based on both economic interests and the wish to avoid being left too much alone with the United States. It can be argued that there is no real reversal because the bilateral agreement strengthens the multilateral system. This might seem to be an exclusively Canadian issue, but it is not. The assessment of Canadians on these matters will influence the shape of the agreement, its operation, its durability, and how adaptable it is to changing circumstances. Moreover, the United States could make serious mistakes if it did not correctly understand the attitude of its partner.

Canadians can turn the tables and ask what assurance there is of a sustained American interest in the bilateral arrangement. Perhaps even more serious is whether the workings of the unpredictable American system will always impose conditions on the smaller partner. There are no clear answers to these questions but they are real and inescapable, so they will be asked, if not answered as we proceed.

There are also questions about the connection between the bilateral agreement and the activities of Canada and the United States in the multilateral trade negotiations with the rest of the world in the Uruguay Round. It is quite possible that some of the issues described above in what may seem rather academic terms will appear in one form or another on the daily agenda of the negotiators. Even if we were to reach relatively clear answers to some of the questions, they might provide only general guidance as to what ought to be done. It is attractive to let one's imagination play over the possibilities, but serious discussion is difficult. Such matters are, by their nature, partly tactical and contingent. The contingencies are numerous and are usually surrounded by uncertainty, especially concerning the motives of third countries, but also with respect to the consequences of what appeared to be *faits accomplis* when the bilateral agreement was adopted. Even then there may well be unfinished bilateral business. It may prove necessary to consider the risks that somehow the multilateral trade negotiations could tempt Canada or the United States to draw back from the active pursuit of the bilateral arrangement. In any case, the unfinished business of the bilateral agreement is bound to affect, and be affected by, the future course of the multilateral negotiations.

It follows, that our basic theme, how a bilateral agreement between two major trading countries will affect the multilateral trading system, always in flux and currently perhaps approaching a crisis, is best looked at as a somewhat long-term prospect.

Notes

1. Jacob Viner used the term plurilateral for agreements that were not limited to countries with some special affinity—geographical or otherwise—and that were open to adherence by others. For him the term was interchangeable with "multilateral" and, indeed, GATT would fit the definition. Such agreements claimed exemption from MFN not because, like regional arrangements, they had a narrow territorial limitation, but because of the "wide and potentially even unlimited territorial scope." Jacob Viner, *The Customs Union Issue* (New York: Carnegie Endowment for International Peace, 1950), pp. 21, 22.

2. The exchange rate between the Canadian and American dollars, and how future changes will take place, are matters that have a bearing on the acceptability and operation of the bilateral trade agreement, but are unlikely to be dealt with in it.

3. Richard C. Snyder, *The Most-Favored-Nation Clause* (New York: King's Crown, 1948), pp. 34, 214.

4. U.S. Tariff Commission, *Summary of the Report on Reciprocity and Commercial Treaties* (Washington: Government Printing Office, 1919), p. 8. Other quotations come from this source. There is a good summary of the history of MFN in Hugh O. Davis, *America's Trade Equality Policy* (Washington: American Council on Public Affairs, 1942). The language of the 1778 treaty with France was lapidary on conditionality. If either country granted "any particular Favour to other Nations in respect of Commerce and Navigation" it should "immediately become common to the other Party, who shall enjoy the same Favour, freely, if the Concession was freely made, or on allowing the same Compensation, if the Concession was Conditional." Even so, there were disputes about the meaning. Text from Davis, p. 7.

5. The quotation comes from Culbertson's introduction to Davis, *America's Trade Equality Policy, op. cit.* See also William Culbertson, *Reciprocity, A National Policy for Foreign Trade* (New York: Whittlesey, 1937), Appendix 6, p. 34.

6. Jacob Viner, "The Most-Favored-Nation Clause in American Commercial Treaties," originally published in *The Journal of Political Economy*, vol. 32 (February 1924); reprinted in *International Economics* (Glencoe, Illinois: Free Press, 1954), p. 25.

7. Frank W. Taussig, "Necessary Changes in our Commercial Policy," *Foreign Affairs*, vol. 11, no. 3 (April 1933), pp. 397–405. Other quotations come from this article.

8. I have a sense that Taussig or the editors may have made some late changes in the text, perhaps in response to news coming out of Washington, without pulling everything together.

9. Frank W. Taussig, "Reciprocity," *Quarterly Journal of Economics*, 1892; reprinted in *Free Trade, the Tariff and Reciprocity* (New York: MacMillan, 1920).

10. Cordell Hull, *The Memoirs of Cordell Hull, Vol. I* (New York: Macmillan, 1948), p. 356. I am grateful to I.M. Destler for calling my attention to this passage when I once said that Hull had no interest in multilateral measures.

11. William Diebold, Jr., *New Directions in Our Trade Policy* (New York: Council on Foreign Relations, 1941), p. 19.

12. John W. Evans, *The Kennedy Round in American Trade Policy* (Cambridge, Ma: Harvard University Press, 1971), p. 7.

13. Manuel Fox, a member of the Tariff Commission, said in 1940, "Not more than 3 percent of our imports from Japan have received the benefit of concessions granted in the trade agreements." Quoted in Diebold, *New Directions in Our Trade Policy, op. cit.*, p. 80. There was a protectionist element in this reclassification, but it should be remembered that in those days Japan's biggest export by far to the United States was raw silk (nearly two-thirds of 1938 imports) and it was on the free list. The extent to which Japan was the target of tariff reclassification in the agreement with Britain is detailed in Carl Kreider, *The Anglo-American Trade Agreement* (Princeton: Princeton University Press, 1943), pp. 212–18, 254, 255.

14. The British agreement covered the colonies and Newfoundland as well as the United Kingdom. London conferred with the Dominions about the terms of the American negotiations. Australia and Canada gave explicit go-ahead signals. In the first Canadian agreement the United States reduced the tariff on whisky even though Britain was the principal supplier. (It is not clear to me why this was not a justification for tariff reclassification so as to differentiate rye from scotch.) See Kreider, *The Anglo-American Trade Agreement, op. cit.*, pp. 39–41, 104–7. Writing before the agreement was signed, Percy W. Bidwell also stressed the Commonwealth dimension, saying that the agreement would involve "not a single bargain, but a series of bargains with a federation of self-governing states." See Percy W. Bidwell, *Our Trade with Britain* (New York: Council on Foreign Relations, 1938), p. 96.

15. Henry J. Tasca, *World Trading Systems: A Study of American and British Commercial Policies* (Paris: Institute of Intellectual Co-Operation, 1939), pp. 152, 157.

16. The last few sentences have been borrowed with some editing from a paper in which I have discussed some of these issues in a wider setting. See William Diebold, Jr., "The United States in the World Economy: A Fifty Year Perspective," *Foreign Affairs*, vol. 62, no. 1 (Fall 1983), p. 84.

17. Gilbert R. Winham, *International Trade and the Tokyo Round Negotiation* (Princeton: Princeton University Press, 1986), p. 386.

18. Archives of the Council on Foreign Relations. Studies of the American Interests in the War and the Peace. Economic and Financial Series. Digest of Discussion, 55th meeting, April 29, 1944. EA 55, pp. 3, 4. (Mimeographed.) Summary of discussion by Arthur D. Gayer.

19. I have simplified matters by leaving out other provisions of the various proposals. The whole story is told by Clair Wilcox, *A Charter for World Trade* (New York: MacMillan, 1949), pp. 161–64.

20. John Jackson surmised that "relatively few Latin-American countries have become members of GATT" because through "an MFN bilateral treaty with its principal trading partner"—the United States—a country "obtains most of the advantages of GATT without granting anything to those GATT members with which it has no trade agreement." John Jackson, *World Trade and the Law of GATT* (Indianapolis: Bobbs-Merrill, 1969), p. 258.

21. Viner, *The Customs Union Issue, op. cit.*, p. 127.

22. Howard Ellis, "Bilateralism and the Future of International Trade," originally a Princeton Essay in International Finance, reprinted in the American Economic Association's *Readings in the Theory of International Trade* (Philadelphia: Blakiston, 1950). His definition was that "a trading arrangement is bilateral when it involves an effort to achieve a predetermined quantitative ratio of the exports of country A to country B to the exports of country B to country A." Thus the capacity of the smaller trade flow set the limit.

23. Gardner Patterson and Judd Polk, "The Emerging Pattern of Bilateralism," *The Quarterly Journal of Economics*, vol. 62 (November 1947), pp. 118–42.

24. Ragnar Frisch, "On the Need for Forecasting a Multilateral Balance of Payments," *The American Economic Review*, vol. 37 (September 1947), pp. 535–51.

25. Charles P. Kindleberger, "European Economic Integration," originally written for a *Festschrift* for John H. Williams published in 1951, reprinted in Charles P. Kindleberger, *Marshall Plan Days* (Boston: Allen & Unwin, 1987), p. 59.

26. These sentences unduly compress and oversimplify the carefully balanced conclusions reached in a detailed and realistic analysis by Gardner Patterson, *Discrimination in International Trade: The Policy Issues, 1945–1965* (Princeton: Princeton University Press, 1966), especially pp. 60–66, 110–13.

27. Patterson, *Discrimination in International Trade, op. cit.*, p. 385.

28. Evans, *The Kennedy Round, op. cit.*, p. 318 ff.

29. Snyder, *The Most-Favored-Nation Clause, op. cit.*, pp. 214, 215.

30. Atlantic Council of the United States, Trade Committee, Special Advisory Panel, *GATT Plus: A Proposal for Trade Reform* (New York: Praeger, 1976).

31. We pointed out that the same kind of consideration applied to the way in which bilateral agreements to settle disputes before the GATT procedure had run its course could affect the interests of third countries. Miriam Camps and William Diebold, Jr., *The New Multilateralism* (New York: Council on Foreign Relations, 1983 and 1986), pp. 28, 49–56 in 1983 edition and pp. 44, 65–72 in the 1986 edition.

32. *Trade Policies for a Better Future*, GATT, March 1985, p. 47.

33. See Camps and Diebold, *The New Multilateralism, op.cit.*, and Diebold, "The United States in the World Economy," *Foreign Affairs, op. cit.* Although Aho and Aronson convey a more optimistic impression, their clear explanations

of the complexity of the issues to be faced, the difficulties each major negotiating country has in dealing with them, and the length of time it is likely to take to achieve very much, all seem to me to do a good bit to confirm the earlier assessments. "These negotiations could last a decade and could take on the appearance of being continuous and never-ending." C. Michael Aho and Jonathan D. Aronson, *Trade Talks: America Better Listen!* (New York: Council on Foreign Relations, 1985 and 1987) p. 135.

34. See Murray Smith's chapter herein.
35. The debate about bilateral and multilateral approaches is very well summa-
    · rized in Helena Stalson, *Intellectual Property Rights and U.S. Competitiveness in Trade* (Washington: National Planning Association, Committee on Changing International Realities, 1987).
36. Snyder, *The Most-Favored-Nation Clause, op. cit.,* p. 215.
37. The quotations are from John W. Holmes, *The Shaping of Peace: Canada and the Search for a World Order 1943–1957,* Vol. I (Toronto: University of Toronto Press, 1979), p. 166. Holmes quotes other Canadians and Americans and gives a revealing account of this and other wartime relations as they affected thinking in Canada.
38. The words are those of Congressmen McCall of Massachusetts, as quoted by Davis, *America's Trade Equality Policy, op. cit.,* pp. 102, 103, who says they are "typical of the American discussion . . . " Snyder, writing much later and as a scholar takes much the same view, without reference to the 1911 issue. See Snyder, *The Most-Favored-Nation Clause, op. cit.,* p. 192.
39. Rodney de C. Grey, *Trade Policy in the 1980s: An Agenda for Canadian–U.S. Relations* (Montreal: C.D. Howe Institute, 1981), and *United States Trade Policy Legislation: A Canadian View* (Montreal: The Institute for Research on Public Policy, 1982).
40. A number of passages in the last seven paragraphs have been taken, with some editing, from earlier writings of mine. These are, principally, *The United States and the Industrial World* (Praeger for the Council on Foreign Relations: New York, 1972), Ch. 4; *Canadian-American Relations in a Changing World Economy* (Center for International Relations, University of Toronto, 1979), a lecture given in Toronto in January 1979; "Canada and the United States: Twenty-five Years of Economic Relations," *International Journal* (Toronto), (Spring 1984); "U.S.–Canada Free Trade: An American View," in John Whalley, ed., *Canada–United States Free Trade* (Toronto: University of Toronto Press, 1985), a paper prepared for a conference sponsored by the MacDonald Commission in October 1983.

2

Why Canada Acted

GILBERT R. WINHAM

I N TAKING THE INITIATIVE for trade talks with the United States, the
Canadian government seems to have departed from its traditional
preference for multilateralism. Since World War II, Canada has
followed a multilateral policy both in its security relations and in its
international trade policies. In the former sphere, Canadian policies
supported collective security and the North Atlantic Treaty Organization (NATO); in the latter sphere, the preference was for multilateral
trade liberalization under the General Agreement for Tariffs and Trade
(GATT). Canada rejected the notion of closer economic relations with
other countries (especially with the United Staes) along the lines char-
ted by the Common Market in Europe, and it explicitly tried to diversify
its economic relationships with the "Third Option Policy" of the Trudeau years. The attempt to negotiate a bilateral free trade agreement
with the United States appears to be a sharp reversal of recent Canadian policy. Why has this occurred?

To respond to this question, this chapter will first briefly survey the
background of Canada–U.S. economic relations, particularly since the
Canadian bilateral initiative has its precedent in the past. Second, I will
examine the reasons behind Canada's bilateral initiative, taking into
account both the historical and the contemporary factors which motivated the policy. Finally, this chapter will consider some probable
implications of the Canadian bilateral initiative.

Background

Free trade is not a new issue in Canada–U.S. relations. A review of the
history of this issue reveals a great deal about the broader relationship

between Canada and the United States, and also about some of the problems faced in the negotiation.

In the past, free trade has been understood in Canada to mean "reciprocity."[1] The historical meaning of the term differs from the way it has recently been used in the U.S. Congress, where it carries the implication of retaliation for unfair treatment of U.S. exports. The earliest embodiment of reciprocity between Canada and the United States was the Reciprocity Treaty of 1854. It is instructive to note that while this treaty was concluded because of Canadian insistence, the reason for the Canadian initiative was a previous action by the British government withdrawing the trade preferences Canada enjoyed in the mother country. In modern times, a similar reaction against Britain's decision to join the Common Market was a determining factor in Canada's increasing attention to the North American economic relationship.

The negotiations for the Reciprocity Treaty took eight years, and the Canadian government found it difficult to arouse much interest in the United States. But Canadian persistence paid off, and a limited treaty covering only natural products was finally concluded. Trade flourished under this agreement, although there were numerous complaints from both sides about violations of the accord. In 1866 the United States unilaterally abrogated the treaty, in part because of certain tariff increases on manufactured goods in Canada which were not covered by the treaty, but mostly because of ill-feeling generated toward Canada during the Civil War. This action left an unfortunate legacy in Canada. Today, even at the highest levels, there are still occasional doubts about whether the United States can be relied upon to carry through an economic treaty with Canada. The fact that Canadians know their country is not a major factor in the U.S. economy makes these doubts all the more difficult to dispel.

The treaty period coincided with an economic boom in Canada, which was probably due more to a natural upturn of the business cycle than to the effects of reciprocity. Nevertheless, the period was remembered warmly in Canada, so the government made a new attempt to negotiate a similar agreement in 1874. This initiative enjoyed wide support in Canada, but again there was little interest in the United States.[2] As a consequence, five years later, a new government under Sir John A. MacDonald brought in the National Policy of 1879 on a strong wave of nationalism and protectionism. The policy was intended to promote manufacturing in Canada, and it was a conscious reaction to the U.S. rejection of efforts at free trade. Indeed, the policy was in part aimed at the United States, for MacDonald argued that it was only by closing Canadian doors to trade that the United States would be induced to accept reciprocity with Canada. As these events are viewed from the modern perspective, it is important to recognize that Canada—which today is a high-tariff country among the Organization for Economic Cooperation and Development (OECD) nations—apparently did not turn to protectionism by choice. Rather it was the absence of an opportunity to establish a more liberal regime with its larger neighbor that started Canada down the road to high protection.[3]

The subsequent history of the National Policy offers nearly a textbook case of the political effects of economic protectionism. Most of Canada's manufacturing sector grew up under this policy, and these interests came to see the trade protectionism of the National Policy as an immutable part of the economic environment. Business supported protectionism, and this politicized the issue of trade in a way that was previously unknown in Canada.[4] The national election of 1891 was fought largely on a Liberal platform calling for "unrestricted reciprocity," and MacDonald, invoking Canadian nationalism and the Empire connection, handily won the contest.

In 1911 reciprocity came up again. This time on a U.S. initiative, a reciprocity agreement had been negotiated by the Laurier government and it became the principal issue in the 1911 election. Manufacturing and financial interests again took strong exception to this plan, and thus became exceptionally active in the campaign. The anti-reciprocity forces made blatant appeals to Canadian nationalism, and to anti-Americanism (then as always a corollary of Canadianism), and these appeals received widespread support. Laurier lost the election to Borden of the Conservatives, and although there were other issues at stake, it was widely regarded as a defeat both for reciprocity and for closer relations with the United States.

Despite these reverses, the Canadian government again made efforts at the ministerial level in 1922 and 1923 to interest the United States in trade negotiations. These made little progress, for the United States was then moving in the direction of more, not less, protectionism. In the 1920s and 1930s little action was taken, except that in 1935 and 1938 Canada and the United States concluded two bilateral agreements pursuant to the Reciprocal Trade Agreements Act of 1934.[5] These agreements were limited to specific tariff reductions and were not reciprocity agreements in the earlier sense; nevertheless, they constituted the first commercial agreements between the two countries since the 1854 Reciprocity Agreement. Finally in 1947–48, on the initiative of the U.S. government, Prime Minister MacKenzie King authorized a secret negotiation of several months duration to draw up a comprehensive free trade agreement. In the end, in part because of uncertainties about the approval process in the United States, King formally decided not to proceed and talks were broken off. This was the last time either country seriously considered a comprehensive bilateral trade agreement.

From this historical summary one can draw several conclusions which are useful for interpreting the current bilateral negotiation. First, caught between the attraction of the U.S. economy on the one hand, and the difficulties of establishing a viable natural economy in Canada on the other hand, successive Canadian governments have returned to the idea of securing a broad-ranging reciprocity agreement with the United States. Admittedly, this idea was less popular with the business community and the public once the protectionism of the National Policy had worked its full effects, but the idea nevertheless remained inviting. One of the important facts about the current initiative is that the Canadian business community, for its own economic reasons, has become far more supportive of the idea than it was even a decade ago. A free trade agreement will still raise nationalist opposition in Canada, but the automatic link between business interests and nationalism seems to have been broken. An important window of opportunity appears to have presented itself on the Canadian side.

A second conclusion is that, with few exceptions, Canadians have found it difficult to arouse enthusiasm in the United States for the idea of reciprocal free trade with Canada. This may have been due to the inherent difficulties of a small state proposing initiatives to a larger partner, or it may have been a matter of inappropriate timing. Nevertheless, the United States has a much larger home market and much less dependence on trade, and an agreement with Canada has apparently not had enough economic value to be worth the administrative and political costs incurred in its negotiation. Today, U.S. indifference is less of a problem, but it is still unclear whether any deal with Canada will be sufficiently attractive to mobilize the necessary support in Congress. The central dilemma is that this is a negotiation between a larger, relatively uninterested party and a smaller highly-interested and inherently conflicted party. As seen from the Canadian side, there is the danger that Canada may have to go a considerable distance in the negotiation to attract interest on the U.S. side; however, if this strategy is carried too far it will certainly risk being counterproductive at home.

A third conclusion from a review of the history of reciprocity talks can be simply stated: in economic terms, and even in political terms, Canadians tend to define themselves in relation to the United States. The U.S. economy is viewed at once as both an enormous attraction as well as a serious threat to Canada, and the same could probably be said for American society in general. All this produces a conflict of purpose, which is compounded by the fact that free trade necessarily incites an enormous dose of Canadian nationalism. As a result, public discussion in Canada often tends to attribute cataclysmic results to trade negotiations which are wholly unrelated to the technical issues involved. Such overstatement is unavoidable, because, for better or worse, this negotiation touches on how Canadians think about themselves. If Canada negotiates a bilateral trade agreement with the United States, it could appear to Canadians and others as a reduction in Canada's stature from an international actor to a regional one. This is important at the symbolic level, and the politics of this issue are bound to be sharp and distracting. If Americans want a domestic analogy to the high politics that this kind of negotiation creates in Canada, they can find it more in their own negotiations of arms control with the Soviets than in any negotiations over foreign trade.

Canada's Initiative

Why did Canada initiate a bilateral trade negotiation with the United States this time? To answer this question, one has to take into account the structure of the country, and its relations both past and present with the United States.

In many respects, Canada's background is like that of the United States. Both countries were settled from abroad and, in the words of American political philosopher Louis Hartz, were "born free." Both countries absorbed immigrants from many different countries; in Canada this left the nation with two founding races and two official languages, and with a regional diversity that in part reflects the settlement patterns of Canada's immigrants. Both the Canadian and American peoples pushed their domain from the Atlantic to the Pacific, and in the process struggled to create an integrated economy and polity from coast to coast. In Canada this process was much more difficult, for against the efforts to integrate the country from East to West there was always the strong pull southward from the large and vital American workplace. And finally, both countries faced and solved problems of democratic government, and evolved similar federal structures coupled with representative governments at the national and regional levels. It is here that the similarities end.

One important historical difference between the two countries is that the United States quickly developed a strong self-sufficient economy, while Canada's domestic economy has always been largely defined by its relationship to the global economic system. There were far fewer people in Canada than in the United States and, as a consequence, they did not create internal markets sufficient for the development of efficient manufacturing. Instead, trade with the "mother countries" of Canada's immigrants and with the industrial centers of Europe and the United States sustained economic activity in Canada, and in turn shaped their domestic demographic patterns and institutions.

Today, the Canadian economy is still heavily influenced by external economic relations, as illustrated by the fact that foreign trade accounts for over 30 percent of Canada's gross national product (GNP).[6] On this dimension, Canada is one of the most trade-dependent of the OECD nations. In contrast, the United States is one of the least trade-dependent of this group. The consequences of these differences have been seen historically in the response of the two countries to hard times.[7] In periods of economic distress, Canadians have tended to look outward to deal with internal problems, and to seek their salvation in international trading relations. On the other hand, the United States could not expect to make major repairs in its economy by external measures. In hard times Americans have been more likely to look inward, and to seek their salvation in the revitalization of the domestic economy. Of course, the position of the United States in economic policy is less independent than it once was, but nevertheless the North American partners remain substantially different in this respect.

A related matter is Canada's history as a hinterland and resource-producing economy. In the colonial period, Canada was situated on the margin of European civilization, and its economic relations with the center were driven by its exports of staples, such as fish, fur, and later, timber and wheat. As the nation grew and technology changed, Canada's minerals and ores were developed for export to more highly industrialized nations. Today Canada is a fully industrialized nation producing a wide range of manufactured goods, but it still has a resource-based economy and its comparative advantage lies in semimanufactured goods fabricated from natural resources. In this respect, Canada has an international economic profile analogous to some of the resource-exporting developing countries, and it has suffered from some of the same problems, such as a high proportion of foreign investment and ownership in the total economy, and uncertainties in the foreign demand for resource-based products. Here, again, are sharp differences between Canada and its larger neighbor, for the manufacturing strength of the United States has made it a more resilient actor in the world economy. Recently the demand for Canada's resource-based exports has been depressed, which has put even more pressure on Canada to increase the competitiveness of its manufacturing sector, and to extend the processing of resource-based products beyond the primary and semi-manufactured stages.

Yet another difference between Canada and the United States is that of the role of the state in the economy. In Canada, governments, both federal and provincial, are important players in the economy, and this affects the bilateral trade negotiation with the United States. What may not be appreciated is the extent to which this role for government is an historical fact. Because Canada traditionally exported raw materials, the Canadian government became intimately engaged in economic activity through providing transportation, finance and other support services. It spent heavily on railroads and canals, and provided large grants and subsidies to support other infrastructural development. Government involvement in the economy began in earliest colonial times with trade in fur and fish, and the pattern reinforced itself with each new staple commodity Canadians produced.

In the United States, things could not have been more different. The American economy, driven by a large domestic market, developed far more independently of the influence of government. Furthermore, American political values came to accept a strict separation between business and government which has no real counterpart in Canadian values. It is often said that Americans trust the market and fear government and that Canadians trust government and fear the market; while this may seem overstated, it does summarize the different historical experience and outlook of the two peoples. Today, involvement of government in the economy has probably gone too far in Canada. To redress this balance is one reason why the Canadian government sought to negotiate bilateral free trade.

One example of the role of government in the economy is in industrial policy. Since Canada's beginning, governments have consciously pursued policies to promote the growth of manufacturing so that Canadians could avoid the condition of being, as it was popularly expressed, "hewers of wood and drawers of water." These policies were not unlike those currently being pursued by governments in the developing countries in South America and elsewhere. In Canada the cornerstone of these efforts was the aforementioned National Policy of 1879. Among other things, this policy instituted a protective tariff for Canadian manufacturing, the main lines of which have never since been fundamentally altered.

Up until this point this chapter has dealt with history, and the extent to which historical factors might have shaped Canada's trade initiative.

There are also factors in Canada's contemporary experience that motivated the government to propose a free trade negotiation with the
United States. First, the role of the government in the economy is now
being sharply questioned in Canada, as well as in other developed
countries. The arguments for less government involvement were laid
out clearly in the recent Report of the Macdonald Royal Commission on
the Economy, which also strongly recommended that Canada negotiate a bilateral free trade agreement with the United States. The commission emphasized the theme of less government as follows: "The
stimulation of competition is key to economic growth and productivity
improvement;" and ". . . we Canadians must significantly increase
our reliance on market forces;" and ". . . we recognize [free trade] as
proposing a fundamental change in the relationship of the state to the
market."[8] What is genuinely intriguing is that although the Commission was ultimately proposing something similar to domestic deregulation, it chose a foreign policy, namely trade policy, as the main instrument by which to achieve its purpose. The Commission stated that
"The National Policy of 1879 (of high tariff protection) has played itself
out" and that "Free trade is the main instrument in the Commission's
approach to industrial policy."[9] The fact that the Macdonald Commission turned to an international solution (and indeed to the United
States) to solve what is essentially a domestic problem is consistent
with the traditional external focus of Canada's political economy.

The report of the Macdonald Commission was embraced by the
Mulroney government because it was in tune with the philosophy and
broader concerns of that government.[10] Likewise, the main policy
recommendation of the Macdonald Commission (that is Canada–U.S.
free trade) became and remains the major economic policy of the
Mulroney government, in part because it is a means to accomplish both
a reduction of the scope of government and a revitalization of the
private sector in Canada. The Mulroney government appears to be
using a negotiation with the United States as a stimulus for domestic
reform, which is increasingly a use to which international negotiation is
being put these days. If one wants an analogy from the current GATT
multilateral trade negotiation to what Canada is doing bilaterally, it
would be in the willingness of the European Community (but not
necessarily the French government) to negotiate agricultural export
subsidies in a new GATT round.

Second, it would appear that for Canada economic relations with the
United States may now be reaching a turning point. Despite the efforts
of the Canadian government to diversify trade in the "Third Option
Policy," Canadian trade has become (through natural forces) more

oriented toward the U.S. market, which now accounts for almost 80 percent of Canada's total exports and well over 70 percent of its imports. This situation, particularly the export concentration, creates a dependency on the U.S. market, and ultimately on the U.S. government which can control access to that market. One great concern is that dependency produces fear and uncertainty in Canada: for example, the fear that in any future U.S. action to restrict imports (such as that of August 1971), Canada's exports might not be spared; or the uncertainty that in the ordinary course of international business, Canada's exports could suddenly become subject to the threat or reality of unfair trade actions taken against them by the United States.

These observations help to explain why Canada has attached such great importance to security of access to the U.S. market. It is probable that a free trade agreement would increase even further the proportion of Canadian trade that goes to the United States. Unless this were accompanied by a greater certainty of access to U.S. markets for Canadian producers, it is unlikely that a deal would be acceptable to Canadians. The Canadian position is that access to the U.S. market has already been "bought and paid for" by participation in past trade liberalization under the GATT, but this access is threatened by U.S. administrative practices of countervailing, antidumping and safeguarding which occur across a range of Canadian exports.[11] Since U.S. unfair trade actions have affected major exports from Canada, such as softwood lumber, these actions are a legitimate economic concern as well as being high politics in Canada.

Concern over U.S. unfair trade actions (or contingency protection, as these actions are called in Canada) emerged as the major issue for Canada in the negotiation. One reason is that several cases arose during the negotiation itself. This creates the impression in public opinion of a Canadian government negotiating to reduce protectionism while an American government takes actions to increase it. The politics of this issue have become more important than the economics, which is often the case with economic negotiations. A related concern on the Canadian side is Congress, which has constitutional authority over international trade, and which is now rife with protectionist sentiment. Congress is an unpredictable force, for Americans as well as Canadians, but this unpredictability has vastly more frightening implications on the Canadian side of the border than on the American side. As a result of this uncertainty, an important objective of the Canadian government is to arrive at an understanding that would lessen the possibility that Canadian interests would be damaged by future actions of Congress.

A third reason why Canada proposed this negotiation is to increase access to the U.S. market in order to help Canada overcome some of the inherent weaknesses of a small, widely-dispersed home market. There are instances where U.S. barriers inhibit full Canadian participation in the North American market, thereby preventing Canadian companies from achieving the efficient large-scale production that is necessary to meet current international competition. Just as freer trade would open the doors to a beneficial competition at home, the Canadian government seeks to ensure that new opportunities are made available for Canadians to sell in the U.S. market.

Canada's manufacturing sector in particular stands in need of new opportunities. Although the Canadian manufacturing sector has fared better than the resource sector, its return on equity is below its average before the 1981/82 recession. Furthermore, the comparative performances of the Canadian and U.S. economies during and after that recession were not encouraging. In Canada, the rate of unemployment was much worse, the decline in inflation was slower, and the rate of recovery was also much weaker.[12]

Additionally, Canadians are now concerned that recent changes in the economy of the United States will make that nation a more competitive partner in the North American relationship. These changes are consistent with the marketplace ideology of the Reagan administration, but their effects go beyond the impact any single administration might expect to have on U.S. society. The United States is moving toward decentralization, deregulation and less unionization. Economic life is shifting from old industries to newer, more entrepreneurial, and more competitive industries. In making U.S. business more competitive, these developments have brought increased pressure on Canadian businesses, such as transportation and telecommunication companies.

In summary, an influential strand of opinion in Canada, including the Mulroney government, believes that the nation will have to develop a more competitive economy simply to continue to enjoy the economic advantages it now has. A secure free trade arrangement with the United States is viewed as the best way to promote Canadian economic development in the future, and incidentally to promote the greater competitiveness that the United States has achieved largely through its own internal actions. By negotiating free trade with the United States, the Canadian government is implicitly prepared to use accommodations to a trading partner abroad as a catalyst to achieve the necessary economic reforms at home.

Implications

As noted earlier, a bilateral trade agreement between Canada and the United States would represent a substantial departure from the multilateral character of Canada's postwar trade policy. A bilateral agreement would have implications for Canada's future trade policy, and more important it could have consequences for multilateral trade relations within the GATT. These consequences are more likely to be of concern to the United States and to third parties in the GATT than they apparently have been to Canadian policymakers.

The basic obligation of the multilateral trading system is Article I of the General Agreement, which requires GATT members to extend unconditional most-favored-nation (MFN) treatment to the trade of all other members. Preferential arrangements are generally prohibited, except (as provided in Article XXIV), where members seek to establish customs unions or free trade areas. Article XXIV sets down conditions for the latter arrangements, the most important of which are that they must cover substantially all trade between the parties, and that they must be achieved within a reasonable length of time. It is assumed that GATT members would demand that any Canada–U.S. agreement must meet the conditions of Article XXIV. (The complete text of Article XXIV appears in the Appendix.)

A Canada–U.S. trade agreement would cover the largest bilateral trade flows in the GATT system, therefore it will probably have some effect on that system. Exactly what the effect would be is a matter of conjecture. In legal terms, the effect would most likely be minimal, since both sides appear to be moving in a direction that would comply with Article XXIV. Even if compliance with Article XXIV were problematic in some areas (that is because of the exclusion of one or more sectors from the agreement), the rules are likely not clear enough to sustain a major challenge to the North American partners. Similarly, in economic terms, a Canada–U.S. agreement may not have great impact because of the already existing concentration of trade between these two countries. More than three-fourths of Canada's trade is with the United States, and much of the remainder is agricultural and primary products (especially wheat) that will be little affected by the agreement. Some distortion of trade could occur on America's exports to Canada, but again it would be a relatively small issue.

The most important effects of a Canada–U.S. trade agreement would be political and symbolic. The United States continues to play a leadership role in the GATT, and it has vigorously supported the values of universality and nondiscrimination in the organization. It has also voiced objections to the expansion of the European Community (EC), and to the preferential ties the Community has established with selected developing countries. By moving to establish a preferential arrangement with its major trading partner, the United States might be seen as contributing to an attack on the universal character of the GATT. Certainly this action would nullify any argument the United States might raise against other nations' attempts in the future to further bilateralize (or plurilateralize) the system.

It should be recalled that the tension between multilateralism and bilateralism is fundamental in the trading system; as one example, this tension has always been implicit in the choice between MFN tariff rates and preferential tariff schedules. There is a cost to multilateralism and MFN rates: namely, that one cannot pursue as discriminating a trade policy as one can through bilateralism or preferential rates. Previously, nations sought to use discriminatory trade policies to achieve protection, and opposition to discrimination went hand-in-hand with opposition to protectionism. Today, however, the purpose of a discriminatory trade policy may be to promote greater liberalism, and an argument currently popular in the U.S. government is that liberalizing agreements should be concluded between whatever nations wish to join them. A Canada–U.S. free trade agreement would be an obvious example of this contemporary policy direction.

Despite the best of intentions in both Canada and the United States, there is a nagging worry that history has shown a relationship between universalism and liberalism on the one hand, and particularism and protectionism on the other. Liberalism is almost never expedient, and once the world is broken up into trading blocs, there is a greater possibility that expedient policy will come to replace principled policy in the relations between groups of trading nations. The GATT experience appears to demonstrate that protectionism, like racism, is best fought on universalistic grounds. It is undeniably true that progress is slower in universalistic fora, but arguably it is also more durable. If the trading world breaks up into regional blocs, it could leave the Canada–U.S. partnership in a worse position in the long run, and particularly vis-a-vis developing countries.

As a middle power, Canada has clearly benefitted from the multilateral nature of the GATT, and as a trading nation it has benefitted from the liberalism that organization has promoted. These facts should make Canada a strong supporter of the GATT. Despite this, there has been apparently little concern in Ottawa about the effects of a Canada–U.S. agreement on the GATT. One reason for Canada's lack of concern is the recognition that other nations (particularly the members of European Community) have been prepared to pursue discriminatory policies when it served their interests. More important, however, the Canadian position is motivated by the hard realities of Canada's trade position. Despite popular ideology to the contrary, Canada is no longer a world trader, but rather a bilateral trading nation with one major partner, the United States. Trade with the United States is not only high, but it also includes the highest value-added products (especially auto products) in Canada's total exports. The United States thus represents a market that Canada would hope to expand in the future. The trade concentration undeniably leaves Canada economically dependent on that country, and it is this fact that has given rise to the "realist" position in Canada in support of a trade agreement with the United States. Given that an economic dependency already exists, it is argued that it is better to secure that dependency with a bilateral political agreement than to leave the U.S. government free to apply multilateral policies to an essentially bilateral trading regime.[13]

A debate between multilateralists and bilateralists has taken place in official circles in Ottawa over the past several years. On the multilateral side, it was argued that the GATT forum was the most compatible with historical Canadian policies; that this forum had helped to expand Canadian trade in the past; and that participation in the current GATT negotiation would be the best way to expand Canada's trade with the United States and other countries. On the bilateral side, the argument was simply that the GATT forum no longer corresponded to Canada's unique trading position, and that trade policy (and trade negotiation) should take its direction from actual trade flows. Bilateralists went so far as to argue that by missing the true nature of Canada's trading position, multilateralism was incapable of producing (or worse, was never intended to produce) a genuine liberalization of Canada's overall trade policy. Both the multilateral and bilateral positions were extensively debated in the Macdonald Commission process, and the bilateralist's position was confirmed in the subsequent report of that Commission. As noted earlier, this position coincided with that of the Mulroney government, and later became official policy.

It is tempting to conclude from Canada's bilateral initiative that it has lost confidence in the GATT, or that it doubts it could obtain improved access to U.S. markets on a nondiscriminatory MFN basis. While there is no indication that the Ottawa trade bureaucracy has officially retreated from the GATT, or that Canadian officials are any more cynical about the GATT process than officials anywhere, it is nevertheless true that multilateral negotiation in the GATT has inherent limitations as a mechanism for achieving Canada's particular trade policy goals. These limitations have more to do with Canada's size than its particular trade structure, and they are also ones which Canada shares with other middle and smaller powers.

Multilateral negotiations in the GATT are a more satisfying arena for large powers than they are for middle or smaller powers. In tariff negotiations, for example, it has long been recognized that it is necessary to give concessions in order to receive concessions from other countries. Nations with large trade volumes normally have a broad range of potential concessions to offer trading partners, while, conversely, nations with smaller volumes have little to bargain with, particularly in their negotiations with other smaller countries. This basic reality is compounded by the GATT practice of negotiating mainly with "principal suppliers" of goods, since there are not many products (especially industrial products) on which middle or smaller countries will be the principal supplier. In negotiations over nontariff measures (NTMs), the correlation between bargaining power and trade volume is less precise; but the main action in the negotiation still occurs first between large powers, and then it is extended to middle and smaller powers after the major issues have already been decided. This is how the Tokyo Round negotiations on the subsidies and customs valuation codes proceeded.[14]

The difficulty Canada has in achieving its commercial policy goals through multilateral negotiation can be seen in several instances drawn from the Tokyo Round. First, Canada entered the Tokyo Round with a demand from its Western-based petrochemical industry to secure a lowering of U.S. tariffs on petrochemical products. This demand was not attained because the trade volumes between the United States and the European Community were higher than those between the United States and Canada. If the United States had lowered its petrochemical duties in negotiations with Canada, it would have been required to extend the same rates to EC products, but the Europeans were not prepared to grant something in return. As a result, Canada was unable to achieve its objectives in this area.[15]

A similar example of immobility occurred on subsidies and countervailing duties. The Canadian delegation invested a great deal of time and expertise in the preliminary period of the subsidies negotiation, but when meaningful talks finally began, the basic tradeoffs were made essentially between the United States and the EC. The result was not that detrimental for Canada, since both Canada and the EC sought the same concession from the United States, that is to introduce a material injury test into U.S. countervailing duty legislation. However, the lesson was similar to that of the tariff negotiation: namely, that multilateral negotiation may not be a good vehicle to achieve directly the goals of Canadian commercial policy, even though those goals might be achieved when they correspond to the objectives of other (especially larger) parties.

Another instance where multilateral negotiation did not seem to serve Canadian commercial policy is paradoxically an area where Canada appeared to be a "winner" in the negotiation. It is well known that when MFN concessions are exchanged between large nations, it creates a possibility for smaller nations to receive unreciprocated benefits. In the competitive environment of trade negotiations, it is expected that negotiators from smaller countries will pocket whatever MFN benefits they can without making reciprocal concessions. Consequently, multilateral negotiations may not be the best vehicle for achieving trade liberalization among middle and smaller countries. There is some evidence that in the Kennedy Round, Canada used its position as a middle trading power to avoid extending full reciprocity to its trading partners.[16] Furthermore, even after the Tokyo Round, where Canada participated more fully in the tariff negotiation than previously, Canada's average duties remained about twice as high as those of the United States. If Canada's current commercial policy goals are to liberalize its tariff structure, as has been argued earlier, it is difficult to see how this could be achieved in further multilateral negotiations under the GATT, given that such negotiations are based on MFN and reciprocity.

In conclusion, Canada's turn toward bilateral negotiation did not imply a rejection of GATT principles or of the GATT as an organization, but rather a recognition that the technical mechanism of multilateral negotiation does not address the fairly unique circumstances of Canadian trade. The reality of Canada's trade is *bilateral,* and the initiation of a bilateral negotiation simply had the potential to address more Canadian issues than did a multilateral negotiation.

Throughout the bilateral negotiation Canada has continued to participate vigorously in the GATT multilateral negotiation (the so-called Uruguay Round). From the Canadian perspective, negotiation at the bilateral level is not incompatible with negotiation at the multilateral level. If the bilateral negotiation is successful, one might expect the Canadian and American positions to be closer on most of the "old" issues, such as subsidies, countervailing duties, and government procurement, and closer as well on some of the "new" issues, such as services, investment, and the protection of intellectual property. This could be a distinct benefit to the multilateral negotiation. The sharpest divisions in the Uruguay Round tend to be between the industrial and developing countries, and Canada—with its high volumes of primary and semi-manufacturing exports and a high level of foreign investment—has a trade structure (and some trade policies) similar to those found in developing countries. Any blending of the Canadian and American positions would be a valuable pre-negotiation exercise for the Uruguay Round. However, if the bilateral negotiation is not successful, it will at least have exposed some of the difficulties that will be faced in the multilateral negotiation. Presumably, a failure at the bilateral level would also give Canada even more reason to demonstrate it could achieve trade liberalization in the multilateral round.

Conclusion

As stated at the outset, the Canadian initiative to negotiate bilaterally with the United States was a major departure from Canada's traditional preference for multilateralism in foreign policy. If the initiative is successful, it will undoubtedly create a major change in Canadian trade policy in the coming decade. Curiously, however, if the initiative fails it could leave very little impact on Canadian policy. There seems to be an "all-or-nothing" aspect to the negotiation that is in and of itself a troubling departure from the normal, more incremental nature of Canadian policymaking.

There is an element of stability in the notion that Canadian trade policy would revert to a multilateral stance in the absence of a bilateral agreement with the United States. However, there has been little attention given to how a multilateral policy would deal with Canada's biggest trade problem of the future: namely, its large, unsecured export concentration with the United States. Canada's export concentration with the United States creates an economic dependency on that country, and unless that export trade can be secured in some measure by a political agreement, it will continue to be subject to restrictive actions (either bilateral or multilateral) by the U.S. government. This could create the potential for instability in the North America economic relationship which would not be good for either party.

For Canada, there is the prospect that an economic downturn could translate what is undeniably an economic dependency into an acute (and ultimately unacceptable) political dependency; while for the United States, there would be an awkward problem of whether to accept Canada as a special case for the purpose of U.S. commercial policy, or to apply ordinary multilateral trade policies to that country. The real concern is that economic dependency between allies creates policy instability. One way to avoid this problem is to establish an international structure (such as was done in the Auto Pact) that manages the relationship, and to some extent conceals the true extent of the dependency. In this sense there are political, as well as economic, stakes at issue in the Canada–U.S. trade talks.

Epilogue

On December 11, 1987 the final legal text of a Canada–U.S. free trade agreement was released. The agreement was described by the Canadian government as "the most important trade agreement Canada has ever concluded," and "the culmination of almost one hundred years of Canadian efforts to secure open and stable markets."[17] As an indication of Canadian perceptions, this statement speaks for itself.

A preliminary analysis of the text suggests two conclusions. The first is that in the areas of tariffs, energy, investment, services, and agriculture, Canada offered substantial economic benefits to the United States. One major *quid pro quo*, as perceived on the Canadian side, was getting the United States to move toward a binational dispute-settlement process. This juxtaposition of economic versus institutional benefits indicates how deeply concerned Canadians had become over U.S. contingency protection; and how much Canada needed a liberalizing trade agreement with the United States for its own domestic reasons.

The second conclusion is the agreement is indeed pathbreaking (as so described by the Canadian government) on issues like services, investment, and a related problem, immigration policy. For this reason the agreement could well become a symbolic point of conflict in the multilateral Uruguay Round negotiation in the GATT.

Notes

1. Simon Reisman, "Canada–United States Free Trade" (Paper presented at a Brookings Institution Conference on U.S.–Canadian Economic Relations, Washington, April 10, 1984).
2. J. L. Granatstein, "Free Trade between Canada and the United States: The Issue That Will Not Go Away," in Denis Stairs and Gilbert R. Winham, eds., *The Politics of Canada's Economic Relationship with the United States* (Toronto: University of Toronto Press, 1985), pp. 11–54.
3. Ibid., p. 17.
4. Crawfurd D. W. Goodwin, *Canadian Economic Thought: The Political Economy of a Developing Nation 1814–1914* (Durham: Duke University Press, 1961), especially pp. 53–59.
5. *A Review of Canadian Trade Policy* (Ottawa: Department of External Affairs, 1983).

6. Thomas d'Aquino, "A Canada–United States Free Trade Association: Economic and Legal Perspective" (Paper presented to a Symposium on Private Investments Abroad, Southwestern Legal Foundation, Dallas, Texas, June 16, 1987).
7. See, generally, Reisman, "Canada–United States Free Trade," *op. cit.*
8. *Report of the Royal Commission on the Economic Union and Development Prospects for Canada, Volume I* (Ottawa: Canadian Government Printing Centre, 1985), pp. 58–63.
9. Ibid.
10. See *Competitiveness and Security: Directions for Canada's International Relations* (Ottawa: Department of External Affairs, 1985).
11. Alan M. Rugman and Andrew Anderson, *Administered Protectionism in America* (London: Croom Helm, 1987).
12. Richard G. Lipsey and Murray G. Smith, *Taking the Initiative: Canada's Trade Options in a Turbulent World* (Montreal: C.D. Howe Institute, 1985), especially Chapter 2.
13. For further discussion, see Earl H. Fry, "Canada–U.S. Free Trade Discussions Within the Context of U.S. Economic Competititveness," in Earl H. Fry and Lee H. Radebaugh, eds., *Canada/U.S. Free Trade Agreement* (Provo, Utah: David M. Kennedy Center for International Studies, Brigham Young University, 1986), pp. 70–82, especially pp. 79–82.
14. Gilbert R. Winham, *International Trade and the Tokyo Round Negotiation* (Princeton: Princeton University Press, 1986).
15. Rodney de C. Grey, *Trade Policy in the 1980s: An Agenda for Canadian–U.S. Relations* (Montreal: C.D. Howe Institute, 1981).
16. David W. Slater, "Canada in the Kennedy Round," *Canadian Banker*, vol. 74 (1967).
17. Department of External Affairs, "The Canadian–U.S. Free Trade Agreement: Synopsis," released December 12, 1987, p. 5.

3

What the GATT Says (Or Does Not Say)

ANDREAS F. LOWENFELD

THIS CHAPTER IS DESIGNED to provide some background for the international legal aspect of the negotiations between Canada and the United States looking to a free trade agreement. I write as a child of the 1960s—the early 1960s—not quite as enthusiastic about the postwar world of Bretton Woods, San Francisco, and Geneva as the children of the 1940s, but not as cynical or disillusioned as the children of the 1980s. I believed in European unity and the Common Market; I believed in the Kennedy Round—not the sectoral negotiations and the last minute packages—but the idea of trading partners of equal strength leading a multilateral effort to reduce trade barriers, and to reduce some of the negative effects of creation of the European customs union. The Tokyo Round left me disappointed—by the failure to adopt a Safeguards Code, and by adoption of a "fair trade" package that looked better from a distance than close up. Still, the Tokyo Round was a reaffirmation of multilateral approaches to trade problems, and it stemmed to some extent the tide of managed trade. Clearly, "success," however defined, is better than failure.

At this stage, disillusion with the General Agreement on Tariffs and Trade (GATT), with the European Community (EC), and with multi-lateralism in general, is everywhere. Unilateral action is seen as the only effective instrument of foreign economic policy, even as a new GATT round is commenced. Enter the Canadians, with the initiative of a bilateral trade agreement with the United States, looking to free trade between the two countries, though not right away and perhaps not in every product. Such an agreement raises many questions—of principle, of numbers, of short- and long-term gains—but only rarely have the implications for the trading system as a whole been considered. Some of these questions are addressed in this chapter, not out of idealism fed by nostalgia, but with the thought that the unprecedented prosperity of the four decades following World War II may well not be unrelated to the ideas and institutions of the founding fathers of the postwar economic system.

Compatibility of a Bilateral Free Trade Agreement with the GATT

One of the questions arising from the U.S.–Canada bilateral initiative is whether it is compatible with, or a threat to, the multilateral trading system of the GATT. To address this issue from a legal perspective, I ask the following questions: does the GATT matter as a multilateral institution; what does compatibility in fact mean; and what are the legal obligations which must be complied with in order for a U.S.–Canada free trade arrangement to be "GATT-legal?"

Does it Matter?

It has become fashionable to snicker at the GATT when viewed as law. Like international law in general, so goes the argument, the GATT has no sheriff nor even a strong director general.[1] Furthermore, to any given criticism, whether from the Community, from Japan, or from the developing countries, a ready answer is "look who's talking;" that is the "pot calling the kettle black;" or comparable slogans that may or may not fend off the complaint (recall the lengthy dispute about DISCs[2]), but somehow salve the conscience and avoid introspection. I believe that is a very foolish attitude. If a majority of Americans (or Canadians) were prepared to say today that the GATT has outlived its usefulness and that the time has come for us to withdraw (as we did from the United Nations Educational, Scientific, and Cultural Organization, UNESCO), I would be unhappy—as well as surprised. If, on the other hand, there is a consensus in the United States—Congress, the administration, the business and farming communities, the legal/economic/academic communities—that on balance, adherence to and leadership in the GATT is desirable, then to treat the GATT code as a formality to be measured by the likelihood and severity of punishment for its breach is shortsighted and counterproductive. It is true that the European Community has to some extent taken this attitude, especially with respect to the web of association agreements and to the Common Agricultural Policy. But I believe the Community always acted on the basis that it could not topple the GATT as long as the

United States was holding it up. If the United States now decides that the principles do not matter and that we can avoid the sanctions, that might serve the European Community right, but would serve the world—including the United States—ill.

Perhaps we take the benefits of GATT too much for granted—universal most-favored-nation (MFN) treatment on trade in goods; regular, multilateral trade negotiations; tariffs and other trade restraints bound in published schedules; and quotas in principle outlawed. The exceptions which presently exist, it seems to me, prove how fragile the system is, *not* that it has become worthless. A good standard for comparison is the situation with respect to matters not covered by GATT, such as trade in services. Given all the known shortcomings in the present GATT system—agriculture, textiles, association agreements, and so forth—would it be seriously advocated in the United States or Canada that the legal regime for trade in goods be assimilated to that prevailing for banking, insurance, shipping, finance, or other service industries?

What Does it Matter?

Compatibility with the GATT can be described in several ways:

1) Conduct wholly in conformity with the provisions of the General Agreement, for example a tariff applied uniformly to the products of all member states in accordance with Article I and pursuant to a published schedule notified to, and bound under, GATT in accordance with Article II.

2) Conduct that may depart in some way from the General Agreement but does not injure any other member state. In general, the idea that a violation exists only upon a showing of injury—*nullum damnum absque injuria*—borrowed from civil (as contrasted with criminal) law has tended to be accepted within the GATT. Not infrequently, the reluctance of states to come forward to assert actual or potential injury is influenced by economic or political inducements that may or may not be related to the action subject to challenge. In the long run, however, the code of conduct, and the reliance member states place in the GATT, may well be weakened.

3) Conduct pursuant to a waiver in accordance with Article XXV(5) of the GATT. Article XXV(5) speaks of "exceptional circumstances not elsewhere provided for . . . ," but over time, the understanding seems to have grown up that any departure from the GATT may be the subject of a waiver, provided that two-thirds of the votes cast, comprising more than half of the contracting parties, are recorded in favor of the waiver. To some extent waivers have been negotiated between the applicants

and the Contracting Parties. For instance, in connection with obtaining a waiver for creation of the European Coal and Steel Community (ECSC), agreement was reached on a variety of assurances of market access and continuing supply for third parties, as well as on a requirement of an annual report by which compliance with these assurances could be verified.

In some instances, including the application by the United States for a waiver with respect to the U.S.–Canada Automotive Agreement, the action was taken first, the waiver applied for afterwards.[3] Faced with a choice between granting a waiver and finding one or more member states in violation, the GATT Contracting Parties have tended to grant waivers, usually upon a finding that injury was unlikely, and subject to reporting and periodic review. Waivers are usually subject to revocation, but the experience has been that once granted, they will not be revoked, except on request of the parties. The consequence of a waiver is that the beneficiary state is not deemed in violation, and that other states are not authorized to retaliate. Thus, conduct pursuant to a waiver is similar to conduct pursuant to one of the "grandfather clauses" in the GATT. Conduct pursuant to a waiver clearly is not conduct in defiance of the GATT; whether it can be said to be compatible with the GATT is not, I submit, so clear. In part the answer depends on whether the waiver concerns a fundamental, as contrasted with a peripheral, obligation under the GATT; in part on whether the waiver was approved on the basis of understandings (express or implied) that the state granted the waiver this time will support a waiver next time for the states that supported the first waiver in question.

The implication of the preceding paragraphs may surprise the casual observer. It turns out that compatibility with the GATT is often not a yes or no question, or even just a legal question. To answer the question with another question, suppose the United States and Canada concluded a free trade agreement which is otherwise in compliance with the GATT but excludes agriculture and fishery products, and the Contracting Parties granted a waiver of the "substantially all the trade" provision of Article XXIV(8)(b). 1) Would such an agreement-with-waiver be compatible with the GATT? 2) Would it lead to a further unraveling of the GATT as a code and institution? What if the United States and Canada asserted that a waiver was not needed for an agreement omitting agriculture and fishery products?

The Legal Obligations

The most basic principle of the GATT, set forth in Article I, is, of course, unconditional most-favored-nation treatment for export and import of goods from other member states. Joined to that obligation is the under-taking to meet regularly in a multilateral setting to negotiate reductions of barriers to international trade (Article XXVIII bis). Preferences of any kind (except those that come in under grandfather clauses[4]) are ex-cluded. Customs unions, however, and by extension free trade areas (that is agreements to eliminate trade barriers among the members, but not to adopt a common external commercial policy), are permitted. The creators of the GATT realized that there was a certain contradiction between the requirement of MFN and the permission to form a cus-toms union or free trade area, but they understood the desires of the BENELUX states to join GATT while maintaining their own links agreed to during the war, and they appreciated even in 1947 the prospects for solving the German question through some sort of eco-nomic link with France and the other states of Western Europe. To have made no provision for customs unions or free trade areas would indeed have been shortsighted.

Clair Wilcox, the principal American negotiator of the GATT, wrote:

> Preferences have been opposed and custom unions favored, in principle, by the United States. This position may obviously be criticized as lacking in logical consistency. In preferential arrangements, discrimination against the outer world is partial; in customs unions, it is complete. But the distinction is nonetheless defensible. A customs union creates a wider trading area, removes obstacles to competition, makes possible a more economic allocation of resources, and thus operates to increase production and raise planes of living. A preferential system, on the other hand, obstructs economy in production, and restrains the growth of income and demand. It is set up for the purpose of conferring a privilege on producers within the system and imposing a handicap on external competitors. A customs union is conducive to the expansion of trade on the basis of multilateralism and non-discrimination; a preferential sys-tem is not.[5]

Thus it was important to establish conditions that would maintain the distinction between customs unions and free trade areas on the one hand, and preferential arrangements on the other. Article XXIV of the GATT, as revised and developed in the course of the 1945–48 negotia-tions, set down four principal conditions for custom unions and free trade areas:

1) A customs union or free trade area must be designed to facilitate trade between the constituent territories and not to raise barriers to the trade of other contracting parties with such territories. (Para. 4).

2) A customs union or free trade area must cover substantially all the trade between the constituent territories. (Para. 8(a) and (b)).
3) If the customs union or free trade area is to be implemented in stages, there must be a plan and schedule to complete the transition within a reasonable length of time. (Para. 5(c)).
4) The duties and other regulations of commerce maintained by a customs union, or by the constituent members of a free trade area vis-a-vis nonmembers shall not on the whole be higher or more restrictive than the corresponding duties or other regulations existing before the arrangement. (Para. 5(a) and (b)). (The complete text of Article XXIV appears in the Appendix.)

Applying these conditions in the context of a possible free trade arrangement between the United States and Canada, it would seem that excluding large sectors of the economy, such as agriculture or lumber, would be incompatible with Article XXIV; excluding smaller subsectors, such as uranium, as to which plausible concerns of national security might be adduced, would seem to be permissible.[6] The criterion by which exclusions must be tested would be to distinguish between a preferential arrangement, which is *incompatible*, and an arrangement meeting the definition of a free trade area, which is *compatible* with the GATT. Moreover, while staging is permissible, and possibly even staging for different sectors at different rates, the requirement of covering substantially all the trade could not be evaded by staging with excessive or indefinite deadlines.

Other Kinds of Agreements

The United States and Canada, with similar economic systems and a common 3000-mile border, have an opportunity to reach bilateral arrangements which go beyond the GATT. This section attempts to the answer the question of just how far the United States and Canada can go.

Agreements on Subjects Not Addressed in GATT

Agreements that do not address the subjects with which GATT is directly concerned would not, *a priori*, be regarded as inconsistent with GATT, even when they might have trade effects. For example, no one would challenge bilateral agreements concerning double taxation, though these might well have trade effects. Similarly, so long as the GATT has not addressed trade in services, there would seem to be no objection to an agreement between the United States and Canada on the exchange of services (or particular services). Of course, to the extent that the Uruguay Round actually addresses services, a U.S.–Canada agreement might be regarded as impermissibly preferential, unless its provisions were generalized.

Agreements genuinely linked to the unique 3000-mile border between the two countries could be concluded, probably without the need to generalize either under GATT or under either country's expressed policy of nondiscrimination. Trans-border television (including cable) and airline services are among the topics that come to mind; in the past the so-called "overland exemption" from the U.S. Oil Import Program (1959–73) is an illustration of a special arrangement that was not universally welcomed but not, so far as I know, challenged on legal grounds.[7] The United States has thus far resisted opening up intra–U.S. air services to foreign-flag carriers, and a change in the Federal Aviation Act would be required to permit such services. I think an amendment to accommodate Canadian carriers could be justified, without admitting KLM, Swissair, Lufthansa, or carriers from other states to services between, say, Chicago and Los Angeles. I doubt that a regional subsidy intended to make an industrial enterprise viable by permitting access to the nearby market across the border would fit within an implied trans-border exception.

Agreements in Implementation of GATT Provisions

An agreement on definitions and notifications with respect to action taken under Article XIX of the GATT concerning emergency import relief would seem to be acceptable, provided that the agreement did not call for discrimination against third parties. For example, a joint definition of "serious injury" for escape clause purposes, or even of "causation" by imports or of what constitutes an "industry" for purposes of escape clause action would *a priori* be unobjectionable, though not binding on third parties. If, however, a safeguards agreement authorized or required the two countries to impose restraints on imports from third countries before imposing them on imports from each other, that would be contrary to the MFN requirement of the GATT.[8]

Bilateral Agreement and the MTN Codes

The MTN Codes, concerning Subsidies and Countervailing Duties,[9] Dumping, Technical Standards, Government Procurement, and so forth provide for international dispute-settlement channels, but also permit unilateral determinations, subject to specified guidelines, for example with respect to subsidies and countervailing duties. The international dispute-settlement mechanisms are not stated to be exclusive, and have not in fact been used much. There would seem to be no impediment to a U.S.–Canadian agreement on joint resolution of disputes over such subjects as what is a subsidy, how it should be measured, how much of a countervailing duty is justified, and so on. If another country expressed interest in a similar agreement, Canada and the United States might both find it awkward to refuse, or indeed to adopt different interpretations of the same provisions of the particular code. No GATT violation could be charged, however, for failure by either the United States or Canada to enter into a "joint commission" agreement with a third country. Again, of course, if a pattern of discrimination could be shown—say if a regional development grant by Canada were found not to be countervailable by the joint commission while a similar grant by Italy did lead to imposition of a countervailing duty, the fact that in the first instance the decision was made pursuant to a bilateral agreement would be no defense.

As to government procurement, the general principle of nondiscrimination is the same. Unique conditions, for instance concerning the North American Defense Command, might justify some preferences not open to third countries. On other types of procurement, a joint mechanism for fact-finding or dispute resolution might be justified, but preferential arrangements would not be.

Waiver of GATT Obligations

Since some provisions of a U.S.–Canada free trade agreement would only be possible if a waiver of GATT obligations is granted, what are the arguments for and against seeking a waiver?

Arguments and Precedents

It is difficult to discuss a possible waiver without knowing what provisions of the GATT would be infringed by a possible U.S.–Canada free trade agreement. In general, as noted earlier, arguments for a waiver have rested on the contention that no third party would be injured by a given measure or agreement, or that if such injury did occur, steps would be taken to take care of the interests of the injured party. The no-injury contention might well support a waiver for a free trade agreement that excluded all cereals, since no country (as far as I know) is a present or prospective exporter of cereals to either Canada or the United States. If the waiver were sought to permit exclusion of all agricultural or fishing products from the free trade agreement, one might want to see what arrangements for such products were contemplated, and how they fit within the waiver granted to the United States in 1955 (and never revoked) concerning import restrictions imposed under Section 22 of the Agricultural Adjustment Act of 1933.[10]

The fundamental point stressed at the outset of this chapter—that each important waiver undermines the integrity of the GATT as a whole, and that each waiver of an agreement meeting some but not all of the requirements of Article XXIV of the GATT blurs the distinction between free trade areas and preferential arrangements—does not turn up in formal GATT documents, because the GATT has never felt itself strong enough to frontally oppose a major initiative by important member states.[11] When the European Coal and Steel Community came before the GATT, a waiver was granted after some eighteen months of negotiations, subject to a variety of assurances about market access, security of supplies, regular reporting, and consultation—plus, of course, the unspoken understanding that the ECSC was the first step in the task of integrating Germany into the Western alliance.[12] All subsequent waiver applications to some extent derive from that case. When the proposed European Free Trade Association (EFTA) came before the GATT following conclusion of the Stockholm Convention in 1960, a working party expressed a good many doubts, particularly about the exclusion of agriculture from the agreement.[13] In the end, the working party recommended neither a waiver nor condemnation, and the Contracting Parties made no decision, stating simply that "there remain some legal and practical issues which would not be fruitfully discussed further at this stage."[14]

When the United States–Canada Automotive Products Agreement came before the GATT in 1965, members of the working party again expressed concerns of various kinds, particularly "concern that the granting of a waiver in the present case might constitute a precedent and lead to a proliferation of similar agreements on other products and in other parts of the world." Eventually, eleven months after the agreement had been signed, and after hearing demonstrations by both the United States and Canada about the uniqueness of the agreement (see below), the Contracting Parties did grant a waiver to the United States, and accepted the contention that Canada did not need a waiver because it was granting the benefits of the agreement to all countries on an MFN basis.[15] The waiver was conditioned upon an assurance by the United States that the Automotive Products Agreement would not cause any trade diversion, and on a requirement of consultation by the United States with any country claiming that trade diversion had occurred or was threatened.[16]

It seems clear that a free trade agreement limited to specified sectors on the model of the Automotive Products Agreement would run into major difficulties with the GATT. An agreement that purported to be comprehensive, but excluded certain products or postponed effectiveness as to such products for extended time periods might well be approved, though not without cost. Among the costs not previously discussed would be the perception, expressed in the working party report on the Automotive Agreement, that if two major industrial countries cannot now observe the rules as written, there is no reason for developing countries to pay attention to these rules either. If the EFTA precedent were followed, that is neither condemnation nor grant of a waiver, this and related consequences from the agreement would, it seems, be even more costly. It seems fair to conclude that the United States has never stopped paying for the 1955 Section 22 waiver, which disabled—or at least discouraged—it from challenging the Common Agricultural Policy of the European Community for more than two decades.

The "Uniqueness" Argument

In negotiations looking to a waiver in connection with the Automotive Products Agreement, the point was stressed that both the manufacturers and the labor unions in the United States and Canada were integrated across the border, and that consumer tastes (for large cars) were peculiar to the two countries. Even as to automobiles, that point is not as true as it was two decades ago, and its main persuasive value lay in enabling the decisionmakers to say that the agreement was not a precedent that could easily be applied to other circumstances. To the extent that the Automotive Products Agreement serves as a precedent for further U.S.–Canada arrangements, applicable to sectors where the industrial integration is not as pervasive, the argument about uniqueness is obviously undercut.

For certain other kinds of arrangements, the uniqueness of the long border and the common language and tastes may be persuasive. Transborder television and airline services, already mentioned (and not presently covered by GATT) raised considerations not replicated among other countries, or addressed in regional arrangements elsewhere (such as Rhine River transport). Clearly arrangements for combatting trans-border pollution, transport in the Great Lakes and the St. Lawrence Seaway, though they have trade aspects, are not deemed to infringe on the global trading rules. Once an arrangement concerns access to markets in one country for the products of another, however, it does not seem that the uniqueness argument can overcome the basic requirement of most-favored-nation treatment for all members of the GATT. Trade experts still recall the 1904 treaty between Germany and Switzerland which permitted Germany to reduce its duties on cattle reared at least 300 meters above sea level and having at least one month's grazing each year over 800 meters above sea level, qualifications unattainable by Dutch or Danish cattle. Uniqueness, in other words, is to some extent a suspect category.

Conclusions

The GATT reflects a fragile compromise between universal MFN and acceptance of customs unions and free trade areas. The conclusion is that a free trade arrangement limited to certain sectors is clearly at variance with the GATT; an arrangement that covers all trade in goods is acceptable; and an arrangement that purports to be comprehensive but makes significant exceptions, or postpones implementation of certain sectors beyond a reasonable and finite length of time, departs from the GATT, but may be eligible for a waiver or a "no decision."

Arrangements outside the present coverage of the GATT (such as about services in general, intellectual property, antitrust, taxation, even foreign investment) would be unobjectionable, whether concluded as separate arrangements or as part of a trade agreement. Such arrangements could be open-ended—that is subject to adherence by third states, or limited to the original parties—though (at least for the United States) some such agreements would require express legislative authorization. Arrangements to hold regular discussions or to resolve disputes—even disputes that would be submitted to a GATT panel—would not seem to be objectionable, though settlements that resolved disputes by granting one state a preference not available to other states might raise concerns under GATT, unless, of course, they were part of a comprehensive free trade agreement meeting the requirements of Article XXIV.

The contradiction between nondiscrimination and special arrangements is not insurmountable, but it is not trivial. The solution of the postwar trading system was to distinguish between arrangements that cover substantially all the trade between parties and therefore can be expected to be trade creating, and those that cover only some of the trade and therefore may be trade diverting and likely to breed other trade-distorting arrangements. Without seeking to verify the economic soundness of that solution, this chapter has tried to suggest some of the institutional costs of undermining it, whether by waiver, by interpretation, or by tolerance.

Epilogue

The agreement, from what I can gather, contains more lawyer's work, and more respect for the GATT, than I had feared. No major sector is omitted, except "cultural industries," which combine elements of both goods and services. Agriculture and energy, in particular, which I feared might be left out, or made subject to staging for such long periods as to virtually be excluded, have, so far as I can tell, been included within the free trading concept. I found particularly interesting—subject to studying the details, if indeed I could understand them—the stated objective of making the agricultural production subsidies (support programs) of the two countries compatible with each other. I don't know yet whether a GATT waiver will be required, and whether if the question is a close one on technical grounds, it would be wiser to seek one or to take the position that a waiver is not necessary. The fact that the agreement recites that it is made pursuant to Article XXIV of the GATT is, of course, not conclusive, but I believe there is evidence that the negotiators did have the code—if not the institution—of the GATT in mind.

The most intriguing aspects of the agreement from a lawyer's point of view are the several dispute-settlement panels, one for antidumping and countervailing duty cases, the other for proposed or actual legislation, regulation, or governmental procedures that might affect the operation of the agreement. In both situations, time schedules are designed to avoid the endless procedures of the GATT, while leaving enough space so that negotiation can overtake legal determination. The idea that one country stays enforcement of an import relief measure based on its unilateral interpretation of the circumstances of an export practice, and the other country postpones its retaliation, strikes me as very attractive. One can only hope that the respective parliaments—national and state/provincial—will accept arrangements that do not fit easily into the structures of government we have grown up with.

Notes

1. See, for example, the following remarks by Donald E. deKieffer, former general counsel, Office of the U.S. Trade Representative, at a conference on U.S.–Canada Trade Relations held at Cleveland, Ohio, April 19–21, 1985. "I would suggest that outside of law review articles, Article XXIV [of the GATT] has been moribund, because the GATT itself is an institution of gentlemen's agreements more than of confrontation. . . . I would not regard any of the relevant provisions of the GATT as impediments to the kinds of sectoral integration we have been discussing." The talk, as well as

the present writer's criticism from the floor, are reproduced in *Canada United States Law Journal*, vol. 10, no. 107 (1985), p. 128.

2. See John H. Jackson, "The Jurisprudence of International Trade: The DISC Case in GATT," *American Journal of International Law*, vol. 72, no. 4 (October 1978), pp. 747–81 and *Journal of World Trade Law*, vol. 16, no. 361 (1982).

3. The agreement was signed by Prime Minister Pearson and President Johnson at the LBJ ranch on January 16, 1965. A working party appointed by the GATT heard from representatives of Canada and the United States in March, but the United States did not formally apply for a waiver until November, following passage of implementing legislation by Congress and proclamation by the president of the duty reductions called for by the agreement. The Report of the Working Party and the Decision of the Contracting Parties by mail ballot are reproduced in GATT, *Basic Instruments and Selected Documents (BISD)*, 13th Supp. (1965), pp. 112–25, and 14th Supp. (1966), pp. 181–90, 37–44.

4. Preferences covered by Article I, cl. 2 include stated arrangements connected with the British Commonwealth, the French Union, colonial Territories of the Netherlands and Belgium, U.S. preferences to the Philippines, all subject to margins of preference no higher than those existing on a date specified.

5. Clair Wilcox, *A Charter for World Trade* (New York: Macmillan Co., 1949, reprinted by the New York Times, 1972), pp. 70–71.

6. The suggestion might be made that the European Community has itself omitted agriculture. Certainly the rules covering trade with the outside world, and also the subsidy arrangements, are quite different from those applicable to all other sectors of the Common Market. Whether the EC's Common Agricultural Policy is compatible with the GATT overall is certainly a problem—an oversized problem, as Professor Robert E. Hudec has called it. I would not think, however, that the CAP offends against Article XXIV; on the contrary, the framers of the Treaty of Rome realized that if the Community had excluded agriculture completely, they could not have made a plausible argument that the European Common Market was consistent with Article XXIV, and they would have had to apply for waivers and subject themselves to periodic scrutiny as the Coal and Steel Community had done.

7. See Kenneth Dam, "Implementation of Import Quotas: The Case of Oil," *Journal of Law and Economics*, vol. 14, no. 1 (1971), pp. 28–35.

8. The United States and Canada did, in fact, conclude an Understanding on Safeguards on February 17, 1984, which requires advance notice and an opportunity to consult before imposition by either country of a safeguard action. In principle the notice should be at least thirty days before the effective date of implementation. While some shared views are set forth in the understanding—that is that safeguard actions are to be temporary, and that compensation by the party imposing the safeguard is preferable to withdrawal of equivalent concessions by the other party—there is no definition of injury in the published text.

9. For example, compare the Agreement on Subsidies and Countervailing Duties Article 4, authorizing imposition of countervailing duties by the importing state, subject to stated conditions, with Articles 12 and 13, providing for bilateral consultation and for conciliation and arbitration, respectively.

10. GATT, *BISD*, 3d Supp. 32 (1955), p. 141.

11. See, generally, Robert E. Hudec, *The GATT Legal System and World Trade Diplomacy* (New York: Praeger, 1975).

12. See, generally, William Diebold, Jr., *The Schuman Plan: A Study in Economic Cooperation 1950–59* (New York: Praeger for the Council on Foreign Relations, 1959), especially pp. 523–32. See also Dean Acheson, *Present at the Creation: My Years in the State Department* (New York: W.W. Norton & Co., 1969), pp. 382–89. The text of the waiver appears in GATT, *BISD*, 1st Supp. (1952), p. 17.

13. Examination of Stockholm Convention, Repeat of GATT Working Party adopted June 4, 1960, GATT, *BISD*, 9th Supp. (1961), p. 70.

14. Conclusions adopted by Contracting Parties, Nov. 18, 1960, GATT, *BISD*, 9th Supp. (1961), p. 20.

15. See note 3 *supra*.

16. So far as I know, no country has requested consultations pursuant to this provision in the waiver. A substantial change in the terms of the Automotive Products Agreement might stimulate some country to request consultations, or even raise the question of the continued effectiveness of the waiver itself. Of course if the agreement on automotive trade were simply folded into an overall free trade agreement, with the special clauses eliminated, the issue would not arise.

4

What is at Stake?

MURRAY G. SMITH

T HE TRADE POLICIES of the United States and Canada are at a crossroads; but which crossroads? The United States and Canada are engaged in bilateral negotiations, which are intended to create a free trade area between the two countries. Both countries have also supported the launch of the multilateral trade negotiations, the so-called "Uruguay Round." Are these two roads to trade liberalization compatible? Some suggest that the bilateral negotiations represent one more step in a process of erosion in the multilateral trading system. Others argue that the bilateral and multilateral negotiations are complementary and although there are tensions between the two sets of talks, the tensions are creative ones, or can be made to be creative.

The debate between the bilateral and multilateral approaches to the liberalization of trade and the resolution of disputes may, however, be irrelevant to the conduct of trade policy in the United States and Canada. U.S. congressional leaders have pledged to enact trade and competitiveness legislation in the 100th Congress which is unlikely to attach much priority to the liberalization of trade. If the proposed legislation (H.R. 3, versions of which have passed the House of Representatives and the Senate) becomes U.S. law, then whether bilateralism or multilateralism are the appropriate approaches to trade negotiations may become a moot question. The United States will instead rely, to an even greater degree, upon unilateral approaches under U.S. trade laws to deal with trade disputes and to redress perceived imbalances or inequities in international commerce. *De facto,* if not *de jure,* the United States will withdraw further away from diplomatic resolution or international arbitral consideration of its trade relations with other countries.

William Diebold's very thoughtful first chapter suggests that the distinction between bilateralism and multilateralism in U.S. trade policy is not a simple one, and that each of these genres is characterized by diversity. For the purposes of this chapter, I will focus on bilateral and multilateral approaches to the negotiation of international agreements and rules which aim to provide a more open and predictable environment for trade and investment. Thus, I will not consider the types of bilateralism which involve barter arrangements, currency exchange agreements or other attempts to manage bilateral trade flows.

The first section of this chapter examines the international economic environment within which the U.S. and Canadian economies are operating and looks into some of the pressures that are acting now, or will act in future, upon the two North American economies. The second section outlines the potential agenda for both the bilateral and the multilateral negotiations, and the third section considers some of the possible parameters of a bilateral trade agreement, which I term a Canadian-American free trade area (CAFTA). The fourth section explores both the implications of a CAFTA for the U.S. and Canadian economies and for the economic interests of third countries, as well as the longer-term consequences for the global trading system. In conclusion, I shall address the strategic considerations for Canada and the United States which arise from the potential interaction between the bilateral and multilateral negotiations.

International Economic Environment

Surely every one would agree that the world economy has changed dramatically over the last three decades. The disagreement comes in answer to the question of why has it changed? And the real question is what should the policy response be to these changes, and to their perceived causes?

Global Competition

The United States emerged from World War II as the world's preeminent economy. Although trade was a small percentage of America's gross domestic product (GDP), U.S. trade policy was an important, if not the dominant influence upon the development of the postwar international trading system under the General Agreement on Tariffs and Trade (GATT) which eventually emerged.

In the last forty years, the world has become much more interdependent. The consequences of this economic interdependence have only been belatedly recognized by policymakers, particularly in the United States perhaps because it has only been since the mid-1960s that international commerce has become more significant to the U.S. economy.

Economic interdependence has increased for some reasons which are unrelated to economic policy. A long period of relative peace and security has fostered the expansion of global commerce. An ongoing revolution in the technology of transportation and communications has reduced, and continues to reduce, the economic impediments to international trade in goods and services.

Economic policy among the industrial countries has contributed to increased interdependence as well. The reduction of tariffs and the liberalization of nontariff barriers, which has occurred under the auspices of the GATT, has made a significant contribution to the expansion of trade and economic growth in the last forty years. In addition, and despite periodic stresses, strains and occasional crises, the conduct of macroeconomic policy in the industrial countries, in association with the resulting balance-of-payments adjustments, has permitted the maintenance of an open trade and payments system.

Let me illustrate the changes wrought during this period by recalling the economic performance of the U.S. and Canadian economies in the 1950s—a period that acquires an increasingly golden hue with the passage of time—and contrast that situation with that which prevails today. In the halcyon days of the 1950s major U.S. manufacturing industries, such as autos and steel, were largely impervious to offshore competition. These major industrial sectors enjoyed economies of scale in production in the American market, which gave them a competitive advantage relative to producers in third countries. Perhaps more importantly for U.S. multinational firms, their involvement in, and exposure to, the large high-income U.S. market meant that U.S. firms were the first to develop and to introduce new products and techniques.

The situation was somewhat similar on the Canadian side of the border. The Canadian market was clearly nowhere near as large as that of the United States, but Canada also, having emerged from World War II with its economy unscathed, enjoyed an improved economic position relative to Europe or Japan. The domestic Canadian market was substantial relative to that of other major industrial economies. For example, in the 1950s Canada was second only to the United States in the size of its domestic market for automobiles. It was during this period that the Canadian tariff played the important role of inducing

U.S. manufacturing firms to set up subsidiaries in Canada, rather than exporting from production facilities in the United States. In addition, the British Preferential Tariff system provided an added incentive for investment in manufacturing facilities located in Canada as a way to serve Commonwealth markets.

Today, however, the world is very different. There has been a dramatic increase in global competition. Three factors account for much of this increase.[1] First, competition has increased among the advanced high-income countries. Since the 1950s Europe and Japan have rebounded vigorously from their depressed economic positions relative to the United States and Canada. European, and especially Japanese, economic growth rates have accelerated and, as a consequence, the relative share of U.S. economic activity amongst the nations of the Organization for Economic Cooperation and Development (OECD) has been substantially reduced. The integration of the European market through the European Community (EC) and the European Free Trade Association (EFTA), and the higher per-capita incomes achieved both in Europe and in Japan, have enabled these economies to now offer many of the potential advantages of economies of scale and innovation to their domestic firms. Thus, European and Japanese industry can now compete much more effectively against U.S. multinational enterprises in the development of new products and new technologies.

Second, high rates of economic growth among the group of newly industrializing countries (NICs) have also altered relative competitive positions in international trade. In conjunction with domestic policies that have shifted from an emphasis on import substitution toward a policy of export orientation, countries such as South Korea, Taiwan and Spain have become powerful competitors in the basic heavy manufacturing industries. Other economies in the newly industrializing group, such as Brazil and Mexico, have continued to pursue more autarkic import-substitution policies, yet high domestic growth rates during the 1970s permitted the creation of a heavy industrial capacity in their domestic markets as well. With the onset of the debt crisis, they have redirected some of this production to export markets. The NICs are a diverse group, with differences in their domestic policies and in their social and economic structures, but several of them have emerged as significant international competitors in industries such as automotive production, steel, and shipbuilding, which were traditionally the preserve of the industrialized countries.

Third, a group of countries consisting of developing economies with large populations are shifting from a heavy agricultural orientation toward more industrial production and trade. Economies such as Thailand, the Philippines, Malaysia, and even India and the People's Republic of China are following the path trod by Hong Kong and Taiwan, by pursuing more outward-looking policies and expanding their production and exports in labor-intensive light-manufactured consumer products.

The increased intensity of global competition in today's world economy has created the perception among North Americans that trade is no longer determined purely by comparative advantage. Instead, it is believed that comparative advantage is now *acquired and influenced* by government policies. And, it is this belief which provides a rationale for more interventionist industrial policies in the United States.

Economists have become more sophisticated in their theoretical analysis and have developed models that explain the potential for government policies to shape or influence a nation's comparative advantage. Quite clearly, under hypothesized circumstances, government can influence the competitive position of domestic firms by imposing trade restrictions or offering production or export subsidies. It is less evident, however, that these types of measures bestow permanent net economic benefits on the nation that engages in such practices, either because the policy interventions are too costly or because of offsetting losses in other sectors of the economy.[2]

Although consideration of strategic behavior on the part of firms and governments may lead to new insights into the factors influencing the actual conduct of trade policy, normative conclusions about how countries should formulate trade policy should be made with considerable caution. There is the possibility—under a specified set of assumptions about the structure of an industry and the response of foreign firms—that the home government and firms, in an attempt to improve national welfare through collusion in the use of trade restrictions or subsidies, cause instead policy measures and rent-seeking activity that are in fact detrimental to national welfare. The actual policy outcome could, therefore, be very different from the "optimal" policy intervention suggested by the theoretical analysis.

I will make just two observations about the potential scope of strategic trade and industrial policies. First, most of the discussion frequently ignores the response of foreign governments. And, beyond the issue of retaliation, the analysis does not consider the possibility that the foreign government might also have opportunities to engage in similar collusive actions which would be detrimental to the home country. Trade negotiations may provide mutually advantageous opportunities for governments to engage in reciprocal disarmament of "strategic" policies inherited from the past. Second, the rent-seeking behavior by competing domestic interest groups can be controlled by the mere existence and negotiation of international trade agreements.

The central empirical hypothesis in the industrial policy debate is that trade is now influenced to a greater extent by government policy and less by the determinants of comparative advantage. Specifically, the hypothesis is that foreign government practices have undermined the competitive position of U.S. industries. As an alternative to this hypothesis, I would suggest that many of the locational advantages enjoyed by the North American economy in the 1950s, in the form of economies of scale in production and advantages in developing and diffusing new technology, have been waning steadily over the past three decades. Indeed, empirical research on the determinants of trade suggest that the factor endowments of the United States are a more important explanation of the pattern of U.S. trade than they were twenty or thirty years ago.[3]

In conclusion, I would suggest that two fundamental developments have altered the competitive position of the U.S and Canadian economies. First, the advantages to U.S. producers from economies of scale in production and innovation have declined at the same time that improvements in the technology and infrastructure of transportation and communications have increased global competition. Since Canadian manufacturing is dominated by U.S. multinational enterprises, the decline in the relative position internationally of U.S. firms has important implications for Canada. Second, the comparative advantage of the North American economies is changing as their share of specialized factor endowments, such as highly qualified manpower or modern technologically-advanced physical capital, are declining relative to the positions of the other high-income countries.

In the longer term the global competitive challenges confronting both the United States and Canada make their respective interests in negotiating a free trade area more compatible. Each country stands to benefit from the rationalization of U.S. (and also Canadian) multinational enterprises which operate on both sides of the border. Furthermore, most of the adjustment to freer bilateral trade will be intra-industry. Thus, adjustment costs will be minimized, while the opportunities for specialization will be significant. Elimination of tariff and nontariff barriers between Canada and the United States would increase the scope for product specialization and enhance the returns from successful innovation. As a result, the U.S. and Canadian economies will become more competitive with offshore rivals if a CAFTA is negotiated.

Macroeconomic Stresses in the 1980s

While the longer-term challenges tend to make trade policy interests in Canada and the United States more compatible, the macroeconomic policy environment has placed severe stress on bilateral economic relations. Both the competitive pressures from growing economic interdependence and the magnitude of the economic adjustments required have been further increased for the North American economy by the overall stance of macroeconomic policy during the 1980s. Although they have been operating more or less in tandem, two distinct macroeconomic factors can be identified which have affected the competitive positions of internationally-traded sectors of Canada and the United States.

The first factor that must be considered is the impact of the shift in monetary policy undertaken by the major central banks at the beginning of the decade. Virtually in concert, they tightened domestic monetary policy in an effort both to contain and to lower inflation. The result was a dramatic slowdown in world economic activity during 1980–82, and the first declines in the value of world trade since the 1930s. Nominal and real interest rates reached historic peaks for most countries during this period. The results were sharp decreases in investment activity, a contraction in household spending on consumer durables, and weak markets for resource commodities.

Over the first half of the decade, this austere and concerted monetary policy program was successful in arresting and lowering inflation in the industrial countries. Indeed, the decline in the rates of inflation in the Canadian and U.S. economies in the 1980s—about 10 percentage points—is comparable to the price deflation experienced in the 1930s. The transition to a low inflation environment was particularly painful for Canada both because of Canada's dependence upon resource commodities which experienced real price declines, and because domestic inflation in Canada proved to be more tenacious than in other economies, notably the United States.

The transition to a low inflation environment would have been painful for the global economy and for industrial sectors in North America even without any other complicating factors. Particularly for the U.S. and Canadian resource sectors, the trend toward lower real commodity prices, which has been associated with the disinflation process, would have caused considerable difficulty.

These pressures on the resource and industrial sectors of the United States and Canada were exacerbated by a second factor—divergences between the fiscal policies of North America on the one hand, and of Europe and Japan on the other. Starting in 1982 the United States, and also Canada, embarked on a policy of fiscal expansion through rising full employment budget deficits. At the same time, the European and Japanese economies were pursuing restrictive fiscal policies by moving toward a surplus in their full employment budgets. Furthermore, associated with this divergence in fiscal policies was significant disparities both in the economic growth rates and in the external balance positions of North America and other major industrial countries.

These two macroeconomic policy divergences affected economic activity in the summit countries through several channels. One channel was the exchange rate. Efforts to finance the U.S. and Canadian budget deficits put upward pressure on interest rates in their capital markets, which increased capital inflows and, in turn, appreciated the U.S. dollar against all major currencies from 1980 to 1985. The Canadian dollar declined against the U.S. dollar during this period, but appreciated against other major currencies. When adjusted for the higher rate of domestic inflation in Canada, the increase in Canada's effective exchange rate was significant although less dramatic than experienced by the United States.

In addition to the exchange rate channel, the transmission of high real interest rates through global financial markets also contributed to the divergences in economic growth and trade performance. The European and Japanese economies were experiencing contractionary effects on domestic demand from the move toward budget surplus, but they did not enjoy the declines in real interest rates that might have been associated with these changes in their domestic fiscal policies. Instead, the high real interest rates emanating from North America acted both to slow the pace of recovery in their economies, and to curtail the increase in private sector capital spending which ordinarily would have been associated with their own fiscal policy measures. Indeed, the liberalization of Japanese capital markets raised Japanese interest rates inhibiting domestic investment, and the resulting capital outflows contributed to the short-term expansion of Japan's trade and current account surpluses.

During the early to mid-1980s the global trend toward disinflation, combined with the strong U.S., and to a lesser extent Canadian, dollar and the divergence in economic growth performance placed severe stress on those parts of the North American economy which were producing primary resource commodities or capital goods. Canada found itself in a position not unlike that of other highly indebted resource-producing nations in the Western Hemisphere, where it had to sustain large trade surpluses, despite the deterioration of its export prices, in order to service its foreign liabilities. The problems of the debtor countries only served to deepen the crisis in the North American resource sector.

Disparities in the macroeconomic policies of the major industrial countries predictably produced a substantial divergence in external current account positions. Japan and Western Europe moved toward larger and larger trade and current account surpluses while the United States, and also Canada with a lag, moved toward large current account deficits.

In the case of the United States, these macroeconomic stresses fanned protectionist fires. There was greater pressure for the application of U.S. fair trade laws as well as increasing resort to escape clause actions and voluntary export restraints, which were used to institute managed trade regimes in major industrial sectors.

The delayed response of the U.S. trade deficit to the declines in the U.S. dollar against the currencies of some of the major industrial countries since March 1985 has heightened protectionist pressures. Yet, this delayed response was entirely predictable for several reasons. First, the pattern of relatively weak economic growth in Europe and Japan has persisted, in part due to the cautious monetary and fiscal policies of those countries. Second, the adverse effects of the appreciation of the U.S. dollar through the first half of the decade had not been fully reflected in the U.S. trade position. Therefore, the traditional J curve effect—which is a short-term deterioration of the trade balance in response to a depreciation in the currency—was exacerbated by the lag in the response to the previous appreciation. Third, the U.S. dollar has declined dramatically relative to the currencies of Japan and Germany, but movement has been much less dramatic against other currencies. A broad-based measurement of effective exchange rates suggests that the devaluation of the U.S. dollar has been about 20 percent from March 1985 to March 1987.

Trade policy factors have also influenced the response of the U.S. trade account to the depreciation of the U.S. dollar. The voluntary export restraint arrangements in key industrial sectors have reduced the impact of exchange rate movements on trade volumes in the short term. Under the export restraints, foreign producers were limiting their export volumes and taking higher profit margins from their sales in the United States. As their costs rise, because of appreciation of their domestic currencies, foreign producers tend initially to absorb the impact by lowering their profit margins. It is only when the exchange rate has moved a sufficient amount—to where their domestic costs necessitate a price increase in the U.S. market up to a level that makes the export restraint arrangements no longer binding—that the exchange rate movement begins to have a significant effect on trade volumes.

The slow response of the U.S. trade balance to exchange rate movements does not provide a basis for pessimism about the long-term competitiveness of the U.S. economy. Many believe that the movement in the exchange rate will not restore external balance in the U.S. economy. Views were similar during the 1970s when there were those who thought that energy prices would rise exponentially, and that demand and supply would not respond to those price increases.

Americans can learn from an examination of the Canadian economy. During the 1970s Canada ran a large current account deficit relative to the size of its gross national product (GNP) and increased its net foreign indebtedness considerably. Today, Canada's foreign debt amounts to about 30 percent of GNP. Presently, Canada is simultaneously running a substantial surplus in merchandise trade along with a large deficit its current account.

Current projections suggest that U.S. net foreign liabilities will be approximately 15–20 percent of GNP by about 1990. As a consequence, the United States will be obliged to run surpluses on trade in merchandise and services in order to service their international debt. Thus, even if the United States persists with a current account imbalance, there will be a substantial swing in the trade balance. This swing will be attained through whatever realignment of exchange rates and interest rates is required to achieve equilibrium in financial and goods markets. And, the swing in the competitive position of those sectors in the U.S. economy most exposed to international trade will be considerable indeed. As a result of shifts in the global macroeconomic environment—which can be anticipated—the United States will undoubtedly have a renewed interest in developing an open and predictable regime for global trade and commerce in the 1990s.

During the 1980s, however, unilateral measures under the U.S. trade laws have appeared to Congress to be the most effective vehicle for resolving trade disputes, and the best means to discipline the unfair trading practices of trade partners. The global imbalances of the 1980s, and the associated rise in U.S. protectionism, have put severe pressure on bilateral economic relations and have stretched the fabric of the world trading system. Since U.S. protectionism has been channelled through complaints about unfair foreign practices, the threat to impose penalty duties adversely affects the investment climate in Canada, and unleashes pressures on Canadian governments. For example, in the 1986 softwood lumber cases U.S. industry succeeded in obtaining a reversal of the 1983 ruling that Canadian stumpage practices were not a countervailable subsidy. As a result, Canada was forced to impose a 15 percent export tax on lumber. Thus, the rules and procedures governing the bilateral application of import relief laws have been a central Canadian concern in its economic relations with the United States, and have influenced that country's objectives in the bilateral negotiations.

Although for Canada the impetus for the talks came from fears of U.S. protectionism, the bilateral trade negotiations present longer-term strategic issues and opportunities for both countries.

Comparison of the Bilateral and Multilateral Objectives

Since Canada made its proposal to initiate bilateral trade talks with the United States, members of the General Agreement on Tariffs and Trade have formally launched the Uruguay Round of multilateral negotiations at Punta del Este in September 1986. Embarking on both sets of talks simultaneously introduces important opportunities and constraints into the bilateral negotiating strategy. This section identifies those opportunities and constraints and indicates their implications for both sets of negotiations.

Bilateral Objectives

Canada's objectives in the bilateral negotiations were outlined by the Honorable James Kelleher, minister for international trade, in a report that was tabled in the House of Commons on September 26, 1985.[4] They are:

- to reduce the potential of U.S. trade laws to frustrate or prevent market access to the United States;
- to eliminate U.S. tariffs that inhibit the further processing of Canadian resource products and the development of Canadian world-scale manufacturing industries;
- to remove "Buy-America" procurement practices that inhibit Canadian exports; and
- to improve mechanisms that deal with trade disputes and the interpretation of international agreements.

The U.S. objectives in the bilateral negotiations were summarized by U.S. Trade Representative Clayton Yeutter in his report to the president.[5] They are:

- to eliminate high Canadian tariffs on a large variety of products, which act as major impediments to U.S. exports;

- to remove Canadian nontariff barriers to trade at both the federal and provincial levels of government;
- to eliminate or reduce bilateral barriers to U.S. exports of services; and
- to obtain clarification and liberalization of Canadian policies toward U.S. direct investment in Canada.

Protection of intellectual property rights has emerged as an additional U.S. objective in the bilateral negotiations. Otherwise the initial statements of objectives continue to be accurate reflections of the goals of each side in the ongoing bilateral negotiations.

Multilateral Objectives

Canada's objectives in the multilateral negotiations are similar to those in the bilateral talks, but subtle differences exist in their priorities and in the opportunities for realization of those objectives. In the multilateral negotiations, the Canadian government attached a high priority both to improving market access through the elimination of tariffs that inhibit the development of resource-based industries, and to eliminating nontariff barriers that impede the development of secondary manufacturing industries. Canada would also like to obtain tighter international rules on policies affecting agricultural trade. In particular, Canada seeks curtailment of European agricultural subsidies, improved access to the Japanese market for agricultural products and concomitant reductions in U.S. subsidies. Canada also seeks to limit the effects of contingent-protection measures under U.S. trade laws and to strengthen mechanisms designed to resolve trade disputes.[6]

The objectives of the United States are to strengthen trade rules dealing with subsidies (in particular to limit European subsidies) and intellectual property, and to improve the effectiveness of the application of these rules, particularly to sectors such as agriculture. As in past GATT rounds, the United States will also seek improvement in the terms of export market access, but since nontariff barriers have become more important in constraining the expansion of trade, "negotiations should aim primarily at eliminating such barriers."[7] The United States will also press for the removal of policies which affect direct investment and which indirectly distort trade flows; the promotion of a freer flow of direct investment; and the reduction or elimination of barriers to trade in services.

A key to the development of momentum in the multilateral talks is the interests of the other major parties. The European Community's declaration on the trade negotiations suggests that it has only a limited interest in improvements in export market access. Rather, its most prominent export concern is to obtain more effective means of entry into Japanese markets for manufactured products. The EC supports strengthening trade rules and their application to problems of intellectual property and counterfeit goods, as well as the principle of freer trade in services. In important respects, however, the EC is defensive about its trade policies. While the EC is prepared to negotiate about agricultural trade issues, negotiations that might change key elements of the Common Agricultural Policy (CAP) are likely to be extremely difficult. The EC also takes the view that the negotiations should aim for tariff harmonization by reducing some high tariffs, but that they should not involve across-the-board reductions.

Japan's objectives in the Uruguay Round are to obtain greater security of access to markets in general, and to improve access to markets for high-technology products in particular. Japan also supports efforts to promote freer trade in services. Japan is least willing to liberalize trade in agricultural and primary resource products, because of the political clout of that country's rural sector.

A potentially major obstacle in the next round of multilateral trade negotiations is the conflicting objectives of the industrial countries on the one hand, and the developing countries on the other. Developing countries want liberalized trade in import-sensitive industries, such as clothing and textiles, as well as tighter restrictions on the use of quotas or other safeguard measures. Most industrial countries (with the partial exception of the EFTA nations), however, are reluctant to accede to these demands. Yet all the industrial countries, including the United States, Japan, Canada, and those in the EC and EFTA, would like the developing countries to accept more obligations under GATT rules, to participate in reciprocal reduction of trade barriers to goods, and to agree to new trade rules for services, investment, and intellectual property. Yet the developing countries remain attached to the GATT principle of special and differential treatment for merchandise trade. They are also resistant to the extension of GATT rules to trade in services.[8]

The Uruguay Round promises to be the most complex and protracted set of multilateral negotiations ever under GATT auspices.[9] Traditional issues, such as agricultural trade problems and safeguards, appear likely to continue to defy resolution. New issues, such as trade in services, investment and intellectual property, are also likely to present serious difficulties for the negotiations.

It is worth noting that many of the gaps in the current GATT system stem from U.S. actions to weaken the rules for agricultural trade and to prevent the establishment of the International Trade Organization (ITO) in the 1950s. If the United States had not obtained the waiver for "domestic" agricultural policies in 1955, greater disciplines might have been imposed on the European Community's CAP at its inception. Similarly, if the ITO Charter had come into effect, the rules respecting investment and also services—the latter was covered under the restrictive business practices section—might have developed in ways which would have prevented some of the current difficulties.

The Scope and Structure of a Bilateral Agreement

In the U.S.–Canada free trade negotiations, both countries have stressed that they seek to achieve a comprehensive bilateral agreement. Prime Minister Mulroney, in his September 26, 1984 announcement of the bilateral trade initiative to the House of Commons, stated that Canada would seek "the broadest possible package of mutually beneficial reductions in tariff and nontariff barriers between our two countries."[10] He declared that the proposed negotiations would be consistent with GATT rules, and that it would not be Canada's intention to negotiate "a customs union, a common market or any other economic arrangement which would affect our own independence or our relations with the rest of the world."[11] On the U.S. side, the administration has stressed that the objective is to negotiate a free trade area.

Although the structure and precise details of a Canadian-American free trade area agreement remain conjectural, pending the outcome of the negotiations, some of the more likely elements regarding trade in goods can be summarized briefly as follows:

- bilateral elimination of tariffs and quotas in the industrial sector;
- rules of origin to determine which products qualify for duty-free trade; and
- transition arrangements governing the timing of tariff reductions.

In general, the issues involved in removing transparent border impediments to trade in goods are clearly understood and present few conceptual difficulties, although there are technical issues that do need careful attention.

The proposed agreement, if it comes to fruition, will almost certainly be a comprehensive trade agreement or free trade area consistent with Article XXIV of the GATT.[12] However, the precise nature of the arrangement that might be negotiated is less clear. It could be a conventional free trade area analogous to that of the European Free Trade Association, which eliminated tariffs and other border impediments to trade on industrial products among the member countries; but there are a number of issues left out of the EFTA negotiations which will inevitably have to be addressed in the U.S.–Canada bilateral talks.

Sectoral Coverage

Sectoral exemptions from the agreement are an issue on which previous experience with free trade areas amongst industrial countries could be instructive. The precedents for such free trade areas involve the elimination of virtually all tariffs and quotas on industrial products, with selective coverage for agricultural, fish, and food products.[13] The European Community went further than EFTA in removing internal barriers to trade in agricultural products, but the *quid pro quo* was harmonized external barriers and subsidies. Within the industrial sector, the United States and Canada may wish to follow these precedents because, once the exemptions-seeking process gets started, there is a risk that the overall trade deal could unravel.

Both countries could also follow the EFTA pattern and choose to retain quotas on certain agricultural commodities. Under GATT Article XXIV 8(b), a free trade area must provide that "duties and other restrictive regulations of commerce (except, where necessary, those permitted under Article XI, XII, XIII, XV and XX) are eliminated on substantially all trade between constituent territories in products originating in such territories." Thus, Article XXIV, in conjunction with Article XI, could provide a rationale for the longer-term continuation of import restrictions which are an integral part of supply-management programs or domestic support systems for the products concerned. Some of Canada's import restrictions, such as those on poultry and eggs, have been justified as being consistent with Article XI. The maintenance of some other restrictions on bilateral trade, however, such as those in Canada and the United States which predate the GATT and U.S. Section 22 restrictions covered by the U.S. waiver of 1955, would be questionable in the context of the Article XI exception to the Article XXIV rules. (The complete text of Article XXIV appears in the Appendix.)

It might be noted in this connection that Article XXIV does not necessarily require the immediate removal of internal trade barriers by members of a free trade area. These barriers can be removed over a reasonable period of time, in accordance with a formal plan and schedule presented to the Contracting Parties.

Whatever the legalities of the GATT rules, there is likely to be less interest in either the United States or Canada in opening up trade in industries such as dairy products where both countries have complicated support systems. The United States might want to liberalize trade in sectors, such as grains, eggs or broiler chickens, where Canadian marketing boards and import quotas create significant cross-border price discrepancies. At the same time, however, there will probably be strong domestic pressures in the United States to retain its highly restrictive sugar regime which raises domestic prices well above international levels. On balance, therefore, neither country is likely to press for inclusion of all agricultural commodities. The prospect for elimination of tariffs combined with retention of import controls on primary agricultural products does raise problems however for processing industries.

It may seem surprising that the United States (and perhaps Canada) is ostensibly prepared to go further in dismantling agricultural trade barriers and subsidies in multilateral negotiations than it is prepared to go in the bilateral talks. The reason is that many of the problems experienced by agricultural producers in both countries result from the agricultural practices and trade barriers of third countries. There is a real reluctance to start dismantling, or even reducing, the agricultural subsidy programs of the United States and Canada in the absence of progress in curtailing the effects of the CAP or opening up agricultural markets in Japan and elsewhere.

Rules of Competition

The more difficult set of issues concerns nontariff barriers to trade, investment matters, and barriers to trade in services. These issues have been dealt with to varying degrees of effectiveness in earlier free trade area or regional trading arrangements. EFTA, for instance, devised rules of competition to deal with nontariff barriers to trade in goods. Except perhaps for the EC, there is little prior experience in dealing with disputes over subsidies, trade in services or investment issues.

The recently concluded U.S.–Israeli free trade area agreement touched on some of these issues, but it did not adequately address the application of U.S. trade laws—which is of particular interest to Canada—and therefore it is unlikely to serve as a satisfactory precedent. U.S. trade laws have significant implications for the activities of Canadian industries. Those directed against what the United States regards as unfair trade practices by foreign governments also have an indirect influence on Canadian economic policy. Similarly, if Canadian commitments on trade in services and on investment policies were analogous to those in the U.S.–Israeli agreement, American firms that do business with Canada will probably be less than satisfied.

The two models which could be most relevant to the Canadian–U.S. negotiations are the rules of competition embodied in the EFTA agreement and the provisions of the Treaty of Rome governing the pertinent issues. Neither of these models seems to provide a perfectly appropriate analogy for the CAFTA. Instead, the bilateral negotiations, if they are to succeed, seem likely to produce a hybrid, which shares elements of the EFTA and the EC systems as well as some unique elements of its own.

As this chapter is written, the precise form and structure of the bilateral agreement on these contentious trade remedy, investment, and trade in services issues remains highly speculative. Furthermore, there is a large, if not infinite, number of combinations of provisions, rules and procedures that could be drafted to resolve the different objectives of Canada and the United States. Let me suggest two broad options that might prove to be a basis for a bilateral agreement.[14]

Option One: National Treatment The most far-reaching approach to rules of competition would involve a U.S. and Canadian commitment to the principle of national treatment—treatment no less favorable than that afforded domestic firms—in domestic legislation and government practices. Thus, each government would undertake to ensure national treatment with respect to public procurement practices, regulatory policies and other such measures affecting trade in goods and services, policies toward direct investment, and in the application of remedies against unfair competition under domestic legislation.

In effect, the national treatment option would entail a bilateral exemption in the application of import relief laws. National treatment is a very logical approach to dealing with allegations of unfair trade practices by private firms. For example, in the case of dumping each country could allow reciprocal application of domestic laws to provide legal remedies for price discrimination that causes injury to other firms. Similarly, an intellectual property agreement could allow recourse to the courts in patent infringement cases, instead of Section 337 of the Tariff Act of 1930. Dismantling safeguard mechanisms on bilateral trade is more likely to encounter political resistance, but it might be acceptable in the context of an overall agreement which eliminates all barriers to trade and investment, and which would result in a closer alignment of competitive conditions in individual industries.

The greatest difficulty with the national treatment option arises in the case of subsidies. Unless a bilateral agreement can devise an acceptable process for controlling the use of subsidies, there is little likelihood that the U.S. Congress would accept the dismantling of the countervailing duty apparatus for bilateral trade. The European Community has a mechanism for disciplining the use of subsidies by the governments of member states, but it involves yielding authority to a supranational agency which can veto spending programs by national governments. A binational agency which could prohibit subsidy programs by both national and subnational governments in both countries could offer the economic benefits of preventing the bidding wars which currently occur to encourage investment in particular jurisdictions; but because such a mechanism would entail relinquishing sovereignty to a supranational agency, it is unlikely to be acceptable in the Canadian–U.S. context.

Resolving the Canadian and U.S. differences on subsidies and countervailing duties seems to require an innovative approach, such as a less-than-supranational institutional mechanism than that of the European Community, but with tighter disciplines on the use of subsidies than the vague commitments in the Stockholm Convention. One possible solution would be to draft detailed guidelines governing the use of subsidies by both countries. Compliance with the subsidy guidelines could be monitored by a binational agency or tribunal. The tribunal could screen countervailing duty cases by ruling whether or not the alleged subsidies were within the guidelines.

The latter approach would be consistent with U.S. proposals for negotiation of agricultural subsidies during the Tokyo Round. The result would be clear and effective disciplines which provide a more predictable environment both for governments in formulating their policy, and for firms in planning their investments.

Although Canada is likely to press for the national treatment approach regarding the application of trade laws, it will probably be reluctant to commit to national treatment for services trade or for policies toward direct investment. Beyond the Canadian concern about cultural industries, which could be dealt with by focused exemptions from national treatment and investment obligations, Canada is disinclined both to allow untrammelled access to U.S. services firms, and to cease screening foreign acquisitions, because of lingering concerns about the high degree of foreign (U.S.) ownership of the Canadian economy.

Option Two: Revised Bilateral Trade Rules and Procedures This option has many variations, but, in essence, it prescribes for the amendment of each country's national import relief laws to clarify the criteria for application of antidumping and countervailing duties, and escape clause measures. In addition, there could be provisions for joint administration of, and consultation on, some aspects of the trade laws, as well as clarification and tightening of standards for the determination of causation and injury. The objective of this approach would be to ensure that the trade laws serve their stated purpose of providing remedies against only those practices which demonstrably distort trade.

This more incremental approach to the resolution of the U.S. and Canadian negotiating positions on import relief laws would also have implications for other nontariff barrier issues. For example, commitments on investment policies would probably be restricted to those issues, such as performance requirements, that directly affect trade. Similarly, the provisions of the agreement regarding trade in services and intellectual property might be more limited and partial in their coverage.

Accessibility to Third Countries

Questions do arise about the availability of the terms of a CAFTA agreement to other countries. Although third countries are unlikely to want to join the free trade area in the near future, some (such as Australia or Japan) might well seek to do so eventually. This being the case, there could well be problems in negotiating a Canada–U.S. agreement—tailored to bilateral concerns—which would be suitable for third-country membership. A much more likely alternative is that either, or both Canada and the United States, might negotiate their own free trade area arrangements with third countries.

If either, or both, countries concluded a bilateral agreement with a major third country, this could create some problems in the administration of rules of origin, as well as create incentives for trade deflection. Since stated U.S. policy is to promote such bilateral agreements, the possible implications need to be examined when negotiating and designing one between Canada and the United States. Neither partner could seek to prevent the other country from entering into free trade area arrangements with third countries, but each might request the right to review the rules of origin in the CAFTA in light of subsequent bilateral arrangements with third countries.

Global Implications

There are contrasting views about the longer-term effects of a Canadian–U.S. agreement on the multilateral trading system. One view asserts that a bilateral arrangement would contribute to greater fragmentation of an already splintered global trading system. Another view contends that a free trade area agreement, consistent with GATT

Article XXIV, creates tighter disciplines which in fact serve to reinforce the global trading system.

These two contrasting views focus on two quite different concerns which are seldom distinguished. One well-established concern is whether a bilateral arrangement is trade creating and thus enhances world welfare, or whether it is trade diverting and thus only of benefit to the partners and at the expense of the economic interests of third countries. The second concern pertains to the longer-term effects on the trading system—such as the impact of the bilateral arrangement on the behavior of the trading partners in subsequent multilateral trade negotiations, and its effects on the management both of the multilateral trade negotiations and of trade relations and trade disputes in the broader multilateral system.

Trade Creation and Trade Diversion

Economists have long recognized that regional trade liberalization agreements will benefit the partners and that they may also bestow net economic benefits to the rest of the world. The expansion of global trade from the removal of barriers among the partners may more than offset the economic losses from diversion of trade from third countries.

The extensive literature on trade creation and diversion makes clear that there is no *a priori* answer to the question of whether a free trade area or a customs union will be trade creating or not. Instead the impact is determined by the economic structure of the trading partners, the preferences of consumers in the member countries, the height and structure of their respective external trade barriers prior to the agreement, and, most importantly, the external structure of tariffs and other trade barriers facing third countries when the regional trade agreement is implemented. If the the trade agreement provides opportunities for economies of scale, the likelihood that it will be trade creating increases greatly.

The potential for economies of scale in production, or economies of scope at the level of individual firms, determines the magnitude and distribution of the economic benefits of the bilateral agreement. Rationalization of production and firms within the North American market will enhance the capability of manufacturing and services industries to meet offshore competition, as well as provide economic benefits to third countries through the expansion of global trade and improvements in international economic efficiency.

It is frequently assumed that the economies of scale to be obtained from opening up bilateral trade are more significant for Canada than for the United States, because the large U.S. domestic market already provides ample opportunities for economics of scale. This argument, however, ignores the importance of economies of scale or scope at the level of individual firms. For example, the U.S. domestic market for automobiles is a great deal larger than the volume of production by plants of efficient scale. Nonetheless, economies of scale and scope can be extremely important to individual firms. It would have been much more costly and risky for the U.S. government to ensure the survival of Chrysler in the early 1980s if the Auto Pact did not exist, and Chrysler had been unable to rationalize production within, and spread the costs of model development over, its U.S. and Canadian operations.

An additional, but tangential question is which is more likely to be trade creating: a free trade area or a customs union? Under most circumstances, one could design a customs union that was more trade creating than a free trade area depending upon the two countries' pre-existing tariff structures. However, such a hypothetical exercise is unlikely to bear much relation to the objectives and actions of countries that form customs unions.

One practical advantage of a free trade area is that it is possible to monitor changes in the external trade barriers of the member countries. A customs union requires the harmonization of external trade barriers, which makes it difficult to discern whether the newly created common structure of protection is more or less open to trade with third countries. Even if formation of a customs union is trade creating, the erection of harmonized external trade barriers is bound to impair market access for some third countries. Acrimonious disputes, such as the one underway between the EC and the United States over the accession of Spain and Portugal to the Community, is a predictable result.

In summary, the effects of a CAFTA on global trade and economic welfare will depend on the parameters of the agreement, and may vary across sectors. The removal of bilateral trade barriers such as tariffs is likely to be trade creating and beneficial both to third countries and to the partners, particularly since there seem to be unexploited opportunities for economies of scale and specialization. In some sectors, such as agriculture, both countries may wish to retain subsidies and import restrictions for negotiation in the GATT talks, which will have neutral effects on global trade. Perhaps the most problematic areas will involve industries such as textiles, apparel and steel, where managed trade regimes exist on a global basis. If the bilateral agreement leads to more open bilateral competition—not managed bilateral trade and higher external trade barriers—in these sensitive industries, then there is a strong case that a CAFTA will enhance international economic welfare.

Implications for the System

A clear case can be made that a customs union or common market is likely to be, over the longer term, more corrosive to the multilateral trading system than is a free trade area. One reason is that once a common external structure of protection has been erected, the process of reaching a supranational consensus on external trade policy with third countries seems likely to create a bias favoring the retention of preferences among the members of the trading bloc. In addition, it breeds a least-common-denominator approach to trade liberalization, meaning that the degree of liberalization is constrained to the level permitted by the member country least willing to discipline its use of particular trade barriers or nontariff distortions. Certainly, the experience of the EC is consistent with the hypothesis that a common market creates a protectionist bias in the decision-making process of common institutions.[15]

Not only does a customs union appear to attenuate incentives for trade liberalization, but the formation of customs-union-type blocs can perpetuate and reinforce a trend toward a discretionary-power-based system of international trade rules. Such a discretionary system is frequently favored by large countries, while a rules-based system is normally preferred by smaller countries.[16]

Returning now to our concern about the interaction of bilateral and multilateral talks, let us examine the potential effects of a bilateral agreement on the multilateral negotiations and the international trading system. Although a free trade area creates preferences among member countries, these preferences are unlikely to erode the multilateral system in the longer term. Indeed, proponents of free trade area negotiations argue that the creation of such preferences in fact produces incentives for other countries to engage in trade liberalization, just as the purpose of the negotiating innovation of plurilateral or conditional most-favored-nation (MFN) agreements is to ameliorate the incentive problems in trade negotiations referred to by Richard Cooper.[17] Plurilateral negotiations reduce the "free-rider" problem that occurs in MFN tariff negotiations, but the least-common-denominator problem will remain if participation of all the major players is a precondition for achieving an agreement.

The free trade area provision of the U.S. *Trade and Tariff Act of 1984* represented a significant innovation which changes the nature of, as opposed to quells, the incentives for countries to engage in international trade negotiations. It grants the U.S. administration authority to enter into negotiations with other countries to establish a free trade area. The rationale for the new approach of negotiating bilateral free trade areas was explained by U.S. Secretary of State George Shultz:

From a global perspective, a splintering of the multilateral trading system into a multitude of bilateral arrangements would be a backward step. Bilateral free trade agreements, however, such as we have negotiated with Israel and have offered to discuss with other countries, need not have this result; they can stimulate trade and strengthen the multilateral system. Free trade agreements are sanctioned by the international rules and involve a tighter trade discipline; they can promote freer trade than the multilateral system is currently prepared to accommodate. Our hope, nonetheless, is that the example of greater liberalization—and the recognition that the United States can pursue another course—will help motivate a larger group of nations to tackle the job of expanding trade on a global basis.[18]

Elaborating on this theme, the U.S. Council of Economic Advisers argues that "the possibility of FTA (free trade area) negotiations . . . offers the United States and others the option of using a free-trade instrument, rather than protectionism, as a lever against protectionist countries. . . . "[19] Thus, the preferential access available to the free trade area partners provides an incentive for other countries to engage in trade negotiations. The pursuit of trade liberalization through a bilateral or plurilateral approach is preferable to using negative inducements, such as threatening to impose trade restrictions in order to bring other countries to the negotiating table. Because protectionist measures would impose costs on the home country, their threatened implementation lacks credibility. Furthermore, if the threats were in fact executed, it would be an invitation for retaliation.

In its 1986 report, the Council of Economic Advisers echoed this theme when it stated:

> The United States now faces a historic opportunity in the possibility of establishing a free trade agreement with Canada. In September 1985 the Canadian Government proposed that both countries consider bilateral negotiations on the broadest possible package of mutually beneficial reductions in trade barriers. In 1935 Canada and the United States took bilateral steps to reverse the protectionism of that era, steps that became a catalyst for broader international cooperation then. The new Canadian–U.S. initiative offers similar prospects now.[20]

The crucial difference between a free trade area and a customs union, is that in a free trade area each member maintains control over commercial policy for, and trade negotiations with, third countries. From the point of view of each member country, the preferential access created by the regional trade arrangements has the character of a public good. It is the external trade barrier of one country that creates the preference for suppliers in the other country relative to third countries.

To illustrate this point, let us consider the following example. Canada's post Tokyo Round tariff on machinery is 9.2 percent. In the absence of a CAFTA, under GATT rules Canada still would negotiate most machinery tariffs bilaterally with the United States because the United States is the principal supplier of the products. With tariff elimination between Canada and the United States, U.S. machinery suppliers would have an advantage relative to producers in third countries such as Japan or West Germany. Depending upon the type of machinery involved, either Japan or the EC would become the principal supplier after the CAFTA was negotiated. Subsequently, in GATT tariff negotiations, Canada could offer to lower its machinery tariff in order to obtain reciprocal reductions in Japanese or EC trade barriers of interest to Canada.

A bilateral agreement can be expected to shift the focus of multilateral tariff negotiations, promote restructuring of the domestic industry, and improve the industry's capability to meet third-country competition. In general, a free trade area partner has an incentive to negotiate reductions in its external trade barriers in the multilateral fora in order to obtain improved access to third-country markets; whereas in a customs union the maintenance of external barriers becomes the *raison d'être* of the organization. Thus, the preferences created by a free trade area are more likely to be reduced over time through multilateral negotiations than is the case with the customs union.

Similarly, the members of a free trade area have a continuing interest in the international trade rules which provide the framework for managing trade relations and trade disputes. Each member will continue to have separate trade relations with third countries, and important elements of the multilateral rules will continue to govern their trade.

Strategic Considerations

The potential interaction between the bilateral and multilateral negotiations creates opportunities and imposes constraints on the negotiating strategies of the two countries. We turn now to a discussion of the strategic considerations for Canada and the United States in the conduct of the two sets of negotiations.

Comparison of the Negotiating Agendas

Despite the apparent overlap in the Canadian and U.S. objectives for both the bilateral and the multilateral negotiations, two important factors will influence whether the two sets of negotiations will complement or conflict with each other. The first factor is whether just two partners can deal more easily with some issues or whether more countries must be directly involved in the negotiations because their policies have a significant impact on world trade. The second factor is whether third countries will either want to join the free trade area agreement at a future date, or want to be included in some components of the agreement.

In the first instance, different negotiating issues are likely to have different fates. For example, tariff elimination in the industrial sectors is a goal of the bilateral negotiations. The same objective, however, is unlikely to be realized in the multilateral talks because of the negotiating positions of Europe, the United States, and the developing countries. As another example, important elements of agricultural trade (such as quotas necessary to maintain marketing boards) may be exempted from the bilateral negotiations, at least in part because many of the difficulties of Canadian and U.S. agriculture stem from the policies of the EC and Japan. Yet, agricultural trade issues are critical, but contentious issues on the multilateral agenda. Indeed, Canada and the United States might use the bilateral talks to develop common approaches to the GATT negotiations.

In the second instance, Canada's main objective of obtaining greater security of access to the U.S. market is shared by other countries, which means that they are also not alone in their desire to address U.S. trade laws. In the context of a free trade area consistent with GATT Article XXIV, the United States would have no formal obligation to extend equivalent treatment to other trading partners, including those signatory to the GATT antidumping and subsidies codes. But third countries are likely to press for similar arrangements with Canada and the United States. Awareness of this possibility will undoubtedly influence the U.S. position on unfair trade laws in its bilateral negotiations with Canada. Thus, the prospects for progress on subsidies and trade remedies in the multilateral negotiations could influence the outcome of the bilateral negotiations and vice versa.

The major GATT trading partners apparently share the common objective of strengthening GATT rules and dispute-settlement processes, but Canada and the United States may be more willing to give practical effect to these general principles in a bilateral arrangement.

An apparent overlap in the agendas for the two sets of negotiations on issues such as barriers to trade in services and policies toward direct investment may mean that Canada and the United States are better placed to develop trade rules that can accommodate the differences in their domestic regulatory and legal systems. It may prove difficult, however, to complete the bilateral negotiations both within the electoral mandates of the Reagan administration and the Mulroney government and within the tight timetable which must be met if the existing U.S. legislative authority for the negotiation and its implementation is to be utilized. Yet, the potential interplay between the two negotiating agendas suggests that the bilateral negotiations could have important strategic implications for the conduct of the GATT negotiations and the realization of the U.S. and Canadian objectives in the Uruguay Round, particularly if they lead to the achievement of a CAFTA.

Plurilateral Agreements

An earlier section discussed how other countries might participate in the elimination of bilateral tariffs either through multilateral tariff negotiations or through joining the CAFTA. It is also possible that components of the bilateral agreement could contribute to the development of plurilateral agreements among the industrial countries analogous to the codes on nontariff barriers concluded during the Tokyo Round. Indeed, the bilateral agreement could pioneer approaches to, and provide a model for, dealing with the new trade issues, such as barriers to trade in services and investment policies. Yet Canada and the United States may be reluctant to sign agreements which are open-ended and invite third-country accession. Furthermore, other countries might be unwilling simply to accede to an agreement negotiated between Canada and the United States.

At a minimum, potential third-country reluctance suggests that if Canada and the United States are genuine in their desire to have bilateral agreements serve as a model for plurilateral agreements, their bilateral negotiations should give some consideration to the views of third countries. Since the bilateral negotiations must proceed expeditiously if they are to succeed, Canada and the United States could consult with the representatives of third countries during the drafting stages of the bilateral agreement. It is certainly in Canada's interest to anticipate the position of other major trading partners in subsequent multilateral rounds on trade in services and investment issues.

The potential for building on bilateral arrangements on trade in services or investment issues to achieve plurilateral agreements in the GATT context does not imply that the coverage of the plurilateral agreement will necessarily be the same as the bilateral agreement. Since the plurilateral arrangements will be based on conditional MFN, signatories will have obligations and rights only with respect to the practices or activities specifically covered by the agreement.

Let us consider the case of trade in services. The bilateral agreement could contain comprehensive coverage of services industries with focused exceptions to take into account the Canadian concern about cultural policies and the U.S. concern about national security. The plurilateral agreements, however, could be formulated as separate self-standing agreements addressing particular services industries analogous to the Civil Aircraft Agreement concluded during the Tokyo Round. Not only could the sectoral coverage of the plurilateral agreements be less extensive than in the bilateral agreement, but other countries might accede to some, but not all, of their arrangements.

The advantages of the bilateral arrangements on issues such as services trade are twofold. First, they could serve as important precedents for plurilateral agreements and second, the creation of the bilateral arrangements would create incentives for other countries to move ahead with the plurilateral agreements.

Rules of Competition and Import Relief Laws

In considering the relationship between the rules of competition in a bilateral agreement on trade laws and existing multilateral agreements, the first point that must be made is that if the CAFTA agreement is consistent with Article XXIV of GATT, then the two countries are largely unconstrained in the form or structure of bilateral arrangements dealing with remedies for import relief. Nonetheless, subtle interactions are possible between the design of the bilateral arrangements and the multilateral negotiations. Alternative approaches to the rules of competition could have quite different implications for the multilateral talks.

National Treatment If the national treatment approach were adopted for dumping or subsidies, for example, it is extremely unlikely that this option would be available to other countries unless they also wished to enter into the free trade area agreement. In the case of dumping, the rationale for relying on domestic price discrimination laws as a remedy against private practices is that the elimination of bilateral trade barriers removes the potential for a protected cartel to engage in predatory activity. Open borders limit the ability of firms to engage in such predatory strategies and also can constrain subsidy policies. As Banks and Tumlir have observed:

> Analysis of the "impediments" to adjustment and growth reveals the key role of border protection. Without protection against imports, neither cartels (in product and labor markets) nor subsidies would pose such a

problem. (If steel could be imported into the European Community without quantitative limitations, subsidy needs would soon exceed the capacity of national budgets.)[21]

Furthermore, acceptance of the national treatment approach would seem to require a mechanism to discipline subsidy practices analogous to that operating within the European Community. Just as the subsidy regulation mechanism of the EC is not appropriate for application to a larger group of countries, it is unlikely that the mechanism developed by the United States and Canada would be amenable to broader application.

Revised Bilateral Rules and Procedures Yet if the approach to rules of competition involves retaining each country's import relief system while refining the criteria and procedures for bilateral application of antidumping and countervailing duties or escape clause measures, then other countries could press to have the same refined criteria apply to them. For example, if the bilateral agreement requires the removal of "sales-below-cost" provisions in the antidumping laws, other countries might seek to incorporate this approach into the GATT Antidumping Code, although they might be reluctant to take the same approach in their own antidumping laws. Similarly, if the CAFTA yields a more precise agreement which prescribes that subsidies are specific and thus countervailable, then other countries almost certainly will push for incorporation of more definitive criteria in the GATT Subsidies Code.

The approaches taken to the procedural issues will also affect the feasibility of subsequent broader application of the bilateral arrangements. Joint administration of import relief laws is not likely to be amenable to broader application, but revision of procedures for determinations of injury in each country's national import relief laws could be incorporated quite easily in future multilateral agreements which deal with dumping, subsidies, and import disruption.

Dispute Settlement
Mechanisms for the arbitration and resolution of disputes may or may not play a role in the adjudication of rules of competition and thus play a role in each country's import relief laws, depending on the approach taken to negotiation of the agreement. An arbitral mechanism or tribunal is much more likely to be developed to deal with intergovernmental disputes and problems of access to, or discriminatory practices in, the other country. Thus, a dispute-settlement mechanism could replace the Section 301 provision in U.S. trade law and the equivalent provi-

sion, Section 7 in the Canada Customs Act. The bilateral agreements on trade in services and investment issues also could provide recourse to a common dispute-settlement process.

Although the dispute-settlement process would probably be binational at its inception, it might be designed in a way that could facilitate the accession of other countries. For example, John Jackson made a proposal for a plurilateral dispute-settlement protocol.[22] Under Jackson's proposal, a tribunal would issue rulings to interpret the obligations in international agreements registered with that same tribunal. Thus, the character of the dispute-settlement process would be quite different from that of the GATT, which stresses conciliation. Since the objective is to obtain authoritative rulings, the tribunal does not need to be a solely bilateral institution. The rules and procedures in a CAFTA will almost certainly be unique, but the institutional machinery needs to be impartial, credible and authoritative; it need not be exclusive.

The key difference between the Jackson idea and the GATT mechanism for dispute settlement is that Jackson is proposing an expeditious mechanism to obtain rulings interpreting the rules and obligations contained in an international agreement; while the GATT process seeks to conciliate and to mediate between the parties to a dispute. Of course, bilateral conciliation and consultation would be an important element in the overall framework of the agreement, but the consultation between governments should be distinguished from a formal process for interpreting the obligations under the agreement.

Bilateral or Plurilateral Approaches?

It is evident that the potential extension of some of the bilateral arrangements to other countries would not be automatic and would occur through negotiations in the multilateral talks. Yet the possibility that some components of the bilateral agreement might subsequently be incorporated into, or influence the negotiation of, plurilateral or multilateral agreements is an important strategic consideration.

In light of the potential broader application of some of the bilateral arrangements pertaining to import relief laws, import-competing interests in both countries which initially might resist changes in such laws, also may prefer approaches that are tailored to the Canadian–U.S. relationship. As a result, these interests may become more amenable to elaboration of an entirely separate set of bilateral rules and procedures for import relief measures or even the national treatment approach, which could involve a more complete overhaul of the existing bilateral systems.

At the same time, both countries may wish to incorporate provisions into the bilateral agreement that are amenable to subsequent broader application as part of their negotiating strategy for the multilateral trade talks. Other countries could qualify for the more precise application of import relief laws if they were prepared to liberalize their tariff and nontariff barriers to trade. In this way, bilateral negotiation of rules of competition governing import relief laws could shape the agenda for multilateral negotiation of nontariff barriers and import relief laws.

Conclusion

Canadian–U.S. economic relations are at a critical juncture. One path is a perpetuation of the recent trend toward unilateral actions in the trade laws. Although U.S. countervailing duty cases have been the most controversial, Canada has also imposed countervailing duties on U.S. corn. Antidumping cases as well are brought regularly on both sides of the border. With the U.S. trade bill on the horizon, it will become even easier for U.S. industries to obtain import relief. Although we can anticipate an improvement in the U.S. trade balance and a waning of protectionism, the legacy of protectionist import relief laws will linger. Canada—who emulated U.S. trade laws with the 1984 Special Import Measures—is unlikely to resist for long pressures for similar counter-measures. The result will be managed trade and further conflict over differences in economic policies or institutions which are perceived to be unfair trade practices. In turn, faced with a hostile U.S. trade regime, Canada may resort to interventionist investment policies.

The other path is the negotiation of a Canadian-American free trade area. This would create a system of trade rules which would provide a more open and predictable environment for trade and investment. Such a regime would promote orderly economic adjustment, strengthen the international competitiveness of both economies and enhance growth prospects. Perhaps most important from the perspective of a smaller economic partner, a rules-based approach provides a more stable foundation for the conduct of bilateral economic relations and the exercise of economic sovereignty in an interdependent world.

Beyond their significance for bilateral economic relations, the negotiation of a CAFTA will have important implications for the international trading system. Although tariffs are unlikely to be a major focus of the next round of GATT negotiations, tariff reductions achieved as a result of a CAFTA will incidentally create preferences for suppliers in one country who are selling to consumers in the other. The expanded trading opportunities that will result within North America could increase the interest of Europe and Japan in negotiating the reduction of trade barriers in the multilateral talks. At the same time, the opening of the two North American markets will facilitate the rationalization of multinational firms operating in both countries and improve their ability to cope with offshore competition. Since Canadian tariffs are higher than U.S. tariffs and cover more products, U.S. exporters will enjoy higher margins of preference in the Canadian market than will Canadian firms exporting to the U.S. market. In both cases, these margins of preference could be gradually eroded by the multilateral negotiations, but this process is likely to be slow and predictable.

Bilateral agreements to liberalize trade in services, to clarify and liberalize policies toward direct investment and to strengthen dispute-settlement mechanisms could be a stimulus for similar types of arrangements in the multilateral talks. Indeed, key elements of a bilateral trade agreement, such as an establishment of general principles for trade in services, could become core components of a deal between a group of industrial countries. Canada and the United States have the opportunity to play a pioneering role in economic cooperation among advanced industrial societies.

If the bilateral talks fail to achieve a mutually acceptable agreement, however, then the implications for the multilateral talks are more problematic. Yes, the preparatory work by both countries will be extremely useful in the multilateral trade negotiations particularly on issues such as trade in services and policies toward direct investment; but if Canada and the United States cannot develop common approaches to these issues, then it will probably be even more difficult to achieve progress in the multilateral talks among countries with greater differences in their economic systems.

Perhaps the most difficult strategic question associated with a bilateral trade agreement pertains not to the multilateral talks, but to the possibility that third countries may wish to enter into bilateral trade agreements with one or both partners. If a third country wishes to accede to the Canadian–U.S. free trade area, it would most likely require a renegotiation of some key aspects of the bilateral agreement. If, on the other hand, another major trading country entered into a bilateral trade arrangement with one partner of the CAFTA—say, the United States—the result would be an erosion of the relative position of Canadian suppliers in the U.S. market, while U.S. producers would continue to enjoy preferences in the Canadian market. Of course, if either country entered into a bilateral trade agreement with a third country and no bilateral agreement existed between Canada and the United States, then only the third country would enjoy preferential access to its partner's market. Under the former British Preferential Tariff system, for example, U.S. suppliers often faced higher tariffs in the Canadian market than did their rivals in the United Kingdom. It must be recognized that the possibility of either the United States or Canada entering into a bilateral trade agreement with a third country is a direct corollary of each country wanting to preserve its independence in commercial policy.

If the bilateral talks between Canada and the United States are successful in concluding a free trade area agreement, they could provide a much needed impetus to the multilateral negotiations. If the bilateral talks fail to reach an agreement, however, this will not augur well for the multilateral process. Whatever the outcome, both countries can be expected to pursue separate commercial policies for economic relations with third countries. American and Canadian conduct in the bilateral and multilateral negotiations will have important implications for bilateral economic relations and for the global trading system.

The fundamental question is whether the United States seriously wishes to pursue either the bilateral or multilateral negotiations. In the 1930s the bankruptcy of the Smoot-Hawley tariff became quickly evident. The United States embarked on Cordell Hull's policy of reciprocal trade negotiations and one of several such bilateral agreements was concluded with Canada in 1935. Those bilateral trade agreements became the model for the postwar efforts that created the GATT and laid the foundations for an unprecedented period of prosperity.

In the 1980s the United States has maintained a rhetorical commitment to free trade while practicing creeping protectionism under the guise that imports are either unfair or disruptive. Despite the fine words of the Punta del Este Declaration, the GATT system is eroding in a drift toward managed trade. The self-inflicted wound of the U.S. trade deficit has unleashed a mania about unfair foreign trade in the United States which harkens back to the era of the scientific tariff—a doctrine that sought to eliminate all cost advantages among nations thereby destroying the potential gains from trade.

With a large trade deficit, the United States can credibly threaten the reinforcement of its arsenal of trade laws and procedures that provide import relief and involve aggressive retaliation. This strategy has already yielded positive results from the U.S. perspective. If it were not for the threat of such U.S. trade actions, Canada probably would not have offered to negotiate an elimination of its high tariffs, liberalization of trade in services or trade-related investment issues. It is not in the economic interest of the United States, however, to impose the threatened trade restrictions. Yet, the risk remains that Washington will believe its own rhetoric about unfair trade practices and act unilaterally.

This apparently tough-minded approach to the defense of U.S. economic interests ignores one important fact: the inevitable consequence of the massive U.S. trade and current account deficits in the 1980s is substantial foreign liabilities. In the 1990s the United States will be obliged to earn substantial surpluses on merchandise and services trade in order to service this foreign debt. The United States has more negotiating leverage now than it will have in the future. The United States will be well-served by greater emphasis on contractual (whether bilateral or multilateral), not unilateral, approaches to trade and investment relations. Expansion of exports will be vital to U.S. economic welfare during the 1990s and strengthening the trading rules, starting with a trade agreement with Canada, is crucial to U.S. as well as Canadian economic prospects.

Forging new bilateral rules regarding unfair trade practices, import disruption, services trade and investment policies, would have important implications for the world's largest economic relationship as well as for the global trading system. Although unilateral actions under the trade laws now appear attractive to the United States with its large trade deficit, both the United States and Canada share a common interest in achieving effective trade rules which will provide a more open and predictable regime for trade and investment. The Canadian-American free trade area will be unique, but the bilateral rules could serve as a directional beacon offering guidance to a rudderless trading system which is drifting toward a power-based system of managed trade and unilateral trade actions.

Epilogue

Without a doubt, 1988 promises to be a decisive year for bilateral economic relations, with broader ramifications for the global trading system. With the text of the Canada–U.S. free trade agreement complete, the focus will shift to domestic political fora to consider implementation. In Canada, the agreement has already sparked intense public debate, while in the United States the implementing legislation risks becoming entangled in political maneuvering over the trade bill.

The political pressures in each country reflect differing propensities toward unilateral measures. In Canada, criticism is focused on real or imagined constraints on nationalist trade and investment policies. Although October's stock market decline appears to have cooled congressional ardor for a protectionist trade bill, unilateral measures under the trade laws remain seductive with a large U.S. trade deficit.

Although the agreement is shaped by the many pressures and interests impinging on the world's largest bilateral commercial linkage, it is compatible with the multilateral system. Not only are the two proposing a classic free trade area, consistent with Article XXIV, but the agreement is interwoven with their respective multilateral trade obligations and interlinked with the Uruguay Round. The agreement goes beyond GATT and other free trade areas in dealing with services trade and investment. Perhaps not as much has been achieved in rolling back barriers as might have been hoped. The services and investment chapters are significant achievements, nonetheless. They provide clear contractual obligations, provide a basis for future negotiations about derogations from national treatment, and are subject to the general dispute-settlement provisions in the agreement. The latter could have significant precedential value for plurilateral agreements on services and investment.

The most controversial aspect of the agreement involves antidumping and countervailing duties. The agreement will institute an expeditious, binding binational appeal process for such cases and a review process governing changes in the trade laws, while deferring the task of developing common trade laws for five years. Thus the agreement seeks to stop the protectionist drift in each country's trade laws and to buffer the administration of those laws from political influences. Even a "responsible" trade bill, however, could make the agreement unacceptable in Canada.

As debtor nations, the United States and Canada will be obliged to run trade surpluses with the rest of the world in the 1990s. The realignment of trade patterns may facilitate efforts to roll back on a bilateral basis some of the protectionist provisions in each country's trade laws. Furthermore, each country's national interest will impel them to offer negotiated reductions in trade barriers to third countries during the Uruguay Round. Whether each will resist political pressures for unilateralism in 1988, and whether other countries will respond to U.S. and Canadian negotiating efforts in the Uruguay Round are different questions, but the answers are closely linked. Implementation of the agreement will strengthen the negotiating position of both countries, while a failure to do so will undermine their respective international interests.

Notes

1. Peter Morici, *The Global Competitive Struggle: Challenges to the United States and Canada* (Washington and Toronto: Canadian-American Committee, 1984), pp. 11–15.
2. Richard B. Lipsey and Wendy Dobson, eds., *Shaping Comparative Advantage* (Toronto: C. D. Howe Institute, 1986), pp. 138–39.
3. Edward Leamer, *Sources of International Comparative Advantage: Theory and Evidence* (Cambridge: MIT Press, 1985).
4. Report of the Honorable James Kelleher, minster for international trade, September 17, 1985.
5. Report to the President by the United States Trade Representative, Clayton Yeutter, September 17, 1985.
6. Department of External Affairs, "Multilateral Trade Negotiations: Some Initial Canadian Views," reproduced in *Canadian Trade Negotiations* (Ottawa: Supply and Services, 1985), pp. 35–42.
7. United States Trade Representative, "U.S. Goals for Multilateral Trade Negotiations: Statement of the United States to the GATT," September 7, 1985.
8. See Jagdish Bhagwati, "International Trade in Services and its Relevance for Economic Development," Xth annual lecture of the Geneva Association published by the Services World Forum, for a discussion of the interests of developing countries in trade in services.
9. See C. Michael Aho and Jonathan D. Aronson, *Trade Talks: America Better Listen!* (New York: Council on Foreign Relations, 1985 and 1987) and Gary Hufbauer and Jeffrey Schott, *Trading for Growth: The Next Round of Trade Negotiations* (Washington: Institute for International Economics, 1985).
10. Prime Minister Mulroney, Statement to the House of Commons, September 26, 1985.
11. Ibid.
12. In principle, at least, the possibility also exists that the bilateral arrangement could be a series of narrow sectoral deals analogous to the U.S.–Canadian Auto Pact. Negotiation of such arrangements, however, is a very difficult undertaking. For example, when Canada and the United States attempted sectoral trade negotiations in 1983, they found it very difficult to identify sectors in which both countries had a mutual interest in liberalizing bilateral trade. Moreover, such arrangements require a waiver under Article XXV of the GATT, whereby two-thirds of the GATT members approve and endorse the proposed bilateral trade arrangement, and obtaining such approval is likely to be difficult.
13. For example, the agreements between the European Community and each of the former EFTA countries—Austria, Finland, Norway, Sweden, and Switzerland—eliminated virtually all tariffs on products falling within tariff classifications 25–99, but maintained selective coverage of products within tariff classifications 01–24, including agricultural, fish, and food products.

14. See Richard G. Lipsey and Murray G. Smith, *Taking the Initiative: Canada's Trade Options in a Turbulent World* (Toronto: C. D. Howe Institute, 1985), Chapter 8; and Murray G. Smith with C. Michael Aho and Gary N. Horlick, *Bridging the Gap: Trade Laws in the Canadian–U.S. Negotiations* (Washington and Toronto: Canadian-American Committee, 1987).
15. Gardner Patterson, "The European Community as a Threat to the System," in William R. Cline, ed., *Trade Policy in the 1980s* (Washington: Institute for International Economics, 1983), pp. 223–42.
16. John H. Jackson, "The Birth of the GATT-MTN System: A Constitutional Appraisal," *Journal of Law and Policy in International Business*, vol. 12, no. 1 (1979), p. 12
17. Richard Cooper, "The Future of the International Trading System," in David Conklin and Thomas Courchene, eds., *Canadian Trade at a Crossroads: Options for New International Agreements* (Toronto: Ontario Economic Council, 1985).
18. U.S. Secretary of State George Shultz, Address to Woodrow Wilson School, Princeton, N.J., April 11, 1985.
19. United States, Executive Office of the President, *Economic Report of the President, Transmitted to the Congress February 1985, together with the Annual Report of the Council of Economic Advisers* (Washington: U.S. Government Printing Office, 1985), p. 126.
20. United States, Executive Office of the President, *Economic Report of the President, Transmitted to the Congress February 1986, together with the Annual Report of the Council of Economic Advisers* (Washington: U.S. Government Printing Office, 1986), p. 123.
21. G. Banks and Jan Tumlir, "The Political Problem of Adjustment," *The World Economy*, vol. 9 (1986), p. 149.
22. John H. Jackson, "Government Disputes in International Trade Relations: A Proposal in the Context of GATT," *Journal of World Trade Law*, vol. 13, no. 1 (1979), p. 13.
23. See Richard G. Lipsey and Murray G. Smith, *Global Economic Imbalances and U.S. Policy Responses: A Canadian Perspective* (Toronto and Washington: Canadian-American Committee, forthcoming).

5

A Mexican View

GERARDO M. BUENO

A REVIEW OF THE EXISTING LITERATURE on the negotiations between Canada and the United States for the creation of a free trade area reveals an interesting feature: there has been scant attention, until recently, to its effects on the partners' bilateral trade relations with third countries. This appears to be equally valid both for the Canadian and, though a bit less so, for the American sides.

This is not to say, of course, that there has been no concern at all about the effects of the Canada–U.S. trade agreement on third countries. In fact, there have been a number of discussions on the subject. The attention, however, has been focused on the effects of a bilateral agreement upon the positions both of the United States and Canada in the world trading system, and upon the ongoing multilateral trade negotiations within the General Agreement on Tariffs and Trade (GATT). There has also been some concern about what have come to be termed plurilateral trade negotiations, such as those with the European Economic Community (EEC), the European Free Trade Association (EFTA), the Latin American Integration Association (ALADI), and so forth.

The lack of preoccupation with the effects that the U.S.–Canada trade agreement could have on their bilateral trade relations with third countries can be easily explained in the case of Canada whose share of total world trade is not very large (1 percent of world imports in 1984), and who conducts approximately 80 percent of its trade relations with the United States. In the case of the United States, however, such a trade agreement could have more important repercussions for its bilateral trade relations, not only because its share in world trade is much

105

larger (18 percent of total world imports in 1968), but also because it is the main trading partner for a relatively large number of countries. One of these countries is Mexico which, like Canada, shares a long border with the United States and has a heavy concentration of trade there, accounting for approximately 70 percent of Mexican exports and 65 percent of its merchandise imports in 1986.

Accordingly, the main objectives of this chapter are to examine, from a Mexican perspective, some of the implications of the U.S.–Canada trade initiative on Mexico's role in the Northern American economic region; describe some of the main characteristics of Mexico's present trade policies; explore Mexico's trade policy options if the U.S.–Canada trade agreement is concluded; and touch upon some of the trade negotiating issues. In the end, some preliminary conclusions are presented.

The Role of Mexico in the Northern American Region

Trade relations among the three countries of the North American region are characterized by a high degree of assymetry. This is due to differences in their relative size, rates of growth, and factor endowments. However, C. Reynolds has pointed out that "from the viewpoint of demand as well as technology, there has been considerable convergence between the United States and Canada as well as between the United States and Mexico's middle and upper income groups which constitute a growing share of the total population (about one-third in Mexico)."[1] Assymetrical relations are also due to the simple fact that economic, social and political relations with the United States are far more important for both Canada and Mexico relative to the significance attached by the United States to its bilateral relations with either one of them. Table 1 provides some basic data about the three countries making up the Northern American region.

Note that the population of the region in 1985 reached about 344 million, which represents 7.3 percent of the world's population. Mexico's share in the region was 23 percent and it had the highest rate of growth, with 2.1 percent annually in 1984 (versus 0.9 percent and 0.7 percent in Canada and the United States, respectively). By the year 2000, Mexico's population is expected to reach about 100 million, Canada up to 31 million and 290 million for the United States.

In the region as a whole the U.S. economy is the largest—with 88 percent of the total gross national product (GNP), followed by Canada (8 percent) and Mexico (4 percent). The gap has narrowed in recent

Table 1

North American Region: Basic Economic Indicators

	Mexico	Canada	United States
Population (mid-1985; in millions)	79.8	25.4	239.0
Area (000 Km²)	1,973.0	9,976.0	9,363.0
Total GNP (1984; in billions)	177.4	346.0	3,946.6
Country share (percent)	4.0	8.0	88.0
GNP per capita (1985; in dollars)	2,080.0	13,680.0	16,690.0
Average annual growth rate (percent; 1965–85)	2.7	2.4	1.7
Structure of production (1985) (distribution of GDP; percent)			
Agriculture	11.0	3.0	2.0
Industry	35.0	30.0	31.0
(Manufacturing)[a]	24.0	16.0	20.0
Services	54.0	67.0	67.0
Exports of goods and non-factor services (percent GNP)	16.0	29.0	7.0
Merchandise trade (billions)			
Exports (1985)	21.9	87.5	213.1
Imports (1985)	13.5	81.5	361.6

[a] Because manufacturing is generally the most dynamic part of the industrial sector, its growth rate is shown separately.

Source: World Bank, World Development Report 1987 (New York: Oxford University Press, 1987), Table 1, Table 3, Table 5, Table 10, pp. 202–3, 206–7, 210–11, 220–21.

years as both Canada and Mexico have exhibited higher rates of growth for the overall economy and in per-capita terms.

There are, as is well known, sharp differences between Mexico's level of per-capita income and those of Canada and the United States. Mexico's per-capita income in 1985 (lower than in 1982) represented only about 15 percent of the average of the other two countries. Nevertheless, a comparison of Mexico's per-capita income level with that of other Latin American countries in the same year reveals that it was exceeded only by Argentina and Venezuela.

Finally, in terms of openness of its economy, Mexico is very much in the middle, at 16 percent, between Canada (where the ratio of exports of goods and non-factor services to GNP in 1985 reached 29 percent) and the United States (where the figure was only 7 percent). Corre-

spondingly, in both cases, Canada and Mexico account for a larger
share of the total foreign trade of the region than of its GNP.

Turning our attention to trade, we find from Table 2 that in terms of
the structure of commodity exports, primary commodities loom large
in the cases of Canada (45 percent in 1984) and of Mexico; although
with respect to the latter, there have been substantial changes in the
structure of exports between 1984 and 1986—due to the sharp decrease
in the price of oil and an equally dramatic increase in non-oil exports.
Thus, primary commodities, which accounted for 73 percent of total
exports in 1984, declined to 55 percent in 1986. In the United States, on
the other hand, manufactures were 70 percent of total exports, this
being mostly machinery and transport equipment (44 percent).

Regarding the structure of imports, note, once again, that there has
been a drastic change in the case of Mexico: between 1984 and 1986
there was a substantial decrease in the share of food imports (from 17

Table 2

Trade in the North American Region

	Mexico		Canada	United States
Structure of exports (percent)	*1984*	*1986*	*1984*	*1984*
Fuels, minerals and metals	64	42	23	8
Other primary commodities	9	13	22	22
Machinery and transport equipment	16	20	35	44
Other manufactures	12	24	20	24
(Textiles and clothing[a])	1	1	1	2
Structure of imports (percent)				
Food	17	7	7	8
Fuels	3	4	7	22
Other primary commodities	6	4	6	7
Machinery and transport equipment	45	50	51	32
Other manufactures	29	35	30	31
Mexican Trade Relations with the United States and Canada (1986)				
Imports (million dollars)			183	6,347
Percentage			2	65
Rank			6	1
Exports (million dollars)			167	8,460
Percentage			1	67
Rank			6	1

[a] Textiles and Clothing are a subgroup of other manufactures.

Source: World Bank, *World Development Report 1987* (New York: Oxford University Press,
1987), Table 11, Table 12, pp. 222–23, 224–25, Banco de Mexico, *Informe Anual
1986*, Caudro 17 (1987), p. 228; and *Comercio Exterior*, vol. 37, no. 5 (mayo de
1987), p. 431.

percent to 7 percent) thanks to substantial increases in domestic production. It seems clear, however, that Mexico will have to continue to
import sizable amounts of cereals, dry edible beans and oilseeds in
future years. The structure of imports for Mexico in 1986 is strikingly
similar to that of Canada. In the United States, on the other hand,
primary commodities account for a large share of total imports.

Based on Mexican data, we shall now focus on trade relations between Mexico and Canada.[2] As can be seen in Table 2, trade between
the two countries is relatively small. Canada's share in Mexican imports is only 2 percent and in exports even lower, 1 percent. Canada
ranks sixth among Mexico's trade partners in both imports and exports. In turn, Mexico's share in Canada's imports was 0.4 percent in
1984 and it ranked sixth among Canada's export markets. Mexican
imports from Canada include mostly steel products, milk, pulp and
paper, metro cars, motor vehicles, and parts for motor vehicles. Mexican exports to Canada have been mainly petroleum, motor vehicles,
and parts for motor vehicles. The intra-industry trade in motor vehicles, and parts for motor vehicles, suggests that production arrangements by multinational enterprises have played an important role in
trade between the two countries.

To this we can add that in other areas of external economic relations,
such as foreign investment, transfer of technology, external debt and
tourism, the pattern is very similar to that observed in the case of trade
relations. In fact, in several of these areas the significance of the United
States for the Mexican economy looms larger than in the case of trade.

In sum, it is clear that Mexico's place in the North American region is
that of a less-developed country (LDC)—even though it is characterized more as a newly industrializing country (NIC)—living side-by-
side with two of the most advanced economies in the world, and
certainly in the Western Hemisphere. In addition, Mexico has very
complex and intense relations with the United States, but scant economic relations with Canada. It is possible, then, that this latter fact is
one of the considerations that prompted the so-called Canadian initiative to be an essentially bilateral, and not a trilateral endeavor.

Mexico's Present Trade Policies

Notwithstanding the above, there are important issues for Mexico
concerning its trade options and, more generally, its development
strategies. In fact, one could speak of a greater degree of convergence
between Mexico's trade policies and U.S. and Canadian policies, since
Mexico—but with the opposition of vested interests—is gradually

abandoning import-substitution policies in favor of more outward-oriented policies.

Trade and industrial development policies are the subject matter of the National Program for Industrial and Trade Promotion (Programa Nacional de Fomento Industrial y Comercio Exterior[3]) which was released in 1984 and, contrary to similar exercises in the past, has served to guide the Mexican decision-making process in the area of trade. The Program itself is quite comprehensive and in many respects, very different from the National Industrial Development Plan formulated in 1977. For one thing, oil is no longer seen as the panacea that the Plan thought it was.

The Program starts by criticizing past development policies that tended to rely heavily on import substitution under the umbrella of a system of protection that granted excessive protection in an indiscriminate manner, and without due regard for its effects on either the allocation of resources or relative prices. Furthermore, it argued that such strategies had led to the creation of an industrial system which, at the same time that it was heavily dependent on imports, showed a very low export capacity. It was pointed out in this regard that manufacturing exports had been sufficient to cover only one-fourth of the imports by the manufacturing sector itself.

For the industrial sector, the short-term objective, quite understandably, was its preservation and revitalization. And in the medium and long term, the Program found no need to choose between import-substitution and export-promotion strategies. Though it recognized a need to increase exports, it also favored import substitution provided that it was supported by sectoral industrial programs.

However, and in spite of the fact that the Program itself is a vast improvement over past exercises, three problems present themselves. First, the issue of choosing between different development strategies is not resolved as easily as saying that there is no conflict between export-promotion and import-substitution strategies, and that therefore the two can be carried out simultaneously. As experience shows, inconsistencies are bound to appear. Rather than speak of export promotion *per se*, one should speak of outward-oriented strategies that provide a uniform incentive to both import substitution and exports, and thus to saving and to earning foreign exchange per unit of domestic resources added. The emphasis, then, should be on a more efficient allocation of resources, rather than on export expansion *per se*.

Furthermore, in any industrialization process there is import substitution *and* exports, with both contributing to the growth of domestic production. The choice between inward- or outward-oriented strategies does, however, make a difference. Take the experience of many semi-industrial countries as an example; outward-oriented strategies with the emphasis on efficient allocation of resources led not only to the growth of exports, but also to more import substitution than in countries with inward-oriented strategies.

A second problem concerns protection policy where, in accordance with the previous plan, the Program rejects two mutually exclusive positions, an "outmoded" liberalization or, alternatively, an absolute protectionism, and therefore says that the main purpose should be to rationalize protection both to favor efficient import substitution and to promote exports. Rationalization in turn was defined, circularly, as a policy in which protection is gradually adjusted "to permit a selective import-substitution process and to promote exports." The all too apparent problem with this approach is that, once more, it avoids hard choices but, more importantly, it says little about the desirable levels of protection.

Third, the Program makes only fleeting references to a realistic exchange rate policy, perhaps on the grounds that it did not fall under the jurisdiction of the Ministry of Trade and Industrial Promotion. In the case of Mexico, to ignore the importance of the relationship between commercial and exchange rate policies is a serious omission since the hindrances to the development process in the late sixties and, more particularly, the crises of 1976 and 1982 all had as a common element the overvaluation of the peso. Furthermore, the efforts to compensate temporarily for overvaluation through raising tariffs and quantitative restrictions had devastating effects on the role of the system of protection in the allocation of economic resources.

As mentioned above, the actual trade policy measures adopted by the Mexican government have, in several areas, gone beyond those put forth in the Program. In addition, the sharp drop in oil prices in 1986 led to a more explicit outward-oriented trade policy than had been the case before.

The most important trade policy measures actually adopted by the Mexican government have been the following:

- the conclusion of a Memorandum of Understanding with the U.S. government concerning export subsidies and countervailing duties;
- the ongoing discussion with the U.S. government for a more comprehensive trade agreement; and
- the decision to join GATT.

Let us consider each of these in turn. The conclusion of the Memorandum of Understanding on export subsidies and countervailing duties in 1984 became necessary because as Mexico was not a signatory of the GATT code on subsidies, American producers did not have to demonstrate that they had been injured before countervailing duties could be put on Mexican exports. In addition, the 1982 debt crisis drastically changed Mexico's position from a country with large imports from the United States and exports mainly of oil, to a country which must curtail imports and increase its exports of non-oil products. As a result, the number of complaints by American producers against Mexico that had to be investigated by the U.S. International Trade Commission increased very rapidly. In 1982 alone there were six such cases (affecting mainly agricultural products, chemicals and steel), another seven in 1983 (mainly for cement, bricks and tiles, glass and other steel products), and as many as eight in 1984. Mexico became, thus, one of the countries whose exports were most affected by the "threat" of investigative actions by the United States.[4]

The negotiation of the Memorandum of Understanding illustrated, in a sense, the weaker negotiating position of the Mexican government. In the end, it was clear that Mexico would have been better off if it had signed GATT's export subsidy code. One important advantage of the Memorandum, however, was that it served to initiate negotiations between the two governments for a more comprehensive trade agreement.

These bilateral negotiations are still underway and, according to the latest information, advancing at a good pace. Mexico is seeking freer access to the U.S. market and a more explicit recognition of its status as a developing country; while the United States is interested both in strengthening its position in the Mexican market, and in improving conditions for its investments and industrial property rights in Mexico. The latter two issues, as was to be expected, are very sensitive politically.

By far the most important decision has been that of joining GATT. It demanded a certain amount of political courage, since it was only in 1979 that Mexico had decided not to become a member of GATT mainly because of what were termed "political" considerations. The rationale given at the time was that joining GATT would restrict Mexico's freedom of action in following the development policies which it considered to be in its best interests.

Yet it was precisely the choice of development policies that had changed after the 1982 external debt crisis, along with the need for Mexico to change from an inward-oriented to a more outward-oriented approach. After the usual negotiations, whose results were not deemed as favorable as those that might have been obtained in 1979—

reflecting once more the loss of political clout—Mexico became a full-fledged member of the GATT in 1986. The reasons given for this turn around—which, by the way, were also valid in 1979—were that GATT membership would provide:

- access to a forum for solving trade disputes;
- an improvement in the conditions for access to international markets; and
- an opportunity to participate more fully in the forthcoming multilateral trade negotiations, the so-called "Uruguay Round."

In the past Mexico had been regarded as "one of the countries that are commercially integrated into the world trading system even if they stand apart in their institutional arrangements."[5] Now it seems clear that Mexico's full-fledged participation in GATT will certainly give greater weight to the LDCs in the ongoing negotiations in the Uruquay Round.

Concerning external economic policies, as mentioned above, there have been substantial changes both in protection policies and in exchange rate policies. Table 3 provides an indication of those trends. However, at least two words of caution about the figures shown therein seem to be in order.

First, the data on nominal protection are based on direct price comparisons between Mexico's domestic prices and world market prices weighted by domestic production values. Therefore, the figures on the average level of nominal protection are heavily influenced by the degree of overvaluation, or, as has been the case in most recent years, by the degree of undervaluation of the exchange rate and, also, by the lower-than-world-market prices of petroleum products, electricity and basic staples. Nominal tariff protection is then higher than nominal implicit protection. Secondly, the figures on the exchange rate take 1970 as the base year; a more satisfactory period would perhaps have been the first quarter of 1977 when Mexico's balance of payments was in equilibrium. The average corresponding figure of the index for the effective rate of exchange was 130.3.

Concerning commercial policy, there have been several important changes. First, starting in 1986 there was a substantial reduction in the number of products subject to import permits, which thenceforth became protected only by tariffs. In 1982, after the debt crisis, practically all the products included in the trade classification required import permits; at the end of 1986, however, the substitution of tariffs for quantitative restrictions had advanced considerably. Only 638 prod-

Table 3

*Mexico: Evolution of Nominal Protection and the Effective Rate
of Exchange: 1981–1986*

(percentages)

		Nominal Protection I[a]		Nominal Protection II[a]		Index of Effective Rate of Exchange
		Average	Dispersion	Average	Dispersion	
	1981	5.86	44.20			87.3
Jan.	1983	−26.10	33.80			144.5
July	1984	−13.80	27.20			109.9
Dec.	1984	−7.30	24.10			99.9
May	1985	−4.40	26.40	−11.0	29	94.7
Sept.	1985			−22.1	30	116.7
Dec.	1985			−28.0	31	128.2
March	1986			−31.0	27	145.8
June	1986			−33.4	28	157.5
Sept.	1986			−34.9	27	169.9
Dec.	1986			−38.1	26	173.0

[a] The figures in column I are based on direct price comparison observations weighted by the actualized 1980 input-output matrix values. Those in column II are based on direct price comparisons for May 1986, which were then adjusted taking into consideration the evolution of the relevant wholesale price indexes in Mexico and in a group of industrialized countries. Weights are based in the actualized 1985 input-output matrix.

Source: For the figures on nominal protection, Grupo de Estudio sobre Proteccion IMCE-Secofi. For those on the rate of exchange, Banco de México, *Informe Anual 1986*, p. 135.

ucts remained subject to import permits; they represented 8 percent of the products included in the Mexican trade classification, and covered 28 percent of the total value of imports.

The rationalization of protection has also entailed a reduction in tariff levels and in their dispersion. When the program was started there were ten tariff groups whose rates went from zero to more than 100 percent. At the end of the rationalization program in 1988 it is expected that the tariff structure will be as follows: 1) zero for basic raw materials and staple goods; 2) 10 percent for goods not produced in the country or subject to the so-called Eighth Rule (mainly machinery); and 3) 20, 25 and 30 percent for the goods produced domestically according to the amount of manufacturing that has gone into them and their levels of effective protection. Other measures included the abolition of official prices used for assessing the taxes paid by importers—which in many instances served to increase the level of protection—and to prevent dumping; the removal of regulations which, in effect, granted a monopolistic position for the importation of certain commodities; and, in general, a simplification of bureaucratic procedures for importers and exporters.

Exchange rate policies have also become a useful instrument for attaining external balance. This is an important change for in the past there was a tendency to keep the peso overvalued based on considerations of national "prestige" and the wish to reduce domestic inflation. As can be seen in Table 3, except for a short lapse in 1985, the Mexican peso has been clearly undervalued for most of the 1982–86 period. In 1986, in fact, increased undervaluation of the exchange rate was an important element in attaining external balance in the face of very difficult conditions (the loss of foreign exchange earnings due to the sharp drop in oil prices). Increased undervaluation of the peso led to a reduction of imports, to a substantial increase in exports of non-oil products, and to inducing capital repatriation. In addition, as has been noted, it made possible, for the first time in Mexican history, the continuation of the programs to rationalize protection and not a reversal, as had been the case in the past.

Mexico's Basic Trade Policy Options

The changes that have taken place in Mexico's trade policy measures and, more importantly, in commercial and exchange rate policies go in the proper direction. Although there is some vocal domestic opposition to them, there is a consensus of opinion in their favor. Nevertheless, there remain important questions about the future. Some of them concern trade policy options.

Broadly speaking these are three:

1) whether to rely on the results of multilateral trade negotiations;
2) whether to seek a more comprehensive trade agreement with the United States; and
3) whether to join—even if there is no "formal" invitation yet—the so-called Canadian initiative.

To these three, perhaps a fourth could be added, which is whether to create a free trade area between Mexico and the United States.[6]

Obviously one option does not necessarily preclude the others. The first one would correspond to a multilateral approach; the second—and perhaps the fourth—to a bilateral one; and the third to a trilateral approach.

These are, of course, not the only options but they seem to be the most relevant. Other options would be: to continue with the status quo of a gradual movement towards trade liberalization through existing channels; to reverse present policies by turning Mexico inwards; to intensify the efforts in favor of Latin American regional economic integration and of trade with other LDCs; and to seek closer trade ties with Japan and Europe.[7] With the exception of adopting more inward-oriented trade policies, several of these options can be pursued simultaneously with any one of the three basic trade options just mentioned above.

Whatever basic trade policy option is chosen, it seems clear that the negotiating issues for Mexico will be very much the same. It is important to mention in this regard that, as in the case of Korea, the Mexican government has publicly stated its concern about the deterioration of the international trading system and its resolve to contribute to its strengthening.[8]

Issues Raised by the Canadian Initiative: The Third Option

What are the implications for third countries of a U.S.–Canada free trade agreement? The answer to this question is not altogether clear. The issue is certainly more important for the United States than for Canada, because the former is a main trading partner of a larger number of countries. Some questions have already been put forward, such as those dealing with the risk of spreading bilateral arrangements; the possible damage to trade relations with other countries; the effectiveness of the bilateral agreement if other countries join; and its relationship with, and bearing on, the current Uruguay Round negotiations. The list can readily be extended.

The matter is further complicated by the fact that the U.S.–Canada free trade agreement announced on October 5, 1987 has yet to be ratified by the legislative branches of the two countries. As is well known, there are still some important issues to be resolved. Therefore, it is difficult to know which of the options are truly available.

However, from the Mexican viewpoint, the agreement definitely poses important considerations, especially with respect to Mexico's position in the North American market. One of them is the threat of trade diversion in products where Mexico has shown a comparative advantage, for instance in motor vehicle parts. Another is the danger that protectionist pressure could spread from the United States into Canada and vice versa. More generally, what are the implications—not only economic, but also political—of being "left out?"[9]

Contrary to what has happened in Canada and, though to a lesser degree, in the United States, not much thought appears to have been given to the subject in Mexico.[10] This is regrettable because the free trade agreement between Canada and the United States will certainly have implications for Mexico.

The main problem, as was to be expected, stems from Mexico's position as the underdeveloped country of the region. In one of the few analyses of this question, Victor Urquidi, after discarding the idea of a common market between the three countries, stated that "without pleading for the Canadian position—also a protectionist country for its industry—the mere notion that Mexico, from a weaker economic position than the other two, should open its tariff border, would mean the rapid demise of most of Mexican manufacturing industry, before it even had a chance to start making inroads—if it could—into the U.S. and Canadian markets."[11] He then went on to propose negotiated schemes in dynamic sectors on branches where production-sharing could take place.[12]

The sectoral approach to trade liberalization appears attractive for a country like Mexico, both because the risks to domestic industry do not loom so large as in a comprehensive free trade agreement, and because there would be a greater degree of control in the trade liberalization process. These are, indeed, important advantages for Mexico since its level of development is so far behind that of Canada and the United States.

Unfortunately, this approach probably is not feasible in actual practice. First, these sectoral agreements are likely to be open to objection under GATT rules. Second, they presuppose that industrial policies are complementary, when in fact they are not. Mexico's industrial policy, with its high degree of state participation, is very different from that which is followed in the United States and Canada. Consequently, and assuming the sectoral agreements even get signed, there would be serious practical difficulties in the endeavor to put these agreements into operation.

On the other hand, it is overly pessimistic to believe that Mexico's participation in a U.S.–Canada free trade agreement would automatically lead to the demise of the Mexican manufacturing industry. Yes, the prevailing sentiment in Mexico and other LDCs is to distrust trade liberalization initiatives coming from the industrial countries of the North, but at a minimum there needs to be an economic analysis of the gains and costs of such a course of action. This unduly pessimistic view is objectionable for at least three other reasons. First, past experience has shown that no country, no matter what its level of development, has seen its industry "disappear" as a result of its participation in a free trade area or other more complex economic integration schemes. Secondly, there is a negotiating process that precedes participation whose purpose is precisely to find the mutual advantages and minimize the possible costs of participation. Finally, if the result falls far short of expectations, or if the costs prove to be greater than the gains, there is always the possibility of renegotiating the provisions or, quite simply, of denouncing the agreement. There is, then, always a way out.

Turning our attention now to the three basic trade options, we must distinguish between the short, medium and long term. In the short term, the optimal course of action for Mexico seems to remain that of seeking a more comprehensive trade agreement with the United States. For now, it would not be practical, or feasible, to join the U.S.–Canada free trade negotiations. What Mexico needs is assurance that its exports will not be subjected to new trade barriers so that it will be able to service its debt through increased exports, rather than through the application of deflationary policies.

In the medium term, however, the option of joining the U.S.–Canada free trade area could assume increased importance. Of course, this would largely depend upon its characteristics, and especially if it can be joined by other countries and under what conditions.[13] Very briefly, some of the main issues are the following:

Mexico's Special Status as an LDC in the Northern American Region Under GATT rules, LDCs enjoy certain privileges because of their development needs. However, it has been pointed out that the concessions granted to LDCs have been in some cases more nominal than real.[14] On the other hand, it has also been argued that future trade liberalization by the industrial countries would hardly be possible unless the more advanced developing countries liberalize their own important restrictions.[15]

In the context of the U.S.–Canada free trade agreement, this means, in effect, that Mexico should be prepared to undertake substantial obligations. But neither these obligations, nor the time schedule for adoption of trade liberalization measures, should be the same for Mexico and the other two countries.

Market Access It is difficult to foresee whether the U.S.–Canada negotiations will lead to the total abolition of tariffs on the reciprocal trade of the two countries. As it stands now, however, the idea is to eliminate bilateral tariffs within ten years beginning January 1, 1989. Together with this, the agreement set up what has been termed a "strong and expeditious dispute-settlement mechanism."[16] Thus disputes not resolved in consultations will be automatically referred to arbitration panels composed of neutral, independent experts. This was one of the main objectives on the Canadian side, thus seeking, as it were, protection against American protectionism.

A reduction in Mexican tariffs could also be envisioned provided that Mexico's special situation as an LDC is recognized in the negotiations to that effect. There would be problems, however, with nontariff barriers. On the one hand, Mexico, along with other developing countries, has suffered in recent years because of the nontariff barriers imposed outside the GATT framework. On the other hand, as we have seen, Mexico also continues to use nontariff barriers as an instrument of protection.

Therefore, the final results of the negotiations between Canada and the United States on this particular issue will be crucial. If nontariff barriers are well-catalogued and both governments can agree to a formal process of negotiations and consultation for solving disputes, this would be a very significant step in a positive direction. Otherwise, it is difficult to foresee how the problems raised by nontariff barriers can be overcome.[17]

Agriculture According to the latest available information, the two sides also agreed to an elimination of all agriculture tariffs within ten years. The agreement provides more access to the Canadian market for U.S. horticultural products; conditionally eliminates the necessity of Canadian import licenses for grains as soon as subsidies for these products reach the same levels as those in the United States; and liberalizes quotas for imports of poultry, poultry products and eggs. In addition, the two countries will exempt each other from their respective meat import laws.

The Mexican agricultural sector is very different from those of the United States and Canada. The portion of the population living off agriculture is much larger in absolute and relative terms, land holdings are much smaller and productivity is lower. This means that the political problem posed by the agricultural sector may be much more important for Mexico than for the United States and Canada. Therefore, the agreement reached between the United States and Canada with respect to the agricultural sector may not be applicable to Mexico's conditions. Specific negotiations would be necessary if Mexico were to join the Canada–U.S. free trade area.

Still, Mexico would have much to gain in terms of export possibilities for vegetables, fruits, flowers and meat. At the same time, it would remain an important market for exports from Canada and the United States for maize, wheat, barley and other agricultural products.

Unfair Trade Practices In the Annex to the GATT Code on Export Subsidies and Countervailing Duties, there is an illustrative list of the trade-promotion measures which could be regarded as, in effect, export subsidies. A problem arises, however, when the domestic subsidies used to promote other important social and economic objectives also cause damage to the competitive position of the industries of other countries. It is here that defining export subsidies becomes a relatively complex matter.

In connection with this, both countries agreed in principle to retain existing national laws on subsidies and dumping and the procedures to deal with them. They also agreed, however, that national antidumping and countervailing duty decisions may be appealed to the binational dispute-settlement panels. The dispute-settlement procedure will, in fact, replace review by the courts. The panels will review decisions by U.S. and Canadian authorities to ensure that the laws of each country have been faithfully and correctly applied. Accordingly, the U.S. decisions of the Commerce Department and the International Trade Commission can be overturned only if they are not supported by substantial evidence or are otherwise not in accordance with U.S. law.

In the Memorandum of Understanding between Mexico and the United States on subsidies and countervailing duties, Mexico agreed not to use export subsidies or subsidies having a similar effect. This goes beyond the requirements of the GATT code on subsidies.

In the U.S.–Canadian context, it has been said that "unfair methods such as subsidies could be explicitly defined. The two countries could decide which policies are not legitimate to use and develop timetables for eliminating them."[18] Unfortunately, this is more easily said than done.[19]

Notwithstanding the final result of the U.S.–Canada trade talks, it is clear that for Mexico the issue will not be an easy one to resolve. A high degree of participation by the state in the Mexican economy leads also to the utilization of subsidies for many development objectives such as regional development, promoting certain economic activities or favoring certain population groups, and so forth. Many of these instruments of promotion do not have a direct bearing on exports, but a case could be made against them. Where to draw the line is not, then, so easy to determine.

In the case of antidumping, Mexico has recently enacted new legislation. In the past, dumping was prevented both through the legal obligations in general trade legislation and, more importantly, through the utilization of import permits and official prices. However, since the recently enacted Mexican legislation resembles that of the United States in its conceptual provisions, harmonization of the terms of their trade legislations should not present a significant problem.

Services At the September 1986 GATT Ministerial meeting Mexico was one of the LDCs that took a favorable attitude toward the inclusion of this issue in the Uruguay Round agenda. This was in opposition to the positions of other influential countries in the LDC groupings. Mexico's withdrawal from the LDC blocs in this instance was justified by the fact, among others, that trade in services is more important for Mexico than seems to be the case for other LDCs. Tourism, border transactions, revenues from offshore plants (*maquiladoras*) and engineering services are important items in the Mexican balance of payments. In addition, the low cost of Mexican labor could serve to open interesting trade possibilities in services given its proximity to the U.S. market.

However, as is well known, regulating trade in services is a thorny and complex issue. To this day there is no negotiating agenda for the Uruguay Round. The United States and Canada arrived at a more or less solid agreement concerning services trade liberalization, and this has been regarded as a significant contribution to the debate and to the GATT negotiations themselves.

In the case of services, according to the information transcribed in the *Elements of the Agreement*, there is a provision for the right of establishment, the right to cross-border sales, disciplines on public monopolies and, again, a binding dispute-settlement mechanism. In financial services in particular—a much debated issue between the two parties—under the agreement both nations undertake to eliminate discrimination and improve "access and competitive opportunities for financial institutions of the other party consistent with prudential and regulatory requirements." The envisaged changes would affect Canadian law that at present prohibits individual share holders of a bank with a capital base of more than 750 million (Canadian dollars) from holding more than 10 percent of the common shares. The rule, as is obvious, served in the past to limit the size of wholly owned subsidiaries of U.S. banks operating in Canada.

Yet, even before judging the merits of the U.S.–Canada agreement on trade in services, there are two problems regarding the Mexican position on this matter. First, the issue is intertwined with foreign investment policies and legislation. According to informal information, this caused difficulties to the Canadian side in the negotiations. Secondly, Mexico's position cannot be defined in an abstract manner without taking into consideration the consensus of opinion of the other LDCs in the Uruguay Round of trade negotiations.

If these two problems are not deemed insurmountable and Mexico considers joining the U.S.–Canada agreement, another stumbling block in the services trade negotiations could be broken down. Mexico's joining the agreement would prove that it is possible for LDCs both to negotiate and to arrive at mutually advantageous results.

Foreign Investment Paul Wonnacott has said that "International investment, and the policies used to regulate such investment, have been a source of friction in U.S.–Canadian relations. For decades, many Canadians have been deeply concerned that foreign—and particularly U.S.—ownership of their industry might lead to loss of control over their economic destiny."[20]

It is well known that Canadian—and American—regulations on foreign investment have been one of the major hurdles in the negotiations for a free trade agreement. Among the issues that seem to have been the most important are the following: 1) how much foreign investment regulations by Canada should be liberalized; 2) how to deal with the problems of domestic-content and export-performance requirements; 3) how to deal with investment by third countries; and 4) the fact that negotiations on services are to some extent related to foreign investment. All these issues, at least from the Canadian viewpoint, have to be considered in terms of the contribution that U.S. foreign investment could make to Canadian interests and objectives.

The *Elements of the Agreement* document states that "the parties have agreed to provide each other's investors national treatment with respect to the establishment of new businesses, the acquisition of existing businesses, and the conduct, operation and sale of established businesses." It also " . . . provides that the parties will not impose export, local content, local sourcing, or import substitution requirements on each other's investors, and will not place such requirements on third-country investors when any significant impact on U.S.–Canadian trade could result."

As can be seen, then, negotiations between Canada and the United States led to a substantial liberalization of foreign investment flows between the two countries. The only industries excluded from the investment chapter are the cultural industries. In addition, the agreement also defines the conditions under which Canada will continue to review U.S. investment in Canada for both the direct acquisitions (only for those above 150 million Canadian dollars), and the indirect acquisitions (with no review whatsoever after the fourth year).

The situation is very much the same for Mexico. First, it is also an important country for U.S. foreign direct investment, accounting for about 10 percent of the total. Secondly, U.S. foreign direct investment in Mexico represents about 70 percent of the total invested in that country (and a similar percentage in terms of payments for transfer of technology). In turn, Canada's share in Mexico's foreign direct investment is only about 7 percent. Most of the foreign direct investment is concentrated in manufacturing, commerce and other services.

Mexican legislation on foreign investment, in the words of Jaime Alvarez S., is "a phenomenon with a long tradition, just as long as that of foreign investment itself." In his opinion, the operation of the law (issued in 1973) has been satisfactory since the legislation has proven to be supple and flexible, and has varied according to changes in the economic environment.[21]

There have been, however, recent changes in the legislation. Their main purpose has been to clarify the rules governing it and to simplify administrative procedures. There has been in addition greater "flexibility" in the interpretation of the law. This has meant that practically all projects submitted for authorization have been approved by the Commission for Foreign Investment. Moreover, the lapse between admission of the application and its authorization or rejection has been considerably shortened. In the case of *maquila* or offshore firms, authorization is granted matter-of-factly in a period that does not exceed three or four days.

As was to be expected, however, in the bilateral negotiations between Mexico and the United States leading to a comprehensive trade agreement, the Reagan administration has been somewhat negative. At the same time that they have recognized that the interpretation of the law has indeed been more supple and flexible, they still regard it as unduly restrictive. Just as in the case of Canada, domestic-content and export-performance requirements are the most contested restrictions, though, in the Mexican case, the restrictions with respect to entry for foreign investment in certain sectors are also queried.

These issues, in the Mexican view, are considered to be "part and parcel" of the negotiations concerning trade-related investment within the context of the Uruquay Round. According to this view, the present rules on domestic content, or even on export-performance requirements, should not, in principle, have to be modified in the basic foreign investment legislation. This is probably a valid approach, for Mexico, on the one hand, may invoke the exceptions contemplated in Part IV of the agreement and, on the other, it can claim that the legislation is not unduly restrictive, as is shown in practice by the significant recent growth of foreign investment in Mexico. The above discussion illuminates two important facts: 1) that there are similarities between the Mexican and the Canadian positions with respect to foreign investment, and 2) that both countries are politically sensitive about the issues involved. Taking these two facts into consideration, plus the change in Mexican attitudes toward foreign investment, one should also conclude that the U.S.–Canada agreement could, to a certain extent, cover some of Mexico's worries in this regard. Some remaining issues would, however, have to be negotiated duly taking into account Mexico's level of development.

Intellectual Property In a recent contribution to the debate, C. Michael Aho and Marc Levinson wrote the following: "Recent disputes over the protection of intellectual property are a major source of friction between the United States and Canada. Among them are Canada's procedure for compulsory licensing of pharmaceutical products."[22] If one substitutes Mexico for Canada, it would also be a fair description of the disputes between Mexico and the United States. There are similar Mexican regulations concerning radio and television programs emanating from the United States, although these are not covered under the label of "preservation of cultural identity," as is done in Canada.

However, it is worth mentioning that, in the past, U.S.–Mexican disputes on this particular issue have been even more contentious. In certain cases, the U.S. position was justifiable; for this reason, but also taking into account Mexico's own interest, important changes were introduced in the Mexican legislation. The most important disputes concerned trademark regulations (and, more specifically, trademark piracy) and the "patentability" of pharmaceutical products. On the U.S. side, also, pressures for further changes in the Mexican legislation have been stepped up. These have involved, on the one hand, limitations on the benefits of the Generalized System of Preferences (GSP) for the LDCs whose intellectual property law is deemed unduly restrictive and, on the other, more specifically directed against Mexico as a condition for the signature of the so-called comprehensive trade agreement between Mexico and the United States.

Negotiations between Mexico and the United States concerning this complex issue—much linked to technological policy—will not be easy; one therefore cannot be very optimistic about rapid progress in settling differences between the two countries. In addition, this issue will be on the agenda of the Uruguay Round; therefore, Mexico will want to participate and to observe the outcome of these negotiations before it commits itself to changes in its own legislation. One further consideration is that there is yet another forum where the issue has traditionally been dealt with, namely that of the World Intellectual Property Organization (WIPO).

The *Elements of the Agreement* document unfortunately does not shed much light on this issue from Mexico's viewpoint. It only mentions two things: 1) that the parties "have agreed to cooperate in the Uruguay Round of multilateral trade negotiations and in other international fora to improve protection of intellectual property;" and 2) that Canada "has agreed to revise its copyright law to provide protection to the retransmission of copying programming effective no later than the entry into force of this Agreement."

Conclusion

In this chapter we have examined some of the effects that the U.S.–Canada free trade agreement could have on third countries. To this end we have explicitly considered the case of Mexico as a country also forming part of the North American region, with close ties to the United States, and therefore most likely to be affected by such an agreement. As argued here, the question of the effects of the agreement on third countries is a relatively novel one. It is likely to be of more significance for the United States than for Canada, in view of the former's much larger share in world trade, and the fact that it is the main trading partner of a relatively large number of countries.

One basic problem we had to face in this endeavor is that this chapter was written without knowledge of the exact provisions of the possible U.S.–Canada free trade agreement, or the exact extent of its "open-endedness." Nevertheless, the issues are relatively well known; so too the agreed-in-principle positions by the two countries on each one of them.

The significance of such an accord for Mexico is derived not only from its strong commercial, investment and technological ties with the United States, and, to a much lesser extent, with Canada, but also from the fact that there is now greater convergence in commercial and other policies between the three countries than at any other time in the recent past. From this point of view, and given Mexico's large share of intra-trade within the Northern American economic region, it is a fact that this country is *already integrated* in the region. The question then centers, as in the case of Canada, on what are the best ways to maximize the benefits from this integration, as well as for setting up clear, as opposed to volatile, rules of the game.

In examining most of the issues related to the possibility of Mexico joining the U.S.–Canada agreement, three different facts stand out. First, since Mexico has a much lower level of development than the other two, joining the U.S.–Canada agreement would definitely depend upon an explicit recognition of its special status as a developing economy. This is a matter that, again, relates to the question of the "open-endedness" of the agreement. Other LDCs facing the same choice would also confront problems similar to those of Mexico.

Secondly, because of Mexico's special status as an LDC among the three countries, there are significant differences both on the relevance and the nature of various negotiating issues. These include agricultural trade, services, subsidies, as well as others. On all of them, Mexico's position is bound to be different; therefore, they will have to be negotiated separately.

Thirdly, and this is an important consideration, there are some issues where the Mexican and Canadian positions are strikingly similar. These concern, among others, market access, foreign investment and intellectual property. It is here that we can expect that the U.S.–Canada negotiations will shed light should Mexico consider joining the agreement at a later date.

All this, perhaps, poses more questions than answers for Mexico, particularly with respect to its trade options in the Northern American region. One important conclusion, however, is that, if the free trade agreement between Canada and the United States is signed and is interpreted as the start of a trend toward bilateralism, then Mexico— and perhaps other countries as well—will have to consider seriously whether to start negotiations with a view to "joining" the agreement, or to push for a separate trade agreement with the United States.

Notes

1. Clark W. Reynolds, "Patterns of North American Trade and Balance of Payments with Implications for Dynamic Comparative Advantage," 1985, (mimeographed).
2. In some years there are significant differences between Canadian and Mexican statistics on account of re-exports from the United States.
3. *Programa Nacional de Fomento Industrial y Comercio Exterior, 1984–1988*, Secretaria de Comercio y Fomento Industrial, México, 1984.
4. See I.M. Destler, *American Trade Politics: System Under Stress* (Washington: Institute for International Ecnomics and Twentieth Century Fund, 1986), pp. 127–30.
5. See Gary C. Hufbauer and Jeffrey J. Schott, *Trading for Growth: The Next Round of Trade Negotiations* (Washington: Institute for International Economics, 1985), pp. 32–36.

6. This has been discussed in Sidney Weintraub, *Free Trade Between the United States and Mexico* (Washington: The Brookings Institution, 1984).
7. These options are described for the Canadian case in Richard Lipsey and Murray G. Smith, *Taking the Initiative: Canada's Trade Options in a Turbulent World* (Toronto: C.D. Howe Institute, 1985), pp. 54–71.
8. Soogil Young, "A Possible Approach to Fuller LDC Participation in the GATT" (Working paper for a Council on Foreign Relations study group on The Integration of Developing Countries into the World Trading System, New York, October 16–17, 1986).
9. See Gerardo M. Bueno, "La Politica de Comercio y Desarrollo de México en el Contexto de las Relaciones Economicas Norteamericanas," *Medio Siglo de Financiamiento y Promocion del Comercio Exterior de México*, Volume II (Mexico: El Colegio de Mexico, A. C., 1987), pp. 44–46.
10. This was pointed out in C. Michael Aho and Marc Levinson, "A Canadian Opportunity," *Foreign Policy*, no. 66 (Spring 1987), pp. 143–55.
11. Victor L. Urquidi, "Is a North American Free Trade Area Viable? The Mexican Perspective," (Paper presented at The Carter Center of Emory University, Atlanta, Georgia, April 8, 1986).
12. Ibid. I have also made this proposal in Bueno, "La Politica de Comercio y Desarrollo de México en el Contexto de las Relaciones Economicas Norteamericanas," *op. cit.*, pp. 44–46.
13. According to the so-called *Elements of the Agreement,* no such possibility has been explicitly contemplated. However, Mexico could make a case for joining it on the basis of Article XXIV of the GATT and other legal dispositions.
14. See Robert Baldwin, "Fashioning a Negotiating Package Between Developing and Developed Countries," (Working paper for a Council on Foreign Relations study group on The Integration of Developing Countries into the World Trading System, New York, October 16–17, 1986).
15. Bela Balassa; Gerardo M. Bueno; Pedro-Pablo Kuczynski; and Mario Henrique Simonsen, *Toward Renewed Economic Growth in Latin America* (Washington: Institute for International Economics, 1986), pp. 34–43.
16. "Excerpts From U.S. Statement on the Accord," *The New York Times,* October 5, 1987, p. D5.
17. See Aho and Levinson, "A Canadian Opportunity," *op. cit.*, pp. 143–55.
18. Ibid.
19. This has been suggested in Paul Wonnacott, *The United States and Canada: The Quest for Free Trade* (Washington: Institute for International Economics, 1987), pp. 102–8.
20. Ibid.
21. Jaime Alvarez S., "La Inversion Extranjera Directa y los Derechos de Propiedad Industrial en las Negociacio nes Comerciales de México," 1986, (mimeographed).
22. See Aho and Levinson, "A Canadian Opportunity," *op. cit.*, pp. 143–55.

6

The New Bilateralism?

William Diebold, Jr.

W HILE THE PREVIOUS CHAPTERS were being written, and discussed in a series of meetings, Canadian and American
negotiators, in Ottawa, Washington and other places were
talking about the same problems—and many others that we have not
tried to deal with in these pages. On October 3, 1987, minutes before
the deadline set in American law, they concluded that they had
reached sufficient agreement so that President Reagan could give Congress formal notice of his intention "to enter into a free trade agreement
with Canada on January 2, 1988, contingent upon a successful completion of the negotiations. The essential elements have been agreed to
and we expect that final details can be hammered out in the next few
days." The "few days" became weeks; there was more than a suspicion
that negotiations were still going on about some issues. Some people
refused to take a position until they saw the final text, but others in both
countries argued fervently on the basis of the published *Elements of the
Agreement*. Not until December 10 was the text finally established; it
was published a few days later.[1]

The drafters expected the agreement to come into effect at the
beginning of 1989, but for that to happen majorities had to be mobilized
and legislative action taken in both countries. At any time in this
process something might happen in one country that would cause the
other to put an end to the affair on the grounds that new conditions or
interpretations had, in one way or another, been introduced and were
unacceptable. To reduce this risk, the United States was acting under a
procedure that permitted Congress only to approve or disapprove the
draft agreement as a whole, but not change it. The Canadian parlia-

mentary system would ordinarily be expected to avoid serious challenge, but the idea of "free trade" with the United States has always been a contentious and divisive one for Canadians. There could conceivably be defections from the government's substantial majority in the House of Commons; the Senate, dominated by members of opposition parties appointed by previous governments, could block approval of the agreement, at least for a considerable time and in ways that could create major political problems for the government, perhaps even requiring an election.

Before the text of the agreement was published the national leaders of the Liberal and New Democratic Parties announced that if they came into power they would "tear it up." If taken seriously, this possibility would make it difficult to persuade Congress and the American public that there was a lasting national interest in a new trading relationship with Canada. In any case, there was a risk that Congress would delay action on the Canadian agreement—or turn it down altogether—if there were serious difficulties over the omnibus trade bill that was hanging fire at the end of 1987. Another source of uncertainty was the possibility that before the agreement was acted on, pressures would appear that would cause one of the governments to call for a change, perhaps to win the support—or at least overcome the opposition—of some crucial industry or area. Should this happen there would either be a rather different agreement from the one described here, or no agreement at all. To be sure, the agreement was accompanied by an exchange of letters in which both parties spoke of exercising discretion so as not to jeopardize the approval process. How far that caution would be effective remained to be seen.

Time and complexity make it difficult to discuss the agreement in detail, but for the most part that is not necessary for the purposes of this book. As will be seen, the agreement leaves open some important issues about its bilateral/multilateral balance. It also sets in motion processes that make it likely that a number of these issues will be dealt with in the years ahead. What the agreement means will depend on what the governments make it mean. Consequently, the main lines of inquiry pursued in this and earlier chapters are still highly relevant.

Since the previous chapters were written before the agreement was public, this one must give some account of its provisions. An estimate of its bilateral/multilateral mix will lead to a commentary on several of the major problems raised in other chapters. Finally, there is an assessment of the bearing of the agreement on questions about the future of American trade policy and the international trading system. Throughout this endeavor, the basic effort is to see both if answers can be given to the major questions raised at the end of Chapter 1, and if choices can be made between some of the alternatives sketched therein. My judgment on these matters has been greatly influenced by the work of the other authors of this volume and of the study group's discussion of the first drafts of all of the chapters, including this one. The conclusions are, however, entirely my own so no one else should be held responsible for them.

The Agreement

To keep this chapter in its proper focus, one should recall a few basic points set out in Chapter 1.

- Bilateralism versus multilateralism does not present a simple, clear-cut dichotomy and is usually a complex mixture in a country's trade policy.
- The balance of bilateral and multilateral elements is very important to the character of a country's trade policy, and so is the kind of bilateralism or multilateralism it practices.
- Although it may be significant whether an international agreement is bilateral or multilateral in form, its effects are likely to depend on its content with regard to the reduction of trade barriers, the presence or absence of most-favored-nation (MFN) treatment (conditional or unconditional), the extent of discrimination against third countries, and the kind of reciprocity the parties to the agreement are seeking.
- The blend of bilateral and multilateral elements in relations between two countries affects not only their economies but the international trading system as a whole. The significance of this impact usually depends on what countries are involved and what issues they have dealt with.

The Canadian-American negotiations have raised questions about all these considerations. The two countries have been major supporters of an international trading system based on multilateral cooperation, equal treatment, and the reduction of trade barriers on a non-discriminatory basis. That system has seriously deteriorated at least since the early 1970s. The Canadian-American agreement has naturally been tailored to the particular bilateral concerns of the two countries, and has been shaped by domestic economic and political factors in each. There are bound to be some strains—and perhaps some outright conflicts—between what it provides and the interests of some third countries, and the practices, and perhaps even the principles, of the multilateral order. But there are ways in which the agreement, and how Canada and the United States carry it out, could contribute to the multilateral negotiations of the Uruguay Round and, ultimately, help strengthen the international trading system.

The issue of bilateralism versus multilateralism has not been the most important issue in the Canadian-American negotiations, nor will it be foremost in the minds of those who will determine whether the agreement comes into effect and how it will be carried out. This book does not argue that it should be. Our concern has been to explore some dimensions that are more complex than most people seem to realize and that also deserve more attention than they have had. Readers should also keep in mind that when we call some elements in the agreement bilateral, it does not mean that they are "bad" because what is "good" is the multilateral system. That system is indeed something to which a high value should be attached, in my opinion, but it is compatible with a number of kinds of bilateral trading relations—and incompatible with others. Such formal rules as the multilateral system has, notably the terms of the General Agreement on Tariffs and Trade (GATT), allow for bilateral and plurilateral arrangements if they meet certain conditions. Even an agreement that meets these conditions is bilateral in more than form when the two countries agree to treat one another differently from the way they treat others (as they do in creating a free trade area). How exclusive these privileges are, how they may change the course of trade, whether they damage other countries, and under what conditions, if any, others can obtain the same treatment, are all matters of importance for our purposes. What is to be borne in mind, however, is that when we say certain features of the proposed Canadian-American free trade area are strongly, or definitely, bilateral, it is more often than not the exchange of exclusive privileges that is at issue—whether the results are "good" or "bad" is another matter, to which we shall come in due course.

What follows is not a complete summary of the agreement but a kind of profile with commentary. It stresses the features which the analysis in the previous chapters has shown to be most important to the issue of bilateralism versus multilateralism. It is a layman's analysis, not a lawyer's. This kind of selective summary is bound to reflect the opinions of the author, and I have not tried to conceal mine. The interpretation of the agreement is also my own and in some respects differs from the standard official view.

Tariffs

The agreement will create a classic free trade area by eliminating tariffs on trade between Canada and the United States over a period of ten years (with a few exceptions). Most quantitative restrictions will also disappear. Rules of origin will determine what products have a high enough Canadian or American content to be eligible for this treatment.[2] There has been a tendency to play down the importance of tariff removal, which is unwise in judging the probable effect of the agreement on the economies of the two countries, especially Canada's. There is not much that needs to be said, however, about the bilateral/ multilateral aspects of this part of the agreement; they are inherent in the nature of a free trade area that removes barriers between the parties, keeps them in relation to the rest of the world, and thereby introduces discrimination that did not previously exist. What combination of trade creation and trade diversion results is, as Murray Smith has pointed out in Chapter 4, important to the effect of the agreement, but it is beyond the scope of this book. The provisions that do require attention concern specific sectors and the most contentious problems of contemporary trade policy—fair trade rules and nontariff barriers.

Sectoral Arrangements

Although both sides had emphasized the advantages of reaching a general agreement and had more or less condemned the sectoral approach in the first phase of the negotiations, the agreement singles out several sectors for special treatment. These are important not only to the economic effect of the agreement and the politics of its acceptability, but to questions of bilateralism as well.

Agriculture, which many had expected would be excluded from the agreement, is the subject of a number of special arrangements. Many tariffs and quotas are to disappear; others are permitted under certain conditions. The action to be taken on some depends on how far the support programs of the two countries can be brought into line—an interesting recognition of one of the basic problems with agricultural trade barriers. There are to be no direct export subsidies on sales to one another and when subsidies are used to sell to a third country, each "shall take into account the export interests of the other." This is a matter that has often been of great concern to Canada in the past, as well as recently when the United States decided to counter the export practices of the European Community with increased subsidies of its own. Several provisions look toward consultation and cooperation between the two countries on agricultural issues.

An interesting question is whether Canada and the United States can effectively coordinate their positions in the multilateral negotiations that lie ahead. They specifically agree "to work together to achieve . . . their primary goal . . . on a global basis, the elimination of all subsidies which distort agricultural trade . . . " It could be said that by including agriculture in the agreement, the two countries are demonstrating that it is not hopelessly unrealistic to try to reach international understandings on farm trade. Such a demonstration is not exactly a challenge to the European Community and Japan, but relations with those countries are never far from the minds of North American farmers and farm officials. There was also some advantage in seeming to come closer than others have done to meeting the GATT provision for including "substantially all" trade in a free trade area. However, whether such considerations actually played a significant part in the national calculations compared with the pressures on the negotiators from agricultural groups in both countries is impossible for an outside observer to say.

At the other end of the scale are the **"cultural industries"** which are, quite simply, "exempt from the provisions of this Agreement." This sweeping language reflects the extreme importance that the Canadian government attached to avoiding any suggestion that a free trade agreement would diminish Canadian "cultural sovereignty" by exposing the country to the untrammeled invasion of American commercial interests. The industries in question, according to the agreement, are the publishing, distribution and sale of books, magazines, periodicals and newspapers; films; recordings (video and audio); the publication or sale of music; and radio and television broadcasting to the general public, including cable and satellite programming and network services. Investment is more of an issue here than is trade given the Canadian concern about American ownership and control of publishing firms. If a country makes use of this exemption to take actions that would otherwise be inconsistent with the agreement, the partner may respond by taking "measures of equivalent commercial effect." What this provision may mean is likely to remain obscure until it is invoked. It seems simply to reaffirm the state of affairs that exists without an agreement. Although the designation of which industries are "cultural" clarifies some matters, uncertainty about others will stem from the fact that issues which to Canadians (or some of them) are matters of cultural autonomy and national identity are to the Americans most involved simply questions of profitable ways of doing business.

The implications of the exclusion of cultural industries for the relations of Canada or the United States with third countries are far from clear. If Canadians do not feel threatened by cultural incursions from countries other than the United States, they may subject Americans to restrictions that do not apply to others. If the United States took any action "in response," it would seem foolish to apply it to any country besides Canada. (Nothing in the text says that action taken "in response" to the use of the exemption must be confined to a cultural industry.) Language comes into the picture. Quebec may wish to encourage relations with France while anglophone Canada remains indifferent. However, there is no necessary connection between ownership and the language of publication or performance. In 1975 *The Reader's Digest* was treated differently from *Time*, in part because it published in French in Quebec.[3] The agreement avoids political and psychological complications by saying nothing about the reasons cultural industries are exempted from the agreement.

Quite a different set of issues arises in connection with **energy,** another field that incites strong political and psychological reactions in Canada. Very few of the discussions of the possible free trade area gave any special attention to energy (see the chapters in this volume). Whether the negotiators had quietly been talking about these matters all along, or turned to energy at a late stage—and why—are matters that may be of considerable interest but cannot be investigated here. The content of what can properly be called a sectoral understanding on oil, gas, uranium, electricity, and coal goes beyond the "simple" free trade principle of eliminating tariffs and quantitative import controls. It also rules out export controls and governmental measures that would establish differences between domestic prices and those charged in foreign trade. Exceptions are made for national security and also for shortages or conservation, but in the latter cases limited supplies are to be allocated without discrimination between domestic use and exports to the other country. All this is to provide what the *Elements* called "nondiscriminatory access for the United States to Canadian energy supplies and secure market access for Canadian energy exports to the United States." The asymmetry of that statement (which is not repeated in the agreement) is not our present concern and neither is the weighing of the economic effects of the understandings.

In answer to criticisms that it had surrendered part of its sovereignty to the Americans, the Canadian government said that the provisions for sharing scarce supplies did not go beyond the commitments Canada had already made in the multilateral agreements concerning the International Energy Agency (which might even call for an increase in exports). Still, one can imagine that the pressure to live up to such a commitment would be different when it came from a next door neighbor, and perhaps the interpretation of the commitment would vary as well. The other assurances about avoiding export controls and price discrimination apply only to bilateral trade. If the United States decided to put taxes or controls on imports of oil in order to encourage domestic production, it would have to exempt Canada. The United States also agrees to supply Canada with up to 50,000 barrels a day of Alaskan oil which is not otherwise exported. The United States also makes an exception for Canada in its policy of not enriching foreign uranium and Canada drops the requirement that uranium has to be highly processed before it can be exported.

Clearly, the gravamen of the arrangement is bilateral, with each country given a special position in relation to the other. There are some mitigating factors. As both Canada and the United States belong to the International Energy Agency, its rules and procedures concerning the allocation of oil in times of general shortage would, in a sense, "multilateralize" some of the energy provisions of the bilateral agreement. As long as normal conditions prevail, neither country is forbidden to extend the same treatment to others. Presumably it would only do so as part of a bargain, though not necessarily one confined to energy. Japan would probably like some of the Alaskan oil and Mexico might be happy to have assurances of unimpeded access to the American market for its oil.

Canadian reactions to the energy provisions have been more concerned with what might be called the bilateral/unilateral balance than with questions of multilateralism. Language like "nondiscriminatory access for the United States to Canadian energy supplies" was bound to inflame some Canadians, raising historic specters against which much Canadian policy—and much more Canadian rhetoric—had been addressed for many years. The government pointed out that existing laws and policies about Canadian ownership were untouched. It tried to disarm suspicion of the scope of the agreement by stressing the fact that water was not included and announcing that it would forbid large-scale export of water to the United States (for which some Canadians were prepared to reverse the flow of some rivers).

On a more mundane note, some people in eastern Canada thought the agreement jeopardized their future supplies of western Canadian oil and gas which might now flow to the United States as well; they also disliked the prospect of higher prices and looked back to the time when the National Energy Policy had put a ceiling on domestic prices even if the Americans were charged more. Ontario took that position, but was deprived of the support it might have expected from the premier of Quebec who strongly supported the agreement, presumably because it reduces the risk that his province's electricity exports to the United States could be interfered with at some future time by the federal government. Naturally, strong support for the agreement came from people in western Canada and elsewhere who were interested in selling to the United States.[4] The extent to which the fundamental differences of opinion about the bilateral agreement could reflect domestic disagreements was emphasized in a statement by Peter Lougheed, the former premier of Alberta: "The biggest plus of this agreement is it would preclude a federal government from bringing in a National Energy Policy ever again."[5]

The **automotive** sector is another in which the relations of the two countries are exceptional. The bilateral arrangement of 1965 has been the subject of much complaint from both sides but has never been altered. Several of the interested groups in Canada, notably the auto workers' union, thought it should be left out of the free trade negotiations. Many observers found it hard to imagine a far-reaching agreement on trade between the two countries that did not take account of this exceptional arrangement, which had contributed greatly to the increased trade between them. The compromise in the agreement is to make no formal changes in the Auto Pact but to stipulate a number of points that will significantly affect its operation.

The creation of the free trade area disposed of an old controversy by removing duties, after ten years, on replacement parts, as well as on those going directly into new vehicles. A more contentious step oddly echoed the dispute which had given rise to the automotive agreement in the first place. In the early 1960s Canada was trying to expand its exports of automobiles by using practices that under American law amounted to subsidies against which countervailing duties would have to be imposed. In recent years Canada has been encouraging the production of automobiles and parts by permitting Japanese and European companies to import cars and parts free of duty whenever their production in Canada, or their exports (primarily to the United States), reached certain levels. Paul Wonnacott, a close student of the subject, wrote in 1987 that "If Canada does not eliminate the duty-remission program, a U.S. countervailing duty case seems probable by the early 1990s. A graceful way to eliminate the program would be to do so as part of a larger package in the current free trade negotiations."[6]

Whether the action was taken gracefully one may doubt; but important changes were made. New remission schemes are ruled out and existing ones are to end by 1996 or 1998 at the latest. As soon as the agreement comes into effect, exports to the United States are not to count toward the remission of import duties, which will greatly reduce the value of some of the arrangements to the foreign producers. The agreement limits the scope of the Auto Pact to companies already included or that qualify by the 1989 model year. This means that, of the major auto producers, only Ford, Chrysler, General Motors and Volvo can bring into Canada duty-free parts, not only from the United States but from other countries (giving an opening to Mexico in the agreement). The 1965 commitments of the American companies to produce in Canada a high proportion of their North American sales and to maintain the level of their investments remain in force. For other companies to be able to use Canada as a route to duty-free entry into the United States (or vice versa), they must produce over 50 percent of the vehicle—measured by direct cost—in North America.

This tightening of the automotive agreement is one of the more clearly bilateral features of the free trade agreement. One could almost regard the Canadian duty-remission schemes as a kind of multilateralization (albeit one-sided) of the arrangement which has now been ended, presumably because the Americans wanted that done. Both countries remain free to try to encourage investment in automobile production by pressing for export restraints in Europe and Asia. The new agreement goes beyond the old one in recognizing a common interest in the adaptation of the automotive industry to changing international conditions. The two countries will establish "a select panel . . . to assess the state of the North American industry and to propose public policy measures and private initiatives to improve its competitiveness in domestic and foreign markets." Canada and the United States will try to administer the Auto Pact "in the best interests of employment and production in both countries." And, in the Uruguay Round, they are to cooperate "to create new export opportunities for North American automotive goods."

Perhaps the statements of solidarity are not too remarkable, since the major American producers operate on both sides of the border. There are, however, interesting contrasts in approach. While Canada seems to be primarily interested in expanding automotive production in Canada, by firms from any country, the American geographical focus is modified by a concern for the interests of the companies as global producers. The two approaches came together in a change introduced between the *Elements* and the final text of the agreement. General Motors' combined operation with Nissan was added to the list of companies eligible for the benefits of the Auto Pact provided it was in operation by the beginning of 1989 (when the agreement was to come into force). This step also reflected another interesting question raised by the way the changes in the Auto Pact emphasized discrimination according to the nationality of the ownership of a firm. How is this approach to be carried out if major firms continue to form joint ventures and other kinds of cooperative arrangements cutting across national lines?

In contrast to what could be seen as the revision of an old sectoral agreement in automobiles, the United States and Canada broke new ground by negotiating agreements concerning services that can also be called sectoral, although the concept of a sector is somewhat different from the way the term was used in earlier trade policy discussions. One of these agreements, kept separate from the others, covers **"financial services."** This turns out to be largely about banking, although other kinds of financial institutions come into the picture. (Ontario's opening of its financial markets to increased foreign participation while the trade negotiations were going on somewhat leapfrogged over what might have been a more prominent part of the agreement—and may have deprived the Canadian side of some bargaining chips.) Canada has for a long time restricted the activities of foreign banks, but in recent years it has taken some measures to open up the field. The agreement takes a few steps farther in the same direction. The United States, for its part, provides some additional rights for Canadian banks and assures them that if the Glass-Steagall Act is amended, they will receive the same treatment as American banks under that law. Further details are not central to our present concerns. The commitments are strictly bilateral; it is up to either country whether to give the same privileges to banks from other countries. In an interesting turn of phrase the agreement says "This part shall not be construed as representing the mutual satisfaction of the Parties concerning the treatment of their respective financial institutions." Although this language is used to introduce a sort of guarantee of the existing rights and privileges provided the other country reciprocates, the note that is struck is one that might well be applied to many other aspects of the free trade area agreement.

It would be stretching the term sector to apply it to **services in general.** The weakness of that generalization, which has been so common in recent discussions, is brought out by the way the bilateral agreement handles the subject. Some general principles are to apply to all services, but special provisions have to be drawn up for particular services because they vary so much.[7] The general provisions of the agreement call on each country to assure the providers of services from the other national treatment—that is, "treatment no less favorable than that accorded in like circumstances to its persons." Efforts are to be made to bring existing practices into line with these principles, but basically they apply to future regulation of a substantial number of designated services.

More detailed agreements had been arrived at covering an odd assortment of services: architecture, tourism, and "computer services and telecommunications-network-based enhanced services." The *Elements* had a statement about future laws and regulations in transportation that was somewhat hedged, and the agreement dropped the subject altogether in response to pressure from the American shipping industry. Its wish to stave off even the possibility of Canadians being given national privileges under the Jones Act is a reminder that the United States has its own restrictive practices even as it champions the liberalization of international trade in services.

The agreement on telecommunications is the most detailed and probably the most important as it affects a wide range of business and finance, not just the "sector" of companies providing these services. The details (including the long list of exceptions) need not concern us. What is important is that new ground was broken in a field that affects many countries. The agreement on telecommunications might become a model for other bilateral or plurilateral agreements. Another possibility is that other countries might want to adhere to the Canadian-American agreement, accepting the same obligations and gaining the same rights. Here, however, we run into the question of the willingness of the Canadians or Americans—in this case probably the Canadians—to subject themselves to further open competition or to give other foreigners the same privileges. Suppose, for example, that the Canadian acceptance of the telecommunications agreement was induced, at least in part, by an American concession in some quite different field. How much should one read into the fact that there is no mention of the Uruguay Round or of the efforts of the two countries to work together to press on others the principles they have agreed to bilaterally?

There is a rather detailed agreement about wines and spirits intended to end some Canadian practices that discriminate against American products. The implementation depends on the provinces (one of the few parts of the agreement of which this is so), and an Ontario official is supposed to have said, "They can make us bring it in but they can't force us to put it on the shelves." Nothing was done to alter provincial practices which both fragment the Canadian brewing industry and create barriers to the importation of American beer. American sugar practices kept that product out of the agreement.

American import controls on steel are to be dropped when their present term comes to an end. There are interconnected arrangements in the lumber industry concerning plywood standards, export controls on logs, the American escape clause action on cedar shakes and shingles and the memorandum of understanding about softwood lumber (which remains in force for the time being at least). No doubt a study of the timing of tariff reductions would give evidence of the care shown by one side or the other for certain sectors.

The sectoral arrangements are a more important part of the free trade agreement than the official emphasis on comprehensiveness would suggest, but that is not really surprising. On the whole they add weight to the bilateral side of the agreement, both in taking account of the special interests of the two countries and in providing rights and privileges not extended to third countries. For the most part they move in a liberalizing direction.

The main exception concerns the automobile industry. Should there never be any change in the softwood lumber arrangements, that would be a significant departure from the principles of a free trade area so far as relations between the two countries are concerned. It is not, however, directed primarily against third countries as are the changes in the automobile agreement. The exemption of the cultural industries is a true special case rooted in the nature and relationship of the two countries. To what extent any of the sectoral agreements might occasion complaints from third countries is impossible to judge. An economic assessment of the cumulative effect of these arrangements is beyond the scope of this book, as is a calculation of their trade creating versus trade diverting effects. Consequently, we can reach no firm conclusions about the long-run economic effects of the agreement on third countries.

Nontariff Barriers and Fair Trade

It was apparent from the beginning that a key element in the bilateral agreement would be the treatment of nontariff barriers and fair trade rules. As previous chapters have pointed out, one of the main reasons Canada proposed the negotiations in the first place was to try to escape the full impact of American measures of "contingent protection;" an objective observer could hardly believe that the GATT codes on subsidies, government procurement, and related matters, would prove adequate for a long time to come to deal effectively with the kinds of disputes that were likely to become increasingly frequent between Canada and the United States. The Macdonald Commission had stressed the importance of devising a new kind of bilateral dispute-settlement procedure to cover a wide range of issues that would otherwise add to the difficulties of the two countries. The agreement covers

all these matters but, as is not surprising, the effectiveness and durability of its provisions are highly debatable.

Our study of the balance of bilateral and multilateral elements in the
Canadian-American agreement can be excused for not going into the
troublesome complexities of the fair trade question—as it may be called
for short. There can be no doubt that bilateral action on some of these
matters could lead to discrimination against third countries which
would conflict fundamentally with the principles of the multilateral
system. At the same time, the argument that the Canadian-American
agreement might strengthen the multilateral system rests largely on
the possibility of the two countries agreeing on measures that deal
effectively with problems which are not adequately dealt with by the
only kinds of arrangements that have been multilaterally acceptable.
The subsidy question and some of the related fair trade matters are
primary examples of just this sort of issue. Bilateral arrangements that
worked, or at least showed great promise, could then strengthen the
multilateral system either by providing models on which multilateral
arrangements could be built, or by themselves being opened to the
adherence of other countries.

Which of these alternatives is more likely is not something one can
deduce from the agreement. It falls well short of what many people had
hoped, and, so far as one can tell, of what the negotiators tried to
achieve. None of the interesting possibilities outlined by Murray Smith
in Chapter 4 have been accepted, not to mention the range considered
in his earlier work with Richard Lipsey.[8] Instead the main emphasis is
on a set of procedures whose outcomes cannot be predicted. There are
a few clear-cut measures that enhance the bilateral character of the
agreement, but in most cases the full effect of what has been accomplished will only become apparent when some cases are dealt with.
Although the two countries failed to arrive at firm conclusions, they did
not close the door on the process. During five years, and if necessary
for another two, the countries are to try to work out "a substitute
system of rules in both countries for antidumping and countervailing
duties as applied to their bilateral trade." Consequently, many of the
questions raised in previous chapters remain wide open.

One firm provision of the agreement is clearly discriminatory. It
concerns not the usual canons of "fair trade" but the closely related
matter of the right of a country to restrict imports when they are of such
volume that they damage, or threaten to damage, its domestic industry. American law has long had this kind of an escape clause; Article
XIX of GATT permits safeguards to be used when certain conditions are
met; it is hard to imagine countries agreeing to the large-scale removal

of trade barriers without some such provision for emergencies. Now Canada and the United States have agreed that when either one invokes Article XIX it will exempt imports from the partner unless they "are substantial and are contributing importantly to the serious injury or threat thereof . . . "

In making this arrangement, the two countries are tacitly endorsing one side of a longstanding argument as to whether safeguard action should be applied to all imports without discrimination, as GATT seems to provide, or whether the restrictions should apply selectively to the imports from certain countries which are held to be the real cause of the trouble. Largely because of this dispute, the Tokyo Round failed to reach an agreement on what was hoped to be a strengthening of Article XIX. Although positions have shifted some over time, Canada and the United States have generally resisted the argument for selectivity (advocated by the European Community), and it is not clear whether the bilateral arrangement means they will now take the other view in GATT. If they do, it will sanction bilateral practices by others.

The safeguards arrangement reflects a longstanding concern of Canadians who have felt that they were often unfairly hurt by American actions directed primarily at other countries. A separate provision provides for suspending duty reductions made under the bilateral agreement if they cause serious damage. This arrangement applies only during a transition period and is subject to compensation or reprisal. There are also efforts to define the terms describing the conditions in which safeguards may be used. Although useful, this falls well short of proposals that have been made to establish objective indicators of the conditions and provide some international surveillance over the use of safeguards.

So far as fair trade proper is concerned, the agreement does not attempt to define the kinds of subsidies or pricing practices that should be either outlawed or recognized as justified and so exempt from countervailing or antidumping duties. Instead, there is a rather complex dispute-settlement process that is to provide a review of the action of either country in applying its own fair trade laws. Should either country change its antidumping or countervailing duty laws, the change would not apply to the other party unless that was specified in the legislation; there are requirements for notification, consultation, and review of actions by a binational panel that could find the legal changes inconsistent with "the object and purpose" of the GATT codes. In that case, a failure to work out a satisfactory new arrangement would permit the complaining country to terminate the agreement in sixty days.

The details of these arrangements—which are more fully spelled out than most other provisions—are of great importance to how the agreement works out. There is room for much doubt, imagination and difference of opinion. For our purposes, however, there is no need to delve into this. Two things are clear. First, weak as it is compared to what might have been, the commitment puts Canadian-American relations on fair trade matters on a different basis from the relations of either country to any others. They are still bound by their GATT commitments and have their rights and obligations as signatories to the GATT dumping and subsidy codes, but there is a new bilateral commitment, as is natural enough given the fact that a bilateral free trade area has been created.

The second point that is clear is that the extent to which the new provisions will introduce discrimination of any serious importance to other countries cannot now be judged. The kinds of actions which Andreas Lowenfeld cites in Chapter 3 as likely to offend the most-favored-nation clause may or may not be taken. Hardly touched are the methods of coping with unfair trade which Murray Smith discusses in Chapter 4 under the heading of "Rules of Competition." To add to the uncertainty of what kind of "substitute system" may be developed in the seven years is the fact that during that time there might well be multilateral negotiations on subsidies and antidumping arrangments in the Uruguay Round.

Naturally, other kinds of disputes than those over the fair trade laws will arise out of the agreement, just as they already do without one. A Trade Commission is to be established which is, at the top, at the cabinet level, but below it will be a considerable structure of "ad hoc or standing committees or working groups" or, very likely, bodies with other names as well. There are provisions for notification, consultation and dispute settlement. These details are important but need not be discussed here. For our concerns it is enough to say that these features inevitably strengthen the bilateral character of the new arrangements but that, as in the case of the other dispute-settlement procedures, one cannot tell what kinds of measures may be taken or how they will bear on other countries or the international economic system.

There is, however, a clear answer to a question raised in Chapter 1. "Disputes arising under both this Agreement and the [GATT] . . . may be settled in either forum, according to the rules of that forum, at the discretion of the complaining Party." Once the choice has been made, however, "the procedure initiated shall be used to the exclusion of any other." Thus, GATT rights are not given up, but the relationship of the new dispute-settlement mechanisms to the established GATT procedure is that of providing an alternative, not a first bilateral stage from which there could be an appeal to the multilateral body. "Forum shopping" is permitted, but not forum switching. In terms of the relationship of the bilateral agreement to the multilateral system the point is of considerable interest; what its long-run economic effect may be is as impossible to judge as whether the new arrangements will strengthen or weaken the multilateral system.

Government Procurement

Government purchasing that discriminates against foreign suppliers is one of the most prevalent nontariff barriers to trade. It is practiced in both Canada and the United States, by the federal governments, states, provinces and municipalities. In these last three, the discrimination is sometimes against products of the same nationality but from different jurisdictions or localities. Since 1959, the two countries have had a Defense Production Sharing Agreement which eliminates the discrimination in a substantial amount of purchasing by the national military establishments. Still, the Pentagon gives some contracts only to companies in the United States and the government of Canada, when buying military planes, requires that a significant portion of them be produced in Canada.

Although there was little public comment on military procurement during the negotiations, there was much speculation as to what more could be done to end the distinction by nationality or location once a free trade area was created. In the end the results seemed quite meager. There are procedural measures that, it is claimed, will improve on the GATT code on procurement so as to make it easier for nationals of one country to bid in the other and to increase competition. The rules of that code will be applied, as between Canada and the United States, to contracts above U.S. $25,000 instead of the $171,000 specified in the plurilateral code. Canadians attach importance to this change which they believe will open opportunities for small firms, particularly in high technology and consulting. Official estimates are that billions of dollars of "procurement opportunities" will be opened, more in the United States than in Canada. The two governments excused themselves from more extensive steps because they were actively engaged in the multilateral renegotiation of the procurement code. But perhaps the problems of including the provinces, which account for a high proportion of public procurement in Canada, or resistance in the United States to placing orders outside the country, had something to do with the matter.

As far as it goes, the bilateral procurement agreement introduces some discrimination against third countries, but how important that will be is difficult to judge. In any case, this is the kind of thing, which, like the result of removing tariffs, is inherent in creating a free trade area. One could also say that by accepting the limitations of the GATT code—which opens procurement only by specified public entities to international competition—Canada and the United States were leaving their free trade area incomplete and that the main discrimination lay in the fact that each continued to give preferential treatment to its national suppliers.

Investment

Intermingled as the processes of trade and investment are, international convention has continued to treat agreements about one as excluding the other. The inadequacy of this approach has long been apparent, but only limited progress has been made in finding ways of dealing adequately with the most significant interconnections. Proposals for a "GATT for Investment" have not met much response, but the United States successfully challenged in GATT some of the "performance requirements" the Canadian government placed on foreign investors by demonstrating that they imposed trade practices that violated GATT rules. The free trade agreement will follow this line by committing the two governments not to impose export, local-content, local-sourcing, or import-substitution requirements on investors from the other country. The main emphasis of the trade agreement's provisions, however, is on limiting the restrictions each country may put on investments from the other. In effect this amounts to an emphasis on how Canada treats American investment, since there is no regular American scrutiny or regulation of foreign investments (although some fields are reserved for nationals and there are some state regulations). The gist of the provisions is to exempt from investigation transactions under a ceiling that rises over time, and to assure national treatment for permitted investments. Existing laws and regulations and "any published policy" can remain in effect even if they are inconsistent with the new agreement. This "grandfathering" of the status quo regarding investment affects a number of other parts of the agreement and is given great weight by Canadian officials in domestic discussion, especially regarding services, cultural industries and the energy sector.

A more detailed account and an estimate of just what the investment provisions of the agreement add up to are unnecessary for our purposes. The bilateral/multilateral balance is easily summarized. As in several of the other cases, there is now a set of bilateral commitments that entail some discrimination against investors from other countries who are not given equal privileges. Because the United States has treaties providing what amounts to MFN treatment for investments, it will have to assure some countries that they will be as well-treated as Canada. In the absence of such treaties, Canada (or the United States) is free to make such commitments to other countries or to withhold them. GATT's equal treatment rules do not apply to investment. There are, however, two provisions in the bilateral agreement that deal explicitly with third countries. The ban on performance requirements extends to third-country investors when they "could have a significant impact on trade between the two Parties." In addition, the ceilings on transactions that exempt them from review apply when American-owned investments in Canada are sold to buyers in third countries. Both these provisions at the same time extend the range of equal treatment and protect specific Canadian and American interests.

Intellectual Property and Some Other Matters

Intellectual property is another area which many people thought would be a prominent subject in the bilateral discussions. Although international disputes about patents and copyrights—and international conventions covering them—are old stories, it is something new for a broader concept of intellectual property to be included in general trade negotiations. A good bilateral agreement in this field might well provide a model for later multilateral negotiations. To be sure, the sphere of intellectual property is not very well defined; it seems bound to overlap with the activities of the cultural industries which are specifically exempted from the agreement; as in every field there are vested interests that would make it difficult for either government to make large commitments.[9] In the end there were some specific commitments—Canada agreed to protect the copyright on retransmission of programming; a bill on the life of patents in the pharmaceutical industry that was going through the legislative process was not formally part of the agreement but responded (in part) to American representations going back some years. No general principles were set out in the agreement, or procedures to deal further with bilateral issues. The only appearance of the term "intellectual property" was in the description of an agreement the two governments had made to cooperate in the Uruguay Round and elsewhere to improve its protection.

The agreement covers many other subjects that cannot be dealt with here. There are provisions about customs practices and procedures; drawbacks of duties when goods are re-exported; duty waivers for individual companies; admission of business travelers; and the application of standards permitting each country to create its own regulations about safety and health, while preventing the use of standards as surreptitious trade barriers. There are also more exceptions than have been noted to the provisions summarized above. No doubt some of these measures have implications for the bilateral/multilateral mix we are studying, but they will have to be left out of this account for the present.

A Summing Up

Strictly speaking, there can be no summing up as too many of the provisions of interest to us are too unclear or unfinished to be totted up. The meanings to be attached to "bilateral" or "multilateral" in different contexts are incommensurable. And yet, the main points made earlier provide something approaching a conclusion.

The basis is the creation of a classic free trade area with almost no tariffs (except for emergencies), few import quotas, and export quotas only in special circumstances. Government procurement is made somewhat less discriminatory and was already somewhat freer than between most pairs of countries. Limited progress has been made in the handling of fair trade measures. The new mechanism to settle disputes may reduce friction, but there is no guarantee this will not be done by restricting trade by mutual assent. Some progress has been made in reducing barriers to the flow of services across the frontier, at least in certain fields. Investment has been brought into the understanding on a new scale, but how much liberalization will ensue is not clear.

The scope of these provisions is quite extensive, with cultural industries the only broad omission. There is more liberalization of agricultural trade than in some other free trade arrangements. Trade in energy seems likely to be freer than before and probably banking and other financial services as well. The existing automobile agreement is widened in one dimension by the general removal of tariffs, but a block has been put in the way of applying some of its provisions to European or Asian companies producing in Canada or the United States. The extensive provisions for consultation and the settlement of disputes could lead to a substantially greater liberalization if the governments want to move in that direction; otherwise these provisions might have few results or could be used to permit an increase in restrictions if the emphasis were mainly on avoiding friction.

With so much uncertainty about the effects of some arrangements, and the postponement of the potentially most important actions, it is impossible to make a firm statement about the substantive bilateralism of the agreement. As already explained, these uncertainties apply particularly to fair trade issues, government procurement and the agreements on services. Where the steps toward bilateral liberalization are most evident—tariffs, energy, financial services and perhaps investment—there is an inescapable intensification of bilateralism from a sharpening of the difference in treatment between the partners and outsiders; but that is the nature of a free trade area. That is true too of the mutual exemption from safeguarding measures. In the case of the automobile provisions, the bilateral effect is enhanced by the specific limitation of certain benefits to the established companies. How serious the resulting discrimination is from any of these features and their total effect on other countries will depend on two factors: 1) how Canadian and American trade and production are affected; and 2) whether either Canada, or the United States, or both extend to other countries the treatment they have agreed to give one another. Neither of these developments can be predicted with any assurance at present and this chapter makes no attempt to guess.

The agreement looks toward common action by Canada and the United States in the Uruguay Round on agricultural subsidies, automotive exports, investment, intellectual property, and, by implication, government procurement. It would seem logical that the agreement on general principles concerning services would be put forward as some sort of guide, if not a complete model, in the GATT talks. There is, however, some room for doubt. On the one hand, the grandfathering of existing practices falls short of what Americans were hoping to achieve in some fields and with other countries. On the other hand, the need to withdraw American shipping from the scope of the Canadian agreement suggests that the United States would be a bit more honest in subscribing only to the formula of the Israeli agreement to use its "best efforts" to liberalize trade in services. For their part, the Canadians might well not wish to go as far with other countries as they did in the telecommunications agreement with the United States. As Michael Aho has pointed out, "a tension exists between generalizability and uniqueness." When it gets an arrangement it asks for, a country is likely to want the same treatment from other countries; when it has to give up something, it stresses "the uniqueness of the bilateral relationship."[10] The experience of the bilateral negotiations on subsidies, dumping, and perhaps safeguards may be of some help in the Uruguay Round as Gilbert Winham suggests in Chapter 2.

Whether the bilateral agreement is as fuzzy and indeterminate as this description suggests, or whether that picture results from the way the author interprets it, is a matter that must be left to the reader. We turn now to some of the larger questions about the agreement as set out at the end of Chapter 1 and try to answer them in the light not only of the agreement itself, but of the analyses in the previous chapters and of the course of events, as well as they can be discerned, from the time this study commenced until the end of 1987.

GATT and the Uruguay Round

What appeared to be a possibly momentous question seems to have been answered well enough to need little discussion. To a layman, the bilateral agreement seems clearly to meet the conditions that Article XXIV of GATT prescribes for free trade areas. As might be expected, the governments proclaim that, in the preamble, the first article and, in effect, by the frequent reaffirmation of their GATT rights on various subjects. Tariffs and quotas are to be removed in almost all fields, including agriculture. The exclusion of "cultural industries," while it may arouse some complaints, seems unlikely to invalidate the "substantially all trade" formula; much of the concern is with investment. As no new substantive rules have been made about subsidies, there does not seem to be any infringement of either the multilateral code or the equal treatment provisions of GATT. To an objective observer, it seems clear that the Canadian and American governments can present their agreement to GATT for review without great trepidation. (But in his epilogue Professor Lowenfeld, who is a strict constructionist, reserves judgment about the possible need for a waiver. One might also raise a question about the statement that "in the event of an inconsistency" between the agreement and "bilateral and multilateral agreements to which both are Party," the new agreement "shall prevail.") In any case, Canada and the United States have not weakened GATT by straining the interpretation of Article XXIV or taken advantage of several uncertain precedents set by the European Community and the European Free Trade Association.

This does not mean there will not be challenges. The commitment on safeguards comes down on one side of a disputed issue and could require the kind of discriminatory action Andreas Lowenfeld warns against in Chapter 3. It is conceivable that someone might consider the new dispute-settlement provisions as a weakening of GATT's position—but this should depend on what was done under its procedures. What is more likely is that some countries with a special concern about one or another feature of the agreement—or even about the effect of a specific tariff change—might try to use Article XXIV as a way of opening a negotiation and would withdraw their broader case if they got satisfaction on the narrower issue. It is hard to say anything about such a possibility except that if Canada and the United States want to resist, they do not seem to have exposed themselves to legal blackmail on this issue.

A more arcane GATT issue seems also to have been resolved. It occurred to some people that the waiver given the United States to legitimize the automotive agreement of 1965 might be challenged on the grounds that the original premise—that no third-country interests would be significantly damaged—was no longer valid now that the automobile industry has so many centers of production and trade flows in so many directions. The tightening of the rules so that no new companies can benefit from the agreement might be called discrimination on the basis of nationality. There may be complaints along these lines, but the creation of a free trade area makes it unnecessary for the United States to have a waiver to continue the duty-free importation of automobiles from Canada.[11]

Although challenges to the bilateral agreement can be made in a number of different ways, there is little doubt that the multilateral negotiations of the Uruguay Round will have sufficient centripetal force to draw in all sorts of third-country concerns. Negotiations about tariff reductions, for example, will be conducted with an eye on the new situation created by the removal of Canadian and American tariffs within the free trade area over the next decade. As Murray Smith has pointed out in Chapter 4, the creation of a preferred position for the United States or Canada in the other's market may give a third country an incentive to negotiate on that tariff item so as to reduce or eliminate the disadvantage that will result from no longer being on an equal footing with another supplier. There are many ways these influences can work. To a degree, the problems are simply those relating several sets of bilateral tariff negotiations within a multilateral framework. In some respects the questions replay the arguments for or against conditional MFN discussed in the first chapter. What is new, though, is that part of the process will have been put in motion by the earlier bilateral free trade negotiations, which may have had nothing to do with the specific multilateral issues in the first place. There is also the possibility that Canada or the United States might feel it is losing something by the way its partner now responds to the interests of other countries. What this might lead to—and it could go well beyond tariffs—raises questions that have been given remarkably little public attention. We revert to them in the section on third countries.

Not all the connections between the bilateral agreement and the multilateral negotiations are inadvertent. As we have seen, there are several issues on which the two countries have decided to carry their areas of agreement into the multilateral trade negotiations in what appears to be something of a common front. There is even the possibility that the multilateral negotiations will provide an occasion for Canada and the United States to carry further their unfinished bilateral negotiations, or perhaps reopen questions they seemed to have settled. A Canadian expert who was close to the negotiations said he thought the Americans would try to use the multilateral negotiations to go after what they had failed to get bilaterally. This could be damaging, or it could be constructive.

It would be damaging if the United States seemed to be trying to reopen the bilateral negotiations to obtain from the Canadians what they had not been willing to accept earlier, without making any new concessions of its own. That would throw doubt on the value of the bilateral agreement and raise concerns about how the United States expected to use the consultative and dispute-settlement machinery. If, in contrast, the United States—or for that matter Canada—were to reopen one of the issues with new proposals and an indication that it was willing to consider things it had previously turned down, the step could be constructive. The obvious question is why this approach was being made in a multilateral setting rather than in a bilateral one. There might be very practical reasons. Neither country is so well supplied with trade negotiators that it can comfortably contemplate carrying on two sets of major negotiations simultaneously. People talking physically in Geneva could be legally under a North American mantle. Or it might be legislatively easier to handle a bilateral arrangement by attaching it to measures to implement the outcome of the Uruguay Round than to have to amend the free trade agreement. An alternative reason might be that one or the other country would like to obtain a multilateral agreement and for some reason it seemed best to start with a bilateral understanding. For example, a start might have been made on an agreement during the bilateral negotiations, but not carried through either because of lack of time or because one of the parties withheld its consent (due, perhaps, to immediate bargaining considerations). Or the bilateral negotiations may have run into obstacles that were less serious in a multilateral setting. Canada, for example, is sometimes willing to do things so long as the action does not appear to be a response to American pressure. Measures affecting culture are far less sensitive if other countries besides the United States are on the other side of the table.

In one respect the idea that the United States or Canada will pursue multilaterally what they did not achieve bilaterally is quite banal.

Needless to say agreements fall short of wishes; the free trade agreement says that in so many words in several places. Both countries would probably like to see multilateral arrangements embodying some of the same provisions they have agreed to bilaterally. It makes sense to pursue some objectives whenever there is an opportunity. But all these remarks beg the basic questions of this book: When is it better to work bilaterally than multilaterally? Does bilateral action always weaken the multilateral system, or can it sometimes strengthen it?

Strengthening the System?

Beyond the original preoccupation with the reconciliation of the bilateral agreement with the requirements of GATT, there is the idea, as we have seen, that a successful conclusion of the Canadian-American negotiations could, instead of challenging the multilateral system, actually strengthen it. This could occur in three ways. First, the bilateral achievement would, by itself, show that significant steps toward trade liberalization could be taken in a difficult time and when the tide is flowing the other way. Second, some features of the agreement could be taken as models for plurilateral or multilateral agreements. Finally, it might also prove possible for other countries to subscribe to some of the bilateral arrangements, thus widening their areas of application.

The models have fallen considerably short of the hopes. There are no striking new arrangements to deal with subsidies or claims of unfair competition, only a new way of handling disputes between the two countries on these matters. Nothing significant has been achieved on intellectual property. There is a services agreement in which some general principles are set forth that could well be a target in broader negotiations, but the bilateral agreement has been applied to only a few service industries and even here the exact prescriptions are not altogether clear. The most detailed agreement, on financial services, is essentially about banking in the special circumstances of the two countries and is unlikely to have any great impact on other sets of negotiations, which will ordinarily be bilateral and not in a trade forum. Investment, too, is likely to be negotiated bilaterally and not mainly in the Uruguay Round. The bilateral agreement contains features the United States might well want to incorporate in agreements with other countries, but one has to doubt how much influence will flow from an arrangement tailored to the special relations of the United States and Canada. This is not true of the Canadian commitment not to impose trade-related performance requirements on American investors, an eminently generalizable provision. There is, however, nothing very new in that concept; its acceptance is a matter of bargaining strength, and of how a country balances its interest in increased foreign investment against its worries about the trade patterns that might result. Many countries feel strongly about these issues; their willingness to give up the right to impose conditions might depend on their belief that they could get from investors assurances that would produce the same results.

As this last example suggests, one should not altogether discard the point about models. It is certainly true that the bilateral agreement does not provide a vivid picture of a new trading world that would be even more impressive if it could be enlarged. But this does not mean that nothing about it is relevant to the larger scene. Even if the adoption of a ban on performance requirements depends on bargaining power and will not come easily, it may still have value as a target in difficult trade negotiations. The agreement on telecommunications services deals with matters of considerable importance to a number of countries. One would not expect the bilateral arrangements to be applied verbatim to other countries or in a general multilateral agreement; there are always differences in circumstances and results are shaped by negotiations. The general principles on services, unclear as their full import is, go beyond any multilateral agreement in existence today. While the dispute-settlement mechanism in the new agreement falls short of promising a full resolution of the issue (as the agreement itself recognizes), it could suggest to some countries that there are advantages to having arrangements with major trading partners that might be easier to use than the GATT dispute-settlement mechanism and that, without anyone's giving up GATT rights, might concentrate a bit more clearly on the special characteristics of a bilateral dispute. Whether this would do more to strengthen the international economic system than to weaken the GATT dispute-settlement process is something else again.

The bilateral agreement also contains something which, although hardly a model, provides a demonstration that could have an influence. This is the agricultural section. For a long time it has been an article of faith that not much could be done about liberalizing trade in agricultural products, even though a good deal of time and effort has been spent on the subject in the major GATT rounds. Thanks to the United States, Canada, and some other countries, the Uruguay Round is also to give a prominent place to agriculture. There was—and is— room for doubt about how much can be achieved, or whether the key governments will accept the need to make agreements on domestic agricultural policies as a way of reducing trade barriers.[12] Against that background, the very fact that Canada and the United States reached detailed agreement on a number of specific agricultural matters and, in at least some cases, recognized the link between domestic policies and the trade barriers strikes a positive note. The conditions, to be sure, are none too similar to those that pose the central problems between the United States and Canada on the one hand, and the European Community or Japan on the other. On one of those matters, export subsidies, the two North American countries have agreed to join forces in the Uruguay Round and they can do so with the claim that they have dealt with some of their common problems as well.

Perhaps the Canadian-American agreement has other demonstration effects. We may leave aside the now historical question of whether the willingness of Canada and the United States to engage in major trade negotiations helped to overcome the reluctance of some other countries to launch a new multilateral round. Whether there is any reason to believe that the Canadian-American example might set off a new wave of bilateralism among other countries is a question best left until later. There is a possibility, though, of a more subtle influence on the bilateral bargaining that normally goes on within the framework of a multilateral round. Agreements between key countries on key issues have been crucial to past multilateral negotiations. These have been understandings compatible with GATT rules and of a generally trade liberalizing nature with only limited emphasis on discrimination against third countries. Ordinarily they are held in abeyance while bargaining proceeds with other countries or while other issues are being worked out. The Uruguay Round promises to be somewhat different from past rounds. There is less emphasis on tariff cuts that have to be generalized and more emphasis on nontariff barriers and new fields where most-favored-nation obligations do not always apply and some agreements may be plurilateral at best. If the multilateral negotiations prove to be as slow and difficult as many have suggested, there will be a case for concluding some bilateral agreements before the end of the Uruguay Round. The risk is that this process would undermine the broader negotiations, not move them ahead. A way around this danger would be to give these limited agreements a form that would permit other countries to adhere to them, as was done with the Tokyo Round codes.[13]

The argument so far has been that although one cannot see a terribly strong influence of the bilateral agreement on the forces driving the Uruguay Round or shaping the multilateral trading system generally, such influence as there is will most likely be positive. There is, however, another way of looking at the bilateral agreement. One does not have to be a great cynic, only a bit skeptical and world-weary, to say, "If Canada and the United States could not do any better in dealing with the kinds of trade problems resulting from differences in national approaches to subsidies and government regulation of the economy, and if they could not open government procurement more widely, or deal more thoroughly with services and intellectual property, what are the chances of major new breakthroughs on these matters in negotiations with the European Community and Japan, much less with the developing countries?"

This is not an altogether fair assessment. For one thing, it discounts the accomplishment of creating a free trade area and of removing tariffs. For another, it belittles the differences between the United States and Canada in precisely the areas of greatest difficulty for contemporary trade policy; for example, contingent protection, the use of subsidies, and views of the place of the government in the national economy. It is also unwise to overlook the discrepancy in size of the two countries, and the delicacy of some of the issues in Canadian politics which make it more, rather than less, difficult to reach agreement on trade issues. This view also exaggerates the similarities of the United States and Canada (to a degree which would offend many Canadians). Even one feature they have in common, federalism, creates additional problems, not least because of the political and economic differences between the states and the provinces. Nevertheless, in a world where there is great reluctance to make new commitments to trade liberalization and governments are more comfortable trying to deal with "domestic" matters by means they "control," the idea that Canada and the United States showed how hard it was to break new ground will often sound like the kind of caution that is equated with prudence.

The reference to domestic factors suggests another, albeit indirect, way in which the bilateral agreement might strengthen the international system, through its own provisions or as a demonstration. Although domestic pressures often shape what can be done with foreign trade policy, there are times when international engagements make possible action that was previously blocked by domestic forces even though it would have served a broad national interest. In the 1930s it was important to reduce American tariffs, but that could only be done by making international trade agreements. In the 1940s much of the American effort to create GATT was motivated by the conviction that it was important to subject the United States, as well as other countries, to international rules. Gilbert Winham, in Chapter 2, argues that one of the reasons the Macdonald Commission recommended free trade with the United States was to reduce governmental intervention in the

Canadian economy and to foster increased competition which it believed was essential to growth. There are Canadians who see the trade
agreement as a good way to exert pressure against the internal trade
barriers created by the provinces. Peter Lougheed, who was quoted
earlier, is not the only westerner who welcomed an international commitment that would limit Ottawa's freedom of action on oil and gas.
Canadians who despaired of putting any discipline into the use of
subsidies if the last word lay with politicians hoped that the free trade
agreement would set some boundaries. They were matched on the
American side by those who believed that the drive by business and
Congress to make ever stricter rules about "fair trade" was a prescription for permanent and increasing trouble between the United States
and other countries. The best, and perhaps the only, way to avoid
growing unilateralism is to get some agreement on international standards and commitments.[14] Since the Tokyo Round codes fell far short of
what might have been hoped for, the Canadian-American agreement
provided another opportunity. And one could imagine further measures through other bilateral agreements.

The free trade agreement did not accomplish much on this last point
although one may leave open the possibility that the dispute-settlement mechanism may make some progress along these lines in the
future, or even that the effort to draft a new regime of antidumping and
countervailing duty laws might have such an effect. It is an interesting
question, highly pertinent to the main themes of this book, whether
these limited results from the bilateral negotiations might be the consequences of an American fear that if Canada was given any kind of
exemption from the trade remedy laws, the same treatment would
have to be given to other countries. There were, to be sure, other
reasons that could explain the American reluctance to go farther to
meet Canadian wishes on these matters, notably the apparent un-
willingness of Congress to provide any general exemptions from the
laws. But there were other possibilities falling far short of general
exemption that would have made progress toward setting international
standards for subsidies and fair trade. Still, the possibility that multilateralism may have checked experimentation in this important area is
troublesome unless there is more reason than is now apparent to
believe that the GATT codes can be greatly strengthened.

Third Countries

In our study group, when I began a discussion of "open-ended agreements," two of the members with the most experience in trade negotia-

tions almost shouted, "No, no, that's impossible." I was a bit shaken. After all, Miriam Camps and I had argued several years earlier that one of the best ways to strengthen the international trading system would be for those countries that were ready to break new ground in dealing with difficult problems to make bilateral or plurilateral agreements that would be open to other countries to join when they were prepared to take on the same obligations. We recognized the dangers of bringing out the worst elements of bilateralism and of the natural disposition of governments to abuse the principle we were putting forward. We acknowledged that there would be some difficulties in deciding just what was involved in applying the original agreements to new countries. We even noted that "Governments do not like to make such commitments about the terms of as yet unknown new agreements." We made some suggestions for dealing with these difficulties, which did not seem insuperable.[15] After all, the Tokyo Round codes worked on this basis; for that matter, so did GATT itself. Of course there might be problems of the sort connected with conditional MFN, but, as was pointed out in Chapter 1, these are quite different when a whole set of provisions and a number of countries are involved. It was difficult to imagine any kind of arrangement in which the existing members of an organization, or parties to an agreement, did not have some voice over the entry of a new country. No one had told us then that we were crazy; what had made the thought so outlandish now?

Discussion soon clarified the issues and provided a valuable commentary on the relationship between an original agreement and what became of it later on. What the objectors had in mind was that there was no chance that Congress would approve an agreement with Canada with the expectation—much less the specific provision—that other countries could adhere to it in the future. Jealous of their own powers, used to a process in which one gets something for everything that is given, and highly sensitive to the way changes in foreign trade could affect employment and other interests of their constituents, the members of Congress were not about to approve agreements that were "open-ended." There was enough doubt about whether Congress would act favorably on the bilateral agreement without trying to load onto it the possibility of extending some of its benefits to unidentified third countries, on terms yet to be negotiated. The Canadians, too, were not likely to see the agreement as open-ended; they were clearly having to balance gains and concessions with great care and to make tradeoffs between economic and political hazards at home and opportunities in the United States. If they were at all willing to deal on the same terms with any third countries, or later became willing, they would want to look carefully at the implications of each step and not sign any blank checks in advance.

No doubt all this is true and stating it brings into focus issues that must be considered in any discussion of how third countries might react to the Canadian-American agreement. No country, presumably, would think of simply joining the free trade area and accepting all its terms if only because some of the major provisions are tailored to bilateral circumstances. Entry into a free trade area, with either or both the United States and Canada, that covered tariffs and quotas but left other provisions to be worked out separately, is a possible, but not very likely, approach. It is more reasonable to suppose that a third country would be interested in certain aspects of the bilateral agreement, and seek to be treated in the same way by the United States and Canada (or either one).

Then some interesting problems arise. The Canadian-American agreement is, after all, a collection of agreements; the balance of interests of the two countries is sometimes achieved within each section, but at other times, one suspects, one country accepted a somewhat one-sided arrangement in one field as a way of getting its wishes in another. All this may be of no concern to the third country, but is likely to affect the willingness of Canada or the United States to see the agreement extended to it. Indeed, it is quite possible that on many matters the two countries will have opposite reactions. The partner that reluctantly made a concession will surely resist going still further, while the one who gained may be happy to see comparable terms accepted by other countries.

Third-country interest will often be directed at the United States, rather than Canada, simply because of the size of its economy; although there will certainly be instances in which a third country wants to overcome the preferred position that the United States has in the Canadian market. Except for the automotive agreement, there is nothing in the bilateral agreement itself, so far as I can see, that forbids either party to treat a third country as well as it treats its bilateral partner, or that even requires it to consult the other country before doing so. However, the partner being left out would certainly raise the issue and demand consultation or, if it got no satisfaction, make use of the machinery for dispute settlement.

One of the most obvious cases in which one of the bilateral partners might feel it was losing some of the benefits of the agreement would be the lowering of the partner's tariff on imports from third countries. Thus, the mechanism by which a free trade area can stimulate more general tariff reduction is at the same time a potential loss of benefits for one of the parties. The traditional Canadian preference for a free trade area over a customs union, in virtually all past discussions of free trade with the United States, is based in part on the wish to retain the freedom to raise or lower Canadian duties without having to seek the consent of the United States. Since the bilateral negotiations took place while the ground was being prepared for the Uruguay Round, the negotiators presumably allowed for the likelihood of reduced margins of tariff advantage (and might even have reached some understanding as to whether there were any exceptionally touchy items on which no action would be taken without consultation—but this seems fairly unlikely). As the main emphasis the United States has put on the Uruguay Round does not concern tariffs, the question is whether other features of the bilateral agreement will be seriously affected by the multilateral negotiations.

Part of the answer is found in the provisions under which the two countries agree to pursue their larger aims in the multilateral negotiations. That presumably means that in these matters their objectives are the same, but it will be interesting to see if their positions continue to be uniform as time passes or whether they will find divergent interests and take different views as to the kinds of compromises to be made in these fields (and with whom). On other matters there is no assurance of a common approach or even a recognition of common interests. Presumably neither Washington nor Ottawa wanted to tie its hands by the free trade area agreement—but might it have done so inadvertently?

Canadians have always worried that in any kind of partnership the American view will prevail when there are differences.[16] Canadian negotiators believe that they helped pave the way for the Uruguay Round by working out arrangements with a number of middle-sized countries that would not have been accepted if they had been advanced as American proposals. The long intellectual concern with Canada's ability to influence world affairs continues and rests to an important degree on not having to have American agreement, as well as on the choice of issues and forums or organizations.[17]

Although neither country has given up its MFN rights under GATT, there are a number of trade issues to which MFN does not extend. In its negotiations with Japan about high-technology industries, for example, the United States is coming close to saying that certain types of subsidy will not be countervailed against provided the Japanese give up certain other practices and open markets to American exports. Much the same was done with regard to dumping in the 1987 agreement on semiconductors. Is the United States obligated to treat Canada in just the same way? Could Canada hope to use the dispute-settlement or consultation provisions to make its case? How would either country's position be influenced by the effect of the arrangements on American-owned companies in Canada or Canadian-owned companies in the United States?

Since the greatest novelty of the bilateral agreement is the dispute-settlement arrangment concerning fair trade, and since American practices in that field are of great concern to most other countries, it seems likely that the third-country question will at least occasionally focus on this issue. Although some review of the operation of the GATT codes may be undertaken during the Uruguay Round, nothing suggests that the major trading countries are ready to try seriously to improve the subsidies code. Consequently, the unilateral application of American definitions of acceptable and unacceptable practices will continue unless individual countries can find ways of moderating American practice. While the position Canada has gained is less than it hoped for, other countries may see advantages in it, especially if they believe that the discussions with the United States to which it will give rise offer opportunities that the normal GATT procedures lack.

Whether the United States would have any interest in making comparable agreements with other countries is another matter that cannot be explored here. It need not regard the Canadian dispute-settlement arrangement as a precedent since it is part of the apparatus of a free trade area.[18] In November 1987, however, it concluded an agreement with Mexico that consists of little more than a consultation and dispute-settlement procedure, and statements of aims and purposes. (There was an earlier bilateral memorandum of understanding on subsidies and countervailing duties connected with Mexico's entry into GATT.) The new procedure sounds fairly conventional and the agreement does not go as far as the one with Canada in providing for binding settlements even on limited issues. It does, however, provide a place where problems between the two countries can be discussed and perhaps settled; so it is more than a dispute-settlement mechanism and may even provide an antechamber to later understandings (as, indeed, may prove true of the Canadian procedure). Interestingly enough, the chairman of the Foreign Relations Committee of the Mexican Senate, Hugo Margain, then called for a similar agreement with Canada. The reason, he said, was that "An ad hoc mechanism is needed to resolve disputes, a procedure that is quicker than that established in the GATT."[19]

Mexico is the "third country" most intimately concerned with the Canadian-American agreement, even though it is the European Community and Japan that most people have had in mind when they thought about the limitations on the bilateral agreement that might come from concern with the rest of the world. In Chapter 5, Gerardo Bueno has set out very well Mexico's relations with Canada and the United States, and highlights the issues reported in the *Elements* that are of particular interest to Mexico. Bueno's chapter reflects the growing interest in Mexico in what can be accomplished by a fuller engagement in international economic affairs, and not least through GATT. He correctly points out that even if Mexico carries further the more outward-looking trade policy that he advocates, it will still not be in a position to liberalize its trade as much as the older industrial countries have done long since. At the same time his prescription calls for a degree of selective liberalization that foreshadows a rather different trade regime from that of the past. How far this can be carried depends to an important degree on the development of Mexico's exports and that, in turn, depends to an important degree on the import policies of other countries. Therefore, the question of whether Mexico is better off relying primarily on multilateral negotiations or needs special arrangements with its largest customer, the United States, is a very salient one. It is not too different from the question Canada faced and, for a hundred years, found difficulty answering—and may not have settled yet.

Mexico is not Canada and any arrangement would have to be tailored to its special needs. As Bueno suggests, anything approaching Mexican adherence to the Canadian-American agreement is far off. Nevertheless, he finds a number of issues that might usefully be discussed. While Professor Bueno's reminders about different levels of development are certainly correct, it is doubtful whether either the United States or Canada is likely to accept the idea that Mexico should be treated as a Third World country in North America in the sense of being almost automatically exempted from most obligations. Ideas about the homogeneity of developing countries have given way to a focus on their diversity. What is called for, as Bueno makes clear, is a trade regime that is geared to Mexico's economic structure, capabilities and needs. Whether that is best produced on a bilateral, multilateral or North American basis is an interesting question. There is no doubt, though, that relations with the United States are the key for Mexico as they are for Canada.

Bueno is certainly on the right track when he stresses the need for Mexico to examine its relations with the United States sector by sector, and to try to arrange its foreign economic relations to take account of the differences among industries. (It cannot be assumed, of course, that it is only the Mexican view of the needs of the sector that will be taken into account.) Formal sectoral agreements, as he points out, raise difficulties, but it is worth recalling that sectoral arrangements are more prominent in the Canadian-American agreement than many people had expected (and are quite important in U.S. trade policy toward a number of developing countries as well—and not always for the best). The time may well come when balanced bargains within sectors are not possible, when the limits of balancing one sector against another have been reached, so that something broader has to be taken into account. It is also surely going to prove true that, as in the case of Canada, trade will not remain strictly trade, or even trade in goods, and will entail understandings not only about services but investment as well.

Bueno makes it clear that some Mexicans have a sense of being left out as Canada and the United States pursue their trade negotiations. (There is an echo of the Canadians' uneasiness at being left out of trading blocs that were taking shape around the world.) Hovering in the background of this and other discussions is the idea of a North American free trade area or common market. This concept has not been very popular in either Canada or Mexico, for obvious reasons. It sounds to many people like giving free rein to the rich and powerful to take what they want from the economies of the others. American industry is seen as exploiting the raw materials of Canada and Mexico. American finance is seen as controlling the fate of common people and governments, to the north and to the south, from the upper floors of tall buildings on the lower end of Manhattan Island. The softer label, "A North American Accord" is seen as hypocritical or a Madison Avenue fudging of the reality of a wholly one-sided arrangement.

In the nineteenth and in the twentieth century, a number of Americans have thought the concept of a single North American economy natural and desirable. But prudence has prevailed and kept the U.S. government from advocating such a goal or adopting policies intended to promote it. Some years ago the then prime minister of Canada and president of Mexico discussed the issue and released parallel statements saying that each thought it best to pursue relations bilaterally with the United States and with each other. This is basically what has been done, with the focus on the United States since the nexus of each of the other countries with the one in the middle is so much greater than with one another. There is nothing in what has happened in recent years to suggest that a different approach has anything more to recommend it, but as each of the sets of bilateral relations changes, questions have to be asked about the other, and that is what is exemplified in Bueno's chapter and some of the Mexican discussions he reports there.[20]

This discussion of the interests of third countries and how they will affect the bilateral agreement has not been very conclusive. Many of the questions raised have not been given serious thought, but they are of considerable potential importance to the future of American-Canadian relations as well as to world trade. What has been most neglected is the extent to which the two countries, by virtue of the free trade agreement, have created questions about common or divergent action towards other countries and multilateral trade issues. To try to push any of these questions farther would require either close study of products and trade patterns or a series of hypotheses, neither of which has a place in this discourse. Apart from flagging issues so that they will be kept in mind for the future, the most that can be done is to speculate on the larger questions of where Canadian-American relations may go after the agreement, what would happen if the agreement were not accepted by one or both countries, and whether there is a new place for bilateralism in the world, for good or ill.

A New Relationship Between Canada and the United States

Extravagant language has been used about the agreement creating a free trade area. The president of the United States has called it "a new economic Constitution for North America." John Turner, leader of the Liberal Party in Canada commented: "Mr. Reagan is really saying the Canadian economy is becoming a part of the American economy."[21] Other Canadian politicians have called the trade agreement a sell-out which will end Canada's independence and sentence its economy to an eternity of producing raw materials and fuel for the American economy. As our analysis has made clear, neither apotheosis nor apocalypse has been made imminent by what is an ambitious but limited trade agreement. Most of the changes that can reasonably be expected fall into three categories: 1) those concerning the economic structure of the two countries; 2) governmental relations as they concern economic issues; and 3) the approach of the two countries to the international economic system.

As has been apparent for many years, and demonstrated in a number of good studies, a major removal of trade barriers between the United States and Canada would have its principal effect on Canada, both in potential gains and in the adaptation of the economy necessary to take advantage of the freer access to the large American market.

Because important segments of Canadian industry were built up to serve a sheltered Canadian market, changes would be needed to sell competitively in larger new markets; not all firms would survive, but some would thrive. Much of the adaptation would be within industries, some of them American-owned. Changes might vary considerably from industry to industry; in some industries production of some items for the whole North American market would be concentrated in Canada (as happened in automobiles), in other industries plants that once produced primarily for the Canadian market, would become suppliers to the globe, either independently or as units in a multinational complex. Shifts in employment would raise productivity but would also require retraining and very likely other forms of aid to workers displaced in the restructuring. These prospects contributed to both support for, and opposition to, the free trade negotiations, depending on which part of the process most concerned the observer (or participant).

In the United States, where much less attention has been given to the consequences of free trade with Canada, opportunities for gains and threats of losses are far less important to the economy as a whole, but can be quite significant for some industries and some areas. In many board rooms decisions will have to be made as to whether plants built in Canada to get behind a tariff should be kept in production when the tariff disappears. Some may be closed down, but more are likely to be incorporated into new patterns of production and trade. New plants may be opened to supply the American market as its import barriers fall. Canadian companies that once produced in the United States may find it preferable to export from Canada.

There is no way to be certain how these processes will play themselves out, or even, within the scope of this book, to review such studies as have been made. The modesty of the agreement's provisions on government procurement, and the uncertainty as to how the new procedures for dealing with countervailing and antidumping duties will work, are the biggest caveats about the generalizations that one would otherwise make with some confidence. As the trade barriers will be removed fairly gradually, the adjustments can be spread over a period of time (unless businessmen decide, as those in the Common Market did, that it makes more sense to begin operating right away as if there were free trade). That ought to make the accommodation easier, but an effort to make predictions has no place here. The passage of time does, however, underline two considerations of particular importance that will have a bearing on how the free trade agreement helps alter the structure of the American and Canadian economies.

At the same time that they remove barriers on trade with one another, both Canada and the United States will continue to go through a rather difficult process of adapting their economies to changes in the world economy. Peter Morici has shown how many similarities there are in the position of the two countries, along with some differences as well.[22] In both cases there are advantages from the creation of the free trade area, but there can also be conflicts between its requirements and efforts to reduce the pain of exposure to increased competition from the rest of the world. Neither Canada nor the United States is highly skilled in governmental measures to improve the processes of adaptation (although both economies have undergone enormous changes in the last few decades). It is far from clear that they would be able to work any better in tandem. Purely national measures could exacerbate the problems of bringing the free trade area into full operation; for example, a seriously sick industry undergoing special care to bring about adaptation and recovery would be an obvious candidate for exceptional treatment and exclusion from immediate trade liberalization; there is room for much argument about whether subsidies to permit industries to retain workers and to compensate for lower productivity as they learn new jobs should be subject to countervailing duties if they affect the industry's ability to sell to the other country. A wider range of national economic policies than is covered by the free trade agreement might well be brought into the discussion, not least of which are exchange rates and tax measures that favored exports. In the long run the free trade area ought to help make Canadian and American producers more competitive internationally, but in the short run some of them will find the adaptation it calls for an additional burden—and they will let their governments know.

The second consideration with which one must reckon is that, in spite of their limitations, the free trade arrangements will foster the further integration of the Canadian and American economies. That process has been going on for a long time, and has advanced further than between any two major industrial countries. It is a process marked by the linking of productive processes, both in terms of supplying raw materials and energy for industry and in specialization among and within industries. The financial relations of Canadians and Americans, public and private, are highly complex and run back and forth across the border; provinces are financed in New York, Canadian industry is owned by Americans, and U.S. real estate and theaters are held by Canadians. The further removal of barriers will permit the process to continue and may in fact accelerate it. One cannot be entirely sure about acceleration, since the process of integration has gone on so strongly with the barriers in place that are now to be removed, and with even greater barriers in the past. As there are aspects of integration that are not always welcome to everyone, and especially as the process is feared and opposed by some Canadians, the dramatization of the issue by the creation of a free trade area may stimulate reactions that could have an impact on our second category of developments, those concerning the relations between the two governments.

Most agreements affecting trade comprise two kinds of provisions, those that call for action that is irreversible, so long as the agreement remains in effect, and those that provide for future actions. The distinction is blurred when the timing or dimension of the steps in the first category depends on the interpretation of agreement language some years hence. For present purposes, however, there is a convenient separation of the removal of tariffs (and some other actions) from the provisions dealing with most nontariff barriers, fair trade rules and, for the most part, services and investment. The action on tariffs will be relatively clear-cut; on the other matters, the provisions of the free trade agreement will mean what the two governments make of them.

Perhaps it is wrong to say Canada and the United States; it is more realistic to say Canadians and Americans since opinions are usually divided on both sides of the border. The differences are particularly sharp in Canada and can shape crucial decisions. This was dramatized when, in the fall of 1987, the leaders of both opposition parties said that if they came to power they would "tear up the agreement." If believed, those statements were enough to create uncertainty even about tariff reduction—if they did not lead Congress to reject the agreement in the first place. In most democracies, election pledges are not always carried out. In office—or on the way there—a political leader may simply say that "circumstances have changed" and while certain nefarious elements in the agreement are still unacceptable, other features are now seen to be advantageous to Canada and should therefore be kept. *Rebus sic stantibus* is usually invoked to get out of a treaty obligation, but there is no reason why it cannot be turned around. But then there is the question of whether the partner will accept a tacit understanding that it should not react too vigorously if the other is slow to carry out some of its obligations.

Alternatively, one country might pursue its rights under the agreement very actively—others might say aggressively—challenging the other's policies, precipitating disputes that bring the machinery into action, threatening the reprisals the agreement permits when certain problems are not resolved. That can be one way of making an agreement live and, in the long run, of strengthening it. But unless the atmosphere is favorable, and the cases good, the results can be less constructive than troublesome. The opposite risk is that the governments would let the agreement languish, putting its provisions into effect as required and on schedule but with litle effort toward using the dispute-settlement and consultation machinery to find new ways of improving trade relations, much less working to replace it with the new regime for fair trade law called for in the agreement. It is easier to see the United States being negligent in this fashion than Canada which not only has more at stake, but is likely to see itself as the aggrieved party more often.

Naturally, there is another range of possibilities. Both countries might accept the agreement with a sigh of relief that so many old troubles had been ended; they could take advantage of the new opportunities to gain some of the benefits of trade liberalization—in a world where that has become a scarce commodity—and try to use the new machinery to add to their accomplishments. Perhaps the strongest force in favor of this outcome is the fact that in both countries there are many people who can benefit from such an approach. Divisions of interest often cut across national lines so that political leaders in both countries can form coalitions in support of the positive approach, or perhaps duck the political problems of taking sides by saying that the issue is covered by the trade agreement (which in a sense covers everything through its dispute-settlement provisions) and should therefore be worked out in those channels.

If, instead, Canadian-American trade issues continue to be approached in the traditional trade-negotiating way—where every issue is treated as if it involves the national interest interpreted in short-run mercantilistic terms, and agreement to anything asked by the other is viewed as a "concession" that has to be paid for—then sharp limits will be put on what can be achieved. It is also not enough to make common acceptance or harmony the highest goal; this leads to compromises which, as often as not, deny the two countries the benefits of the trade liberalization they have agreed to. The effort, for example, to avoid trouble about the impact of American countervailing duties has led often enough to agreements that limit sales to the United States or raise the price of imports without a real resolution of the question of whether the foreign seller is the lowest cost producer. An argument about government procurement can result in a simple division of the market, at some cost to the taxpayers in the buying country and the producers in the other, rather than encouraging the development of a more efficient structure of production in each.

To be sure, more than economic advantage is involved. As we have noted, both countries have serious problems of structural adjustment. Sometimes help must be given to those hardest hit by change; sometimes it is wise to slow the adjustment process to what is politically tolerable. Even in normal circumstances, there are social and political objectives that clash with pure economic efficiency and which cannot be set aside. The two countries will often have different practices with respect to these matters and there will be conflicts of opinion in each about what arrangements should prevail domestically. As the smaller country, Canada will inevitably feel the need to defend itself against the sheer weight of some American practices. Americans need to understand these issues and Canadian feelings about them better than they have in the past. They should also grow accustomed to the idea that even if the trade agreement works very well, it and the United States will be blamed for a large share of the troubles the Canadian economy is likely to go through in the next decade or so. In addition, it is only too easy for the United States—or some Americans in a position of authority—to throw American weight around without much regard for its effect on others. These are just facts of life against which constructive arrangements like the free trade area have to be defended.

No doubt the durability of the agreement is threatened by the sharp division of opinion in Canada where both its economic and its non-economic effects run deep and touch historical emotions. But there is also a threat to the agreement from the United States, of which many Canadians are well aware. This has two elements. One is the traditional unconsciousness of Americans about Canada and Canadian-American relations. ("I need a badge saying, 'I am a foreign diplomat'" a Canadian ambassador in Washington once said to me.) The other element is not peculiar to Canada. All over the globe, one can find Americans who take their domestic political compulsions as facts that the rest of the world should acknowledge without question or recourse. They are surprised to be thought hypocrites when they say political necessity makes their case exceptional. "Congress will not accept this" has been the final word for American negotiators for many years. Sometimes they were right, sometimes wrong, and sometimes faking. But the truth has been bad enough often enough to make Canadian fears reasonable, whether the source of the trouble was the separation of powers or populism and democracy. The defense that has been built into the agreement is the right to denounce the agreement, a recourse that can be costly but that has some power once the United States comes to feel that it has a stake in the success of the agreement.

In summary, the real meaning of the free trade agreement will depend on what the governments make of it in the years to come. What that is, and the durability of the agreement as well, will depend in turn not only on how well the agreement works, but on quite different factors. These include the divisions of opinion in Canada about relations with the United States; the extent to which Americans keep in mind the value of their relations with Canada; and American recognition of the effect on Canadians of some things that reach well beyond trade and are sometimes done with no thought about Canada at all.

The Consequences of Failure

All of the above is written on the assumption that the bilateral agreement comes into effect. It is, however, quite possible that the agreement will be turned down by Congress or fail to take the hurdles of a more complex and less well-defined political process in Canada. That may already have happened by the time this book has readers, but the author remains in the dark. He need not speculate on the outcome but a word on what might happen if the agreement failed—as we may put it—is important to the main theme of this book.

Some things about the failure are easy to predict. Each side will blame the other. The groundwork has already been laid by the negotiators. At the top, the president and the prime minister may refrain from attributing blame to one another, seeking instead domestic opponents who can be held guilty while they commiserate. But from Ottawa and Washington will come the words of "highly placed sources" explaining what it was that the officials, the legislators or perhaps the journalists of the other country did that caused the trouble. The chief executives will be blamed after all, by implication if not directly.

There will be efforts by journalists, scholars, politicians, and others to inquire into just what really happened. It will be important for the long-run relations of the two countries to get the story straight and write it honestly, but that may take time and some biased or incorrect versions are likely to govern opinion for a while. Not everything will be a simple matter of fact. It will take some analysis to know why the executive branch did such a poor job of laying the groundwork to help Congress and the public understand the American national interest in the success of the agreement. It will be asked whether the Office of the U.S. Trade Representative had the resources to appreciate the ramifications in Canada of some of the concessions the Americans asked for. There will be room for asking what might have been accomplished if

Secretary Baker's injunction to the lawyers to "be creative" had come months instead of hours before the end of the negotiations.

On the Canadian side, a key question will be whether the government could have done anything to prepare the political ground better, if not for specific features of the agreement then for the idea of negotiating it at all. There could never have been any doubt that the proposal to adopt such an agreement would be divisive and controversial—history, psychology, and differences of political perspectives and values made that inevitable. It was also easy to see that honest differences of opinion and of personal preference were bound to be exploited and exacerbated by the political process. Were there no ways of reducing the risk that the agreement would be denounced if the government changed?

The immediate consequences of failure are predictable, but for our purposes more obscure and longer-run questions are more important—and also less predictable. Will either government, or both, take off after the other? Will Washington start a series of actions under Section 301 challenging the Canadian subsidies which it was not prepared to waive the right to countervail? Will Canada scrutinize American investments more sharply, lay down performance requirements and refuse to give American banks the treatment promised in the agreement? Will American businessmen, newly sensitized to the value of the Canadian market, mount trade and investment offensives and call on Congress and the executive to support them? Will the Canadian federal government, and the provinces, put more emphasis than before on domestic procurement? Will the duty-remission schemes for Japanese, Korean and European automobile manufacturers be kept in force with the knowledge that down the road there is bound to be American action on countervailing measures? Will the postures of Ottawa and Washington be properly described by such terms as "trade war," "arm's-length," and "strained relations?"

Such actions and attitudes would not be very sensible; nor are they likely to serve the national interests of either country in the long run. This does not make them any less probable. Perhaps the fact that there are consumers and producers in both countries who would be hurt by such activities, and enough businessmen, politicians and bureaucrats who want to save the results of the negotiations, or at least keep the status quo ante, would work against these reactions. One can hardly imagine anyone wishing to start the negotiations all over again even if the two heads of government (if they were still there) were stubborn enough to try to work out an agreement they could put in effect without legislative support. Might the Uruguay Round provide an occasion for picking up lost pieces? Only if both countries are determined to try.

Perhaps the time has come when enough Canadians are willing to accept the economic costs of not having a free trade area with the United States. They may be satisfied to deal with their problems with such powers and resources as Canada can command, and avoid the political and psychological strains of too much exposure to the United States. If that proves to be the case, there is certainly no American interest in challenging the decision. Such economic gains as the United States can have from freer trade with Canada are well forgone if the price is lasting political dissatisfaction in Canada. What the United States needs is a strong and independent Canada with which it can cooperate, and that can only be provided by Canadians living the way they want to—but they cannot do it alone, so they will continue to face the questions that gave rise to this book.[23] It seems likely that the time would come when once again a Canadian government would think it had the support to work out a closer trading arrangement with the United States—but how could one feel sure they were right?

The United States has acquired a different kind of interest in the success of the free trade area negotiations. Their failure would almost certainly be a setback to efforts to increase multilateral trade liberalization and to find ways of handling the increasingly complex sets of issues that make up contemporary trade problems. No one is going to say, "The failure of the Canadian-American negotiations shows that these things cannot be done bilaterally, therefore only multilateral methods will work." Instead we will hear that the ideas the United States has been endorsing for ambitious new agreements cannot even be worked out bilaterally with a neighboring country that is in many ways like-minded and certainly much weaker than the United States. "And so far as the further reduction of conventional trade barriers is concerned, the Americans have timed things badly; we shall be lucky if we get through this period of slow growth without imposing new restraints on imports. So it is best not to rock the boat." How much influence such views would have is not easily guessed, but they are in harmony with much European thinking; and developing countries are happy if their policies are not challenged; while the Japanese, concerned as they are with keeping world markets open, are accommodating people who are not likely to lead a new crusade. Just because the positive influence of a successful free trade area negotiation on the Uruguay Round may not be great, as argued above, it does not follow that the consequences of a failure will not be greater. Here, as in some other things, asymmetry can be realism.

A question that requires still more imagination is the future of Canadian-American trade relations if the free trade area agreement were rejected, and then there was a marked turn toward bilateralism in the world. Closely related is the question of whether a successful conclusion of the free trade area negotiations would herald a turn in the same direction.

The New Bilateralism?

In the eyes of many people, the willingness of Canada and the United States to try to negotiate a free trade agreement was itself an important turn toward bilateralism. After all, since before the end World War II the two countries had been leading proponents of the multilateral system. Before we speculate about the future, it is useful to explore just why this departure took place—if it was indeed a departure.

There were already many bilateral elements in the economic relations between the two countries. The idea of free trade with the United States was an old subject in Canada. In the sixties and seventies there were major studies of the subject. Some Canadians stresssed the repeated demonstrations of economic advantages for Canada; others resented the degree of economic dependence on the United States that already existed and rejected the idea of seeking even closer ties. Although much trade between the two countries was free of tariffs or moved at low rates, and some defense procurement ignored national boundaries, the major formal understanding that could be called a free trade agreement concerned automobiles. It had been devised to deal with a specific set of problems. The conventional wisdom was that other industries did not lend themselves to the same treatment. At the same time, there were always those who thought that a piecemeal approach was the most practical to broaden the area of free trade with the United States.

Consequently, when in 1983 the Trudeau government proposed explorations with the United States of what could be done in several industrial sectors, it looked as if the older ideas had come to the surface again. This time, though, there was a possibility of something more. Enough sectors could add up to something like a free trade area; the omissions, one could guess, would be the difficult cases where one or the other country was not prepared to expose an industry to strong foreign competition, or agriculture which everyone tended to leave out of account. There was, however, a certain lack of enthusiasm about the talks. Therefore, the decision of the Mulroney government to try to work out a comprehensive agreement (various terms were used for it) was a significant political and economic choice that was bound to stir both opposition and support in Canada. Inquiring why the decision was made, and especially how much of a departure from Canada's traditional commitment to multilateralism it represented, has been one of the most interesting parts of this study. My report has to be highly truncated. Gilbert Winham explains the factors more fully in Chapter 2.

At the time of the Trudeau initiative, the most common answer to the basic question was that times were hard and Canada could not cope with its economic difficulties without improving its foreign trade prospects and modernizing the structure of some industries. There was also an immediate danger from the rise of protectionism in the United States. Although economic conditions improved, those arguments continued to play a part in the Mulroney decision, but significant additions appeared. Many people believed that Canada could not live comfortably with the status quo at a time when conditions of world trade were deteriorating. Others argued that the status quo could not be sustained. As an exporter, the country faced problems all over the world but the chances of doing much about them was poor, at least until there was another GATT round and that would not bring results for several years. American contingent protection was seen as the biggest problem and there was no way to come quickly to grips with that except by bilateral negotiations. Whether any thought was given to an agreement confined to the fair trade rules, I do not know. But the broader approach avoided the major difficulties of the sectoral effort, and would do more to help bring about the restructuring of signficant parts of the Canadian economy. Moreover, a reduction of Canada's relatively high tariffs would also help producers become internationally competitive. In many respects there was nothing new in all these arguments; most of them could be found in Canadian discussions over the years, as was pointed out above.

This time, however, there seems to have been a significant shift in business opinion so that support for the free trade area was strong, whereas in the past important segments of trade and industry were quite protectionist. The report of the Macdonald Commission, headed by a former minister in Liberal cabinets who had been thought of as a nationalist in economic matters, made the case for a free trade area in considerable detail and suggested, if only symbolically, that the climate of opinion had changed. No doubt there were other political factors as well which I do not feel qualified to assess with any assurance.

All this seems quite clear, but what is not so clear is how fully this choice represented a deliberate departure from Canada's traditional adherence to multilateralism. That adherence had at least two major components. One was the natural interest of a middle-sized trading nation in arrangements that gave it an opportunity to buy and sell in many markets on equal terms with other countries. The second component of the Canadian adherence to multilateralism was the feeling that when many countries were involved, it was not quite as dependent on the United States or as exposed to its pressures (whether deliberate or unthinking) as it would otherwise be. Beyond the considerations of national interest was the conviction many Canadians shared with Americans and others that a liberal multinational economic order increased the prospects of peace and prosperity in the world.

Canada's firm commitment to multilateralism was underlined by the country's prominent role in creating GATT and other postwar global economic organizations. The emergence of the European Common Market, and particularly British entry into it, somewhat undermined the faith. For years Canadians have spoken ruefully, and perhaps a little fearfully, of the fact that they were one of the few important trading nations that did not have unimpeded access to a very large market. Some drew the conclusion that a free trade area with the United States was the logical step. That was not a new thought; Gilbert Winham gives an account of recurrent efforts to come to terms bilaterally with the United States. It was also nothing new for such ideas to be strenuously resisted by other Canadians.

A new factor influencing the old argument is the view that GATT has not proved as sturdy in hard times as it had seemed earlier. It has been abused by some of its members—almost everyone has a complaint about someone else. Malefactors have gone relatively unpunished. Much time has passed since there have been major steps forward in trade liberalization. The results of the Tokyo Round raise doubts as to whether the methods that worked to remove tariffs and quotas can cope with the very trade problems most bothersome to Canadians, those stemming from disagreements about the use of subsidies and other measures of industrial policy and their effects on "fair trade."

When the decision to propose a free trade area was taken, what was thought about its relationship to traditional multilateralism? Some claim there was no thought about it at all, or at least no discussion in the quarters where it counted. Others believe that the decision was highly conscious and was dictated by pragmatism. What was needed for Canada could only be achieved by working towards a free trade area with the United States. Canada would continue to fight for its rights and make sure that the agreement provided the best defenses possible—but fears about future contingencies had to take second place to efforts to deal with current realities (including contingent protection).

The other set of worries, about the effect of a bilateral agreement on the international trading system, was not of great concern to Canadian officials, according to Gilbert Winham. He reports an argument between bilateralists and multilateralists which the former won, partly, he believes, because the Canadian economy's increased dependency on trade with the United States has made it less of a multilateral trader. Nevertheless, Canada retains an interest in multilateral arrangements in its relations with the rest of the world even though it makes a bilateral agreement to deal with its unique relationship with the United States. At the same time that it started negotiating with the United States, Canada played an active role in setting up the Uruguay Round. Official statements made clear the continuing interest in strengthening GATT. As we have seen, the bilateral agreement was carefully fashioned to meet the multilateral rules, looked forward to some coordinated American and Canadian activities in the Uruguay Round, and might in the end strengthen the multilateral system in some of the ways we have already discussed.

So much for intentions. Naturally, the case was not watertight. There was also the question whether, whatever the intentions, the working out of the free trade area agreement would not have strong bilateral tendencies. Nothing, it was clear, was automatic or even altogether certain, but that turns out to be true of the United States as well.

For the United States the move to bilateralism with Canada was more a matter of assent than choice. Why should it rebuff the initiative of its principal trading partner with whom so much trade was already free and with whom its economy was otherwise so intertwined? The proposal, after all, came when there had already been talks about sectors and the Americans had added some to the original Canadian list. The Americans surely shared the Canadian view that the sectoral approach had serious deficiencies. No doubt they assured the Canadians privately that their broader overtures would not be turned down. It has been suggested by some Canadians that the Americans really invited the proposal, but perhaps this was a matter of interpreting nods and becks rather than anything clear-cut. An exact account of who said what to whom and when will be important to that honest history suggested above—which will also be needed if the negotiations succeed and everyone claims responsibility for the results.

Most people concerned with Canadian-American relations have argued for years that it would be unwise for the United States to make any overtures that could be interpreted as suggesting that it wished to "take over" Canada. The thing to do was to wait until the Canadians had sufficiently overcome their domestic disagreements to take the first step. That seemed to have happened; but now the matter is in doubt. The situation is immensely complicated by the fact that neither side could possibly make a real commitment without knowing what the terms of the agreement would be, and that could only be settled by negotiations which would give occasion for negative forces in both countries to make themselves felt. And that is what has happened.

Throughout the postwar years, the American attitude toward free trade areas and customs unions was that they were something for other people. Europe forced the United States to pay closer attention; one result was the widespread conviction that Article XXIV of the GATT ought to be strengthened so as to require those creating free trade areas or customs unions to take greater account of outside countries and the multilateral trading system as a whole. But this never became a dominant note in American trade policy. In its 1979 trade legislation, Congress asked for studies of trade with Canada and Mexico. The Trade and Tariff Act of 1984 authorized the president to negotiate free trade areas and provided a fast track procedure. When in 1985 the United States negotiated a free trade area with Israel, few people took it as a serious indication of a new direction in U.S. trade policy. Israel's relations with the United States are as "special" as those of Canada, but completely different in ways that seemed adequate to explain the agreement without much regard to trade policy as a whole. The Caribbean Basin initiative provided one-way free entry into the United States (with limitations) from some very small countries. Although some other developing countries became interested in the possibility of similar arrangements for themselves—and used the term free trade area—the circumstances were too different from the main trading relations of the United States to be given a great deal of weight.

Secretary of State George Shultz, in the speech of April 1985 quoted by Murray Smith in Chapter 4, argued that bilateral free trade areas could "strengthen the multilateral system." So far as I am aware, few people expected the United States to press very far in that direction except possibly with Canada with whom talks were already underway. Still, the thought of a series of bilateral agreements focused on the United States may have stirred reactions in some quarters. References to the possibility of bilateral action were also an indication of American impatience with the delay of so many countries in even agreeing to open new multilateral trade negotiations. That was an authentic reflection of the mood of a number of Americans, in and out of office, since the barren GATT ministerial meeting in the fall of 1982. The then U.S. trade representative, William E. Brock, is said to have expressed a good bit of satisfaction with the Canadian decision to move from sectoral to general negotiations. By responding to that initiative, the United States showed that it could take important steps toward trade liberalization even if other countries dragged their feet.

All of this did not add up to the conclusion that the United States was going to substitute bilateral for multilateral approaches in its trade policy. There were, however, other activities that had to be taken very seriously and that certainly increased the bilateral element in American trade policy in the 1980s. They have been summarized in Chapter 1: pressure on countries to rectify bilateral imbalances with the United States (if they ran one way and not the other); the pursuit of specific trade practices judged unfavorable to the United States on a country-by-country basis; the effort to get commitments about trade in services which often meant dealing with countries one by one; an emphasis on reciprocity, rather narrowly conceived; and import controls which, even if they affected goods from several countries, were imposed on individual countries and took account of overall bilateral relations. The United States became one of the biggest champions of no change in the international textile arrangements, which are havens of bilateralism. Perhaps some of these measures reflect only passing circumstances or are meant as a warning to other countries, and will be dropped when there is a response. However, the pressures behind the bilateral measures will continue and the attitudes supporting these approaches are firmly enough fixed in the minds of many of the Americans who count in the making of trade policy to be lasting factors shaping U.S. trade policy for some time to come.

How strong an influence these factors will have depends on developments in three spheres: the course of American politics; the evolution of the world economy; and the outcome of the multilateral trade negotiations. None of these can be predicted with any confidence. So, once again, we must leave some large issues in limbo. This time, at least, the questions are global and not the province of the rather narrow inquiry that has shaped this book. But to conclude our study we should first go back and try to place the Canadian-American bilateral agreement in the broader setting just analyzed. And then we can take an author's prerogative of prescribing for policy. If that requires saying something about the international trading world as a whole as well as about the newly designed bilateral segment, that is something the reader will have to put up with.

There is nothing about the Canadian-American agreement that forces the United States or Canada to follow a bilateral course from now on. Nor is it the kind of agreement that permits other countries to say that the North American partners have abandoned multilateralism, or gone back on their multilateral obligations, so that other countries are freed of the constraints put on them by past engagements. It is almost beyond reasonable challenge that the agreement meets the GATT requirements set out in Article XXIV. (That all actions under it will meet that test is not to be taken for granted, but this type of question joins a number of others for the future.) Moreover, it is clear that there is a truly special relationship between the two countries (however unpopular that term has become in Canada), and that there is a special need to deal comprehensively with the problems that arise between them. If these problems are not altogether unique (some are), they are much more numerous than in Canadian or American relations with third countries.

In spite of these special features of Canadian-American bilateralism, it is reasonable for third countries to suspect that their interests will be damaged and that they deserve either compensation or equal treatment. This kind of complaint, if well-grounded, ought to be taken up by either Canada or the United States, as the case may require, and worked on with sympathetic realism. For the reasons laid out earlier, some of these cases may be important enough to require consultation between both partners and perhaps an effort to arrive at a common position. In general, it should also be the aim of Canada and the United States to try to settle third-country complaints in a multilateral setting—such as the multilateral trade negotiations or through the GATT dispute-settlement procedure—in the hope that this will further ensconce the bilateral agreement in the multilateral setting, and perhaps help strengthen the multilateral system itself.

As their commitments to limited bilateralism do not force Canada and the United States to adopt bilateral policies in other relations—as often happens when there are truly restrictive bilateral agreements or those that seek a balance in trade—the two countries have a choice. They should not, in my view, turn their backs on multilateralism, much less invite other countries to form free trade areas with them, as long as fruitful multilateral negotiations are still possible.[24]

As nearly as one can formulate a position in general terms, I would prescribe using several key principles as guidance. First, work hard to bring successful results from the Uruguay Round and other multilateral negotiations (success being defined partly in terms of the goals the countries have set for themselves, and partly as anything that in fact strengthens the multilateral process and makes it more effective over a large portion of international trade).

Second, the two countries should not give up their bilateral agreement or do anything that would seriously water it down. This does not
mean that no concessions should be made to third countries with
legitimate grievances, as we have said. And, if the effort to meet those
complaints threatens either to founder or to cause other negotiations to
drag on indefinitely, negotiations should be pushed into whatever
channels will minimize trouble without foreclosing the possibility of
taking them up later on.

Third, when the two governments have broken new ground in fields
where multilateral action would be desirable, they should use their
bilateral agreements as models, so far as possible, and as bargaining
positions ("You, too, could have these rights if you took on the obligations"). This will be difficult and may require some alteration or a
weakening of parts of the free trade area agreement. Weakening should
only be accepted if it assures commitment by other countries important
enough to be of serious interest to Canada and the United States. If by
any chance it should prove possible to reach a multilateral agreement
that goes farther than the bilateral one in liberalizing trade, or produces
a more promising procedure for dealing with the basic difficulties of the
international trading system, the two countries ought to stand ready to
try to incorporate these provisions into their bilateral agreement. If that
is troublesome—for example if it involves the dispute-settlement process—Canada and the United States should try to have things both
ways. That is to say, they should not break their bilateral agreement,
but whichever is willing ought to enter the multilateral agreement with
whatever special conditions the conflict of agreements make necessary.

None of these principles will be very easy to apply. As the last
comment suggests, there may be times when two sets of obligations
conflict. There will certainly be cases in which Canada and the United
States differ about which course to take, or whether to admit a certain
country to more or less equal status. They will also have the traditional
conditional MFN problem of determining what is a fair *quid pro quo*,
especially if one of the two seems to be a greater beneficiary than the
other. So far as I can see, these difficulties are inescapable. If we push
this further and suggest that all of the above applies not only to
multilateral agreements but to plurilateral arrangements—so far as
they do not violate GATT or others' rights to equal treatment—we see
more of the problems that lie ahead.

The assumption thus far has been that the multilateral negotiations
will produce favorable results. But suppose they fail, or collapse? It
would be easy to take refuge in the impossibility of judging the situation then. For that matter, there is room to argue about what failure or

collapse might mean. These are good reasons not to go into detail, but to fall back instead on generalities and alternatives in thinking about this new phenomenon, bilateralism in Canadian and American policy.

These guiding principles for negotiations during the multilateral trade negotiations apply as well to the period after they are over if, as seems more likely than not, "failure" and "collapse" do not mean total disappearance of the multilateral system, just some serious further diminution of its capabilities. Then it will be especially important for Canada and the United States to hang onto what they have achieved bilaterally. They would have good reason to argue that what they have achieved in services and other new fields remains a leading edge of trade negotiation. They would gain some freedom of action toward third countries if the latter had helped weaken the multilateral process or denied other countries the treatment they were entitled to. That freedom ought to be used with caution. Retaliation can be a constructive instrument (it is the underside of reciprocity), but only if it is used with some care and with some reasonable idea of what common ground might be reached by several countries. However, it may not be sensible to stick to the basic principles of equal treatment and multilateralism if most other important trading countries ignore these principles. Since the United States has major interests all over the world, it cannot be complacent about this kind of fragmentation of the trading world or indifferent as to what countries are willing to work with it. Unfortunately, these troubling possibilities cannot be much influenced by what is done regarding Canadian-American free trade. Still, the bilateral agreement could provide a nucleus around which a number of different kinds of cooperative arrangements might be built. This is, however, one of those alternatives that ranks far below the second-best—perhaps least-worst is the most that can be said for it, with the lowest rank given to simple unilateralism.

Are all these recommendations—trying to save what can be kept of the multilateral trading world, aiming to build more where it can be built, using the bilateral agreement if possible and protecting it as well—merely the voice of sweet reason, quite out of touch with the actual trading world? I think not. The multilateral trading world during the years in which it flourished was a highly realistic arrangement. That it also reflected and embodied some ideals is not a contradiction. Nothing worked perfectly, but a surprising amount of the multilateral system worked rather well and a great deal was achieved. In a way, the achievement was so great that it helped mightily—along with international investment and the easy movement of money around the world—to create a quite different kind of world from that for which the system had been designed. When we speak of highly developed interdependence, or the creation of a global economy, we are talking of something that no longer fits the Bretton Woods model very well. That system assumed governments could control their economies as they liked and that links would be mainly at the borders; if they lived up to certain rules about their relations with others, they would be able to achieve very practical results.

Condemnation of GATT for being too weak is really a condemnation of the principal trading countries—including the United States—for not adapting their policies and their agreements to the changing world, except in ways that impeded the operations of the trading system. Whether they can change all that, I do not know. Certainly it will not come about through the Uruguay Round. In *The New Multilateralism* Miriam Camps and I tried to analyze this set of problems and put forth recommendations that went rather far in asking for different kinds of trading arrangements.[25] It is not just a matter of strengthening GATT or of applying its principles more rigorously, although that would be very helpful and might be essential. What we called for were quite a few changes in the international system. We asked whether bilateral negotiations (which we called selective action), or perhaps plurilateral arrangements, might be the way to reform, rebuild, and extend the multilateral system. Canada and the United States have now carried that possibility a good bit further. Hence this book, and if its conclusions are uncertain, that too is probably realism.

Where Are We Now?

Those who recall the first chapter in this book might well ask if we are once again in 1934. Then, the United States embarked on a program of bilateral trade negotiations that did much to pave the way for the multilateral system adopted about a decade later. Look first at the similarities. The world's economy was in a mess. No country, including the United States, was free of part of the responsibility. International agreements were not unknown nor totally ineffective, but governments felt stronger compulsions than international trade obligations. The economy of the United States was undergoing great changes and faced basic problems—not least those of unemployment—for which no one had promising solutions. Exchange rates and the value of the dollar were sources of worry. Bad debts, and debts that were pretty likely to go bad, criss-crossed the world economy.

No one had a clear picture of what the new American government was likely to do, including its major officials who disagreed on the right actions to take. The United States took part in the long-prepared multilateral effort to restore stability, at the London economic conference, but it refused to tie its hands on monetary matters in ways that would limit what it could do at home. In a complex pattern, the idea of reducing tariffs gained a high place on the agenda of some officials in Washington, but was opposed by others. A multilateral approach promised no better results than had been achieved in years of conferences sponsored by the League of Nations. And so the Trade Agreements program was launched, which through bilateral bargaining reduced foreign barriers to American exports and the American tariff itself, which was a significant part of the problem.

There are also differences between now and 1934. At that time multilateral arrangements, such as they were, did not amount to very much. There was nothing approaching the Bretton Woods world with its organizations, rules, and cooperative practices. Bilateral agreements covered a large volume of world trade, and were used either to balance trade between two countries or to give one of them some political advantages. The new American bilateralism was in part a reaction, and through MFN it opened a substantial share of world trade to competition on more or less equal terms. It had more limited results as far as what are now called nontariff barriers were concerned. It is impossible to judge what effect this approach might have had if the war in Europe had not begun five years later. The wartime and postwar move to multilateralism was quite different from present day efforts to save and maybe extend multilateral arrangements.

If this summary seems familiar, do not fail to observe one important feature that it does *not* have compared to the standard version of the story of the decline of the multilateral system built at the end of the 1940s. There is not a word here about the United States as hegemon, or for that matter as a leader. It was neither in 1934. It had to work on nearly equal terms with other countries. Today, the United States is more important to the world than it was in 1934, but it also must rely more on other countries than it did in 1947. That may not be a barrier to results, but they will have to be achieved in a different way.

There is another important difference from the thirties. The bilateralism discussed in this book has almost nothing in common with the kind of bilateralism that caused so much political and diplomatic trouble, and did so much economic damage by its emphasis on balanced trade, payment in inconvertible currencies, discrimination, and sometimes political exploitation. There are elements of such practices in the world today; there have been more in the seventies and eighties than in the fifties and sixties. If the world economy grows healthier, some of these practices will disappear, but some will not. And if the world economy does not show greater growth than it is now reasonable to expect, and if the international trading system continues to deteriorate—as it is likely to do unless the Uruguay Round produces surprisingly strong results—then there is little doubt that bilateralism of the narrow and troublesome kind will increase in amount and intensity.

These are not the issues with which this book has been concerned, but they are not altogether foreign to it. The bilateralism that the United States and Canada are practicing is remote from the bilateralism of Hjalmar Schacht and the Nazis. It has in it some of the flavor of Cordell Hull's approach. It is not, however, as Hull's program was, a calculated attack on bilateralism, but it could, with luck, do something to counter the deterioration of the international trading system. It will take more than luck and Canada and the United States are not immune to what happens in the world economy, nor are they capable of reshaping the trade policies of other countries. Under pressure their bilateral agreement could become more restrictive and discriminatory. They are not likely to call for old-fashioned balancing—but neither would be happy with a persistent heavy imbalance of trade. They would continue to proclaim themselves liberal, but would like to make sure that businessmen conformed to national expectations. They would, quite understandably, pay less attention to the interests of third countries except for those who offer new bargains. More of the compromises between them would be at the expense of other countries. Their behavior would be more discriminatory and there would be less emphasis on improving international competitiveness.

There are good reasons for Canada and the United States to resist such developments, but their governments are no more heroic than those of other countries. Once the need to meet broad international standards of behavior has been thoroughly undermined—are we not almost to that point today?—it becomes unrealistic to expect democratic governments to become very resistant to domestic pressures. Unilateralism becomes the standard. For the United States the temptation is greater than for Canada, because there are more resources to work with and cultural lag obscures the high cost of such a course in an increasingly internationalized economy. Unilateralism can be mitigated if the United States, to its own advantage, pays more attention to Canada where the psychological attractions of unilateralism often give way to the economic advantages of bilateralism (provided that the United States does not abuse its power and size).

Then there is Mexico. On the basis of the limited attention this book has given that country, whose importance is growing, there are grounds for moderate optimism about working out new and special arrangements with the United States and possibly Canada. They will not be either the present-day bilateral relations or those of the Canadian-American agreement, but in a deteriorating international trading system it is to the interest of both Mexico and the United States to find new formulas. This is more likely to be done bilaterally than through a heavy reliance on the multilateral system. It would be unwise, though, not to keep the bilateral arrangements within as strong a multilateral framework as the world permits, and to use that framework for the relations of both countries with the rest of the world.

Gilbert Winham, whose studies of international trade negotiations cover a wide range of experience, reminds us in his chapter that "there is a nagging worry that history has shown a relationship between universalism and liberalism on the one hand, and particularism and protectionism on the other. . . . The GATT experience appears to demonstrate that protectionism, like racism, is best fought on universalistic grounds."

The warning should be taken seriously, but, as we have seen, multilateralism and bilateralism are not always on opposite sides. There can be constructive interplay between them, and it can be started by bilateral action. Alternatively, there can be bilateral or plurilateral measures that give some of the benefits of trade liberalization and cooperation when the multilateral path is blocked. Up to this point, we can say that the United States and Canada have taken a step in that direction. It is a rather small step because its achievements are limited; and they are limited, in part, because each country is subject to the normal but troublesome pressures that all governments are exposed to. Neither has shown itself to be of superhuman size and strength, and that is not simply a matter of who is in office. So praise should be qualified—but there should be praise. What comes next—that is, how the agreement is carried out and made use of—will be decisive and there is nothing in the agreement or the behavior of the two countries that warrants absolute confidence.

Perhaps the best guidance comes from another piece of advice, also based in history. Both countries have benefited greatly from the multilateral trading system. The system is dilapidated and in danger of collapse. Repairs must be principally multilateral and both Canada and the United States accept that. But there is no reason to have great confidence in success, and its absence—or simply a continuation of the status quo—makes it harder for any democratic government to persist on that course. One can see how bilateral measures benefit Canada and the United States economically, and also improve the chances of repairing the multilateral system.

It is not easy to find the right combination. At a minimum it requires consistency and a longer-range view of national interest than is common. Neither Canada nor the United States has yet shown itself able to treat the other entirely as a close partner, but in the adversarial manner that characterizes most trade negotiations they have carried out some measures that neither might have undertaken multilaterally and that other countries would not have accepted. Their relationship will change over time, for better or worse, but there is at least a chance that it will be for the better. There are two acid tests. How they use the elaborate machinery for consultation and dispute settlement is one. The other is whether they make significant breakthroughs in handling the subsidy and fair trade issues. Having embarked on this course, the two countries should carry it further. They should at the same time use the new situation to look after their high stakes in improving the multilateral trading order—which is the only way of saving it.

Notes

1. Quotations are from the text unless otherwise indicated. In interpreting these documents I have also made use of several summaries and commentaries prepared by both governments, newspaper reports and conversations with officials and other well-informed people.
2. The basic rule is that enough must be done to an imported product to move it from one tariff classification to another. Specific provisions requiring a higher North American content apply to automobiles, apparel made with imported fabric, footwear, furniture, chemicals, and rubber plastics.
3. See Janice L. Murray, ed., *Canadian Cultural Nationalism*, The Fourth Lester B. Pearson Conference on the Canada–U.S. Relationship, (New York: New York University Press for the Canadian Institute of International Affairs and the Council on Foreign Relations, 1977), pp. 66, 111, and *passim*.
4. Some people were concerned that the end of dual pricing of oil and gas would be a handicap to the Canadian petrochemical industry in exporting to the United States. It was pointed out that the removal of the relatively high American tariffs on petrochemicals was a considerable advantage and, in any case, an official price discrimination on a basic raw material might well bring on American countervailing duties or reprisals. Some Canadians also made the point that the agreement referred to official action on prices; differential pricing by enterprises, if justified by costs or the conditions of distribution, would not be affected.
5. Statement to the House of Commons committee in hearings on the agreement, *Globe and Mail*, November 19, 1987.

6. Paul Wonnacott, *U.S. and Canadian Auto Policies in a Changing World Environ-ment* (Toronto and Washington: Canadian-American Committee, July 1987), p. viii. I have relied heavily on this pamphlet and another study by Professor Wonnacott, *The United States and Canada: the Quest for Free Trade* (Washington: Institute for International Economics, March 1987).

7. Why this is so, and the inevitability of dealing differently with different services even if there can be agreement on some general principles, is shown in William Diebold, Jr. and Helena Stalson, "Negotiating Issues in International Services Transactions," in William R. Cline, ed., *Trade Policy in the 1980s* (Washington: Institute for International Economics, 1983), pp. 581–609. The issues are more fully developed in Helena Stalson, *U.S. Service Exports and Foreign Barriers: An Agenda for Negotiations* (Washington: National Planning Association, 1985).

8. Richard G. Lipsey and Murray G. Smith, *Taking the Initiative: Canada's Trade Options in a Turbulent World* (Toronto: C.D. Howe Institute, 1985).

9. A valuable guide through the whole field is provided by Helena Stalson, *Intellectual Property Rights and U.S. Competitiveness in Trade* (Washington: National Planning Association, 1987).

10. C. Michael Aho, "Comments on Implementation and Durability" in Mur-ray G. Smith and Frank Stone, eds., *Policy Debates: Assessing the Cana-dian–U.S. Trade Agreement* (Ottawa: Institute for Research on Public Policy, 1987), p. 135.

11. I am grateful to Frank Stone for calling this last point to my attention. Andreas Lowenfeld, in footnote 16 to Chapter 3, takes a similar view, but is making a more general point about the agreement "with the special clauses eliminated" (and some have been left in).

12. There is an excellent analysis of the agricultural trade issues that will arise in the Uruguay Round in Robert L. Paarlberg, *Fixing Farm Trade: Policy Options for the United States* (Cambridge, Ma: Ballinger with the Council on Foreign Relations, 1987).

13. Note the related, but quite different proposal that parts of the multilateral agenda could be broken out to reach agreements to meet intermediate deadlines without waiting for the conclusion of everything. See C. Michael Aho and Jonathan D. Aronson, *Trade Talks: America Better Listen!* (New York: Council on Foreign Relations, 1985 and 1987).

14. The case concerning the fair trade laws and for international standards is made in some comments of mine in *Industrial Change and Public Policy*, A Symposium Sponsored by the Federal Reserve Bank of Kansas City, 1983, pp. 335–37, and in William Diebold, Jr., "American Trade Policy and Western Europe," *Government and Opposition*, vol. 22, no. 3 (Summer 1987), pp. 282–301.

15. Miriam Camps and William Diebold, Jr., *The New Multilateralism* (New York: Council on Foreign Relations, 1983 and 1986), p. 49ff in the 1983 edition and p. 65ff in the 1986 edition.

16. This is eloquently expressed in Mitchell Sharp's paper on the Third Op-tion, "Canada–U.S. Relations: Options for the Future," *International Per-*

spectives, (Autumn 1972). In trade matters the concern has usually been advanced as part of the case against a customs union, but it seems relevant to some of the issues created under the free trade area as well. Sharp himself may have implicitly recognized this when he told the committee of the House of Commons on November 4, 1987 that his objection to the free trade agreement was not to any specific provisions but to the "long-term consequences—political, economic and cultural—of abandoning multi-lateralism and embracing continentalism." He said that Canada could cooperate with the United States and remove trade barriers multilaterally while keeping its independent identity, but that inside a free trade area, "The pressure to bring our laws and customs into line with those of the dominant partner would be continuous. Having decided to adopt a conti-nentalist approach to trade relations, it would be increasingly difficult not to do so in other areas of activity." Mimeographed text of prepared state-ment, courtesy of Mr. Sharp.

17. See, for example, John Kirton, "Shaping the Global Order: Canada and the Francophone and Commonwealth Summits of 1987," in *Behind the Head-lines,* Canadian Institute of International Affairs, June 1987.
18. Israel, which also has a free trade area with the United States, is reported to have asked to have its dispute-settlement procedure upgraded to meet the Canadian standard. I am grateful to Joseph Greenwald for telling me of this.
19. Reuters dispatch from Guadalajara, *The New York Times,* November 12, 1987.
20. For some different views and other comparisons of Mexico and Canada, see Sidney Weintraub, *Free Trade between Mexico and the United States?* (Washington: The Brookings Institution, 1984).
21. *Globe and Mail,* October 15, 1987.
22. Peter Morici, *The Global Competitive Struggle: Challenges to the United States and Canada* (Toronto and Washington: Canadian-American Committee, 1984).
23. The theme of the American national interest in an independent Canada runs through one of the wisest books on the bilateral relationship: John Sloan Dickey, *Canada and the American Presence* (New York: New York University Press with the Council on Foreign Relations, 1975).
24. The official American position as of late 1987 was weaker than this and took no stand on principle, only on opportunities and workload. Speaking in Singapore on October 31, 1987, Clayton Yeutter, the United States trade representative, spoke of ASEAN's "interest in being the next partner in a free trade arrangement negotiation with the United States. We appreciate these expressions of interest . . . but it is premature for us to consider entering into another negotiation of that scope at this time. We must first finish the Canadian FTA process. . . . Then we [have] to evaluate our negotiating priorities in light of the Uruguay Round talks and other rele-vant events. After that we will be in a position to decide on proposals for

negotiating other free trade areas." Statement by Clayton Yeutter, October 31, 1987, (mimeographed).

25. Camps and Diebold, *The New Multilateralism, op. cit.* A less radical but thoroughgoing set of recommendations for strenthening the trading system, from a group of veteran negotiators and GATT experts, is *The Uruguay Round of Multilateral Trade Negotiations under GATT: Policy Proposals on Trade and Services*, Report of the Atlantic Council's Advisory Trade Panel, John M. Leddy, chairman, (Washington: The Atlantic Council, November 1987).

Appendix I
GATT
PART III
ARTICLE XXIV

Territorial Application—Frontier Traffic—Customs Unions
and Free-Trade Areas

1. The provisions of this Agreement shall apply to the metropolitan customs territories of the contracting parties and to any other customs territories in respect of which this Agreement has been accepted under Article XXVI or is being applied under Article XXXIII or pursuant to the Protocol of Provisional Application. Each such customs territory shall, exclusively for the purposes of the territorial application of this Agreement, be treated as though it were a contracting party; *Provided* that the provisions of this paragraph shall not be construed to create any rights or obligations as between two or more customs territories in respect of which this Agreement has been accepted under Article XXVI or is being applied under Article XXXIII or pursuant to the Protocol of Provisional Application by a single contracting party.

2. For the purposes of this Agreement customs territory shall be understood to mean any territory with respect to which separate tariffs or other regulations of commerce are maintained for a substantial part of the trade of such territory with other territories.

3. The provisions of this Agreement shall not be construed to prevent:

  (a) advantages accorded by any contracting party to adjacent countries in order to facilitate frontier traffic;
  (b) advantages accorded to the trade with the Free Territory of Trieste by countries contiguous to that territory, provided that such advantages are not in conflict with the Treaties of Peace arising out of the Second World War.

4. The contracting parties recognize the desirability of increasing freedom of trade by the development, through voluntary agreements, of closer integration between the economies of the countries parties to such agreements. They also recognize that the purpose of a customs union or of a free-trade area should be to facilitate trade between the constituent territories and not to raise barriers to the trade of other contracting parties with such territories.

5. Accordingly, the provisions of this Agreement shall not prevent, as between the territories of contracting parties, the formation of a customs union or of a free-trade area or the adoption of an interim agreement necessary for the formation of a customs union or of a free-trade area; *Provided* that:

    (a) with respect to a customs union, or an interim agreement leading to the formation of a customs union, the duties and other regulations of commerce imposed at the institution of any such union or interim agreement in respect of trade with contracting parties not parties to such union or agreement shall not on the whole be higher or more restrictive than the general incidence of the duties and regulations of commerce applicable in the constituent territories prior to the formation of such union or the adoption of such interim agreement, as the case may be;

    (b) with respect to a free-trade area, or an interim agreement leading to the formation of a free-trade area, the duties and other regulations of commerce maintained in each of the constituent territories and applicable at the formation of such free-trade area or the adoption of such interim agreement to the trade of contracting parties not included in such area or not parties to such agreement shall not be higher or more restrictive than the corresponding duties and other regulations of commerce existing in the same constituent territories prior to the formation of the free-trade area, or interim agreement, as the case may be; and

    (c) any interim agreement referred to in sub-paragraphs (a) and (b) shall include a plan and schedule for the formation of such a customs union or of such a free-trade area within a reasonable length of time.

6. If, in fulfilling the requirements of sub-paragraph 5(a), a contracting party proposes to increase any rate of duty inconsistently with the provisions of Article II, the procedure set forth in Article XXVIII shall apply. In providing for compensatory adjustment, due account shall be taken of the compensation already afforded by the reductions brought about in the corresponding duty of the other constituents of the union.

7. (a) Any contracting party deciding to enter into a customs union or free-trade area, or an interim agreement leading to the formation of such a union or area, shall promptly notify the contracting parties and shall make available to them such information regarding the proposed union or area as will enable them to make such reports and recommendations to contracting parties as they may deem appropriate.

    (b) If, after having studied the plan and schedule included in an interim agreement referred to in paragraph 5 in consultation with the parties to that agreement and taking due account of the information made available in accordance with the provisions of sub-paragraph (a), the contracting parties find that such agreement is not likely to result in the formation of a customs union or of a free-trade area within the period contemplated by the parties to the agreement or that such period is not a reasonable one, the contracting parties shall make recommendations to the parties to the agreement. The parties shall not maintain or put into force, as the case may be, such agreement if they are not prepared to modify it in accordance with these recommendations.

(c) Any substantial change in the plan or schedule referred to in paragraph 5(c) shall be communicated to the contracting parties, which may request the contracting parties concerned to consult with them if the change seems likely to jeopardize or delay unduly the formation of the customs union or of the free-trade area.

8. For the purposes of this Agreement:

(a) A customs union shall be understood to mean the substitution of a single customs territory for two or more customs territories, so that

(i) duties and other restrictive regulations of commerce (except, where necessary, those permitted under Article XI, XII, XIII, XIV, XV and XX) are eliminated with respect to substantially all the trade between the constituent territories of the union or at least with respect to substantially all the trade in products originating in such territories, and,

(ii) subject to the provisions of paragraph 9, substantially the same duties and other regulations of commerce are applied by each of the members of the union to the trade of territories not included in the union;

(b) A free-trade area shall be understood to mean a group of two or more customs territories in which the duties and other restrictive regulations of commerce (except, where necessary, those permitted under Articles XI, XII, XIII, XV and XX) are eliminated on substantially all the trade between the constituent territories in products originating in such territories.

9. The preferences referred to in paragraph 2 of Article I shall not be affected by the formation of a customs union or of a free-trade area but may be eliminated or adjusted by means of negotiations with contracting parties affected. This procedure of negotiations with affected contracting parties shall, in particular, apply to the elimination of prefer-

ences required to conform with the provisions of paragraph 8(a)(i) and paragraph 8(b).

10. The contracting parties may by a two-thirds majority approve proposals which do not fully comply with the requirements of paragraphs 5 to 9 inclusive, provided that such proposals lead to the formation of a customs union or a free-trade area in the sense of this Article.

11. Taking into account the exceptional circumstances arising out of the establishment of India and Pakistan as independent States and recognizing the fact that they have long constituted an economic unit, the contracting parties agree that the provisions of this Agreement shall not prevent the two countries from entering into special arrangements with respect to the trade between them, pending the establishment of their mutual trade relations on a definitive basis.

12. Each contracting party shall take such reasonable measures as may be available to it to ensure observance of the provisions of this Agreement by the regional and local governments and authorities within its territory.

Appendix II

The Steering Committee
The Council on Foreign Relations International Trade Project

Edmund T. Pratt, Jr., *Chairman*
C. Michael Aho, *Director of Project*
Suzanne H. Hooper, *Assistant Director of Project*

Thomas O. Bayard
C. Fred Bergsten
Senator Bill Bradley
William H. Branson
Sol Chick Chaikin
Lindley Clark
Ann Crittenden
June V. Cross
William Diebold, Jr.
William D. Eberle
Geza Feketekuty
Martin S. Feldstein
Murray H. Finley
Orville L. Freeman
Richard N. Gardner
William H. Gleysteen
Victor Gotbaum
Joseph A. Greenwald
Catherine Gwin
Robert D. Hormats
Gary C. Hufbauer
John H. Jackson
Abraham Katz
Paul H. Kreisberg
Harald B. Malmgren

Irene W. Meister
George R. Melloan
Ruben F. Mettler
John R. Opel
Sylvia Ostry
William R. Pearce
John R. Petty
Richard R. Rivers
Felix G. Rohatyn
Howard D. Samuel
Daniel A. Sharp
Ronald Shelp
Leonard Silk
Joan E. Spero
Helena Stalson
John J. Stremlau
William N. Walker
Marina v.N. Whitman
Lynn R. Williams
Alan W. Wolff
Lewis H. Young
John Zysman

Peter Tarnoff, *ex officio*

Members
The Study Group on U.S.–Canada Trade Negotiations: Multilateralism vs. Bilateralism

William D. Eberle, *Study Group Chairman*
William Diebold, Jr., *Study Group Director*

Robert E. Baldwin
Thomas O. Bayard
Stephen Blank
Charles Blum
Gerardo M. Bueno
I.M. Destler
Harry L. Freeman
Richard N. Gardner
William H. Gleysteen
Joseph A. Greenwald
Michael Hodin
Ann L. Hollick
Gary Horlick
Gary C. Hufbauer
Jeffrey Lang
Andreas F. Lowenfeld
Irene W. Meister

Peter Morici
Peter Murphy
Sylvia Ostry
William R. Pearce
Myer Rashish
Susan Schwab
James Sebenius
Joanne Reed Shelton
Murray G. Smith
J. Christopher Thomas
Lawrence A. Veit
Sandy Vogelgesang
William N. Walker
John Whalley
Gilbert Winham
Paul Wonnacott

Glossary of Acronyms and Abbreviations

AAA	Agriculture Adjustment Act
ALADI	Latin American Integration Association
CAFTA	Canadian-American free trade area
CAP	Common Agricultural Policy, European Community
EC	European Community
ECSC	European Coal and Steel Community
EFTA	European Free Trade Association
FTA	Free trade area
GATT	General Agreement on Tariffs and Trade
GDP	Gross domestic product
GNP	Gross national product
GSP	Generalized System of Preferences, United States
IMF	International Monetary Fund
ITO	International Trade Organization
LDC	Less-developed country
MFN	Most-favored nation
MTN	Multilateral trade negotiations
NATO	North Atlantic Treaty Organization
NIC	Newly industrializing country
NRA	National Recovery Act
NTB	Nontariff barrier
NTM	Nontariff measure
OECD	Organization for Economic Cooperation and Development
UNCTAD	United Nations Trade and Development Organization
UNESCO	United Nations Educational, Scientific, and Cultural Organization
UNICEF	United Nations Children's Fund
WIPO	World Intellectual Property Organization

Index

202   *Bilateralism, Multilateralism and Canada*

Oil prices, 108, 111
Open-ended agreements, 31, 156–58
Open-endedness: in the U.S.–Canada free
    trade agreement, 125, 126
Orderly marketing agreements, 19, 21
Organization for Economic Cooperation and
    Development (OECD), 39, 42, 72
Ottawa Agreements of 1932, 24
"Overland exemption," 61
Outward-oriented trade policies: Mexico,
    110–11, 112–13
Ownership: and cultural sovereignty issue, 42,
    86, 133–34, 135

Particularism, 48, 184
Patents, 85, 146
Patterson, Gardner, 15–16, 17, 18, 19
Peace settlement (WWI), 4, 5
Peek, George, 8
People's Republic of China, 25, 73
Per-capita income: North American, 107
Performance requirements, 122, 123, 146,
    152–53
Peso (Mexico), 111, 115
Petrochemical industry, 50, 185n.4
Pharmaceutical products, 124, 146
Philippines, 21, 73
Plurilateral agreements, 2, 94–95, 181; in
    GATT, 18; vs. bilateral 97–98
Plurilateral negotiations, 90, 105
Plurilateralism, 184; dispute settlement in, 97;
    and GATT, 13, 14, 15
Politics: Canada, 45, 155; and Mexican entry
    into GATT, 112; and Mexican trade policy,
    124; and rules of competition, 85; and trade
    agreements, 9; and the U.S.–Canada free
    trade agreement, 47–48, 101–2, 134, 167,
    168, 171; and U.S.–Canada trade relations,
    26, 27, 39, 41, 53, 173; U.S., 10, 21, 177
Polk, Judd, 15–16
Pollution, 64
Population: North American, 106
Portugal, 4, 89
Preferences: in the U.S.–Canada free trade
    agreement, 98–99; Canada/Great Britain, 38
Preferential arrangements, 48, 62; and bilateral
    agreements, 99–100; free trade area and, 63,
    90, 91–92; and GATT, 47, 59–60
Preferential Tariff system (Great Britain), 72,
    100; see also Imperial Preference
Price discrimination, 85, 134, 135
Price discrimination laws, 95
Primary resource products, 81
Private Planning Association (Canada), 26
Production: integration of U.S.–Canadian, 165;
    rationalization of, 88–89
Production sharing: Mexico, 117
Protection: border, 95–96; of new industries,
    11–12; see also Intellectual property (issue)
Protectionism, 48, 116; in bilateral agreements,
    90; Canada, 38–39, 40, 117; Mexico, 110,
    111, 113, 114–15, 114T; particularism and,
    184; U.S., 21, 27, 39, 45, 77, 78, 79, 91, 98,

100, 102, 119, 173; see also Contingent pro-
    tection
Psychological problems: in U.S.–Canadian
    trade relations, 26, 41, 45, 134
Publishing industry (Canada), 26
Punta del Este Declaration, 100; see also
    Uruguay Round

Quotas, 16, 81, 174; agricultural trade, 93; and
    GATT, 57; MFN and, 9; removal of, in free
    trade areas, 82, 83; in the U.S.–Canada free
    trade agreement, 147, 149

Rationalization: of multinational enterprises,
    74; of protection: Mexico, 111, 114–15
Reader's Digest, 134
Reagan, Ronald, 128, 163
Reagan administration (U.S.), 46, 94, 123
Reciprocal Trade Agreements Act of 1934
    (U.S.–Canada), 39
Reciprocity, 2, 12, 180; in GATT, 11; in inter-
    national agreements, 130; multilateral nego-
    tiations and, 51; in U.S.–Canada relations,
    38–41; U.S. concern with, 4, 6, 7, 22–23,
    177
Reciprocity Treaty of 1854 (U.S.–Canada), 38
Regional agreements, 2, 15, 16, 64, 84
Regional blocs, 48
Regional development (Canada), 26
Regional diversity (Canada), 41
Regional integration, 16–17; Latin America,
    116
Rent-seeking behavior, 73, 74
Report on Reciprocity and Commercial Treaties
    (U.S.), 3–5
Resource-based industries, 80
Resource sector: Canada, 42–43, 46, 75, 76–77
Retaliation, 15, 38, 73, 91, 180; fear of, 14;
    threats of, 100–1
Reynolds, C., 106
Rhine River transport, 64
Roosevelt, Franklin, 7
Rules of competition, 143; bilateral negotiation
    of, 96, 98; in bilateral/multilateral agree-
    ments, 95; in the U.S.–Canada free trade
    agreement, 84–87
Rules of origin, 82, 87, 132

Safeguards, 85–86, 148, 149–50; and GATT,
    141–42; U.S., 45
Schacht, Hjalmar, 1, 183
Schultz, George, 21, 90–91, 176
Scientific tariff, 100
Sectoral agreements, 27, 29–30, 95, 103n.12,
    162, 173; in Mexico, 117; in the U.S.–Can-
    ada free trade agreement, 60, 62–63, 64, 65,
    66, 83–84, 89, 132–40, 175, 177
Security relations, 22–23, 37; see also National
    security
Services, 21, 30, 51, 57, 60–61, 126, 177; bar-
    riers to trade in, 80, 81, 82; bilateral agree-
    ments re, 65, 94–95, 97, 98; bilateral/
    multilateral negotiations re, 93–94; bilateral

About the Authors

William Diebold, Jr. was educated at Swarthmore College, Yale Graduate School and the London School of Economics. His long association with the Council on Foreign Relations began in 1939 as a Rockefeller research fellow studying the impact of the war on the trade agreements program, and in 1940 he became research secretary of the Economic and Financial Group of the Council's War and Peace Studies Project. From 1945–47 Mr. Diebold worked at the Department of State in the Division of Commercial Policy before returning to the Council as director of economic studies. He is widely published in the area of U.S. foreign economic policy. His most recent work includes *Industrial Policy as an International Issue*, Council on Foreign Relations, 1980 and with Miriam Camps *The New Multilateralism*, Council on Foreign Relations, 1983 and 1986.

Gilbert R. Winham is professor and chairman of the Department of Political Science at Dalhousie University in Canada. He holds a Ph.D. from the University of North Carolina (1968) and an undergraduate degree from Bowdoin College (1959). He has also served as director of the Centre for Foreign Policy Studies and research coordinator of the Royal Commission on the Economic Union and Development Prospects for Canada (Macdonald Commission). Professor Winham specializes in the analysis of international negotiation and his recent work includes *International Trade and the Tokyo Round Negotiation*, Princeton University Press, 1986.

Andreas F. Lowenfeld is the Charles L. Denison professor of law at the New York University School of Law, where he specializes in public and private international law, international economic transactions, aviation law, and international litigation. He is a graduate of Harvard College (1951) and Harvard Law School (1955). Professor Lowenfeld has frequently served as arbitrator in international cases and has written widely on various aspects of international trade, investment, finance, and dispute settlement. He is the author of a series of books on international economic law.

Since June 1987, **Murray G. Smith** has been director of the International Economic Program at the Institute for Research on Public Policy in Ottawa. Previously, he was with the C.D. Howe Institute where he served as senior policy analyst and Canadian research director for the Canadian-American Committee. He was educated in economics at the Universities of British Columbia and Michigan. He is the author or co-author of several books—including *Taking the Initiative: Canada's Trade Options in a Turbulent World*, C.D. Howe Institute, 1985 and *Bridging the Gap: Trade Laws in the Canadian–U.S. Negotiations*, Canadian-American Committee, 1987.

Gerardo M. Bueno is a senior fellow at El Colegio de Mexico. He has served as director of the Industrial Projects and Programing Division at Nacional Financiera; as director general of Mexico's National Commission for Science and Technology; and as ambassador of Mexico to the European Economic Community, Belgium and Luxembourg. His most recent publication is a book jointly authored with Bela Balassa, Pedro-Pablo Kuczynski and Mario Henrique Simonsen, *Towards Renewed Economic Growth in Latin American*, Institute for International Economics, 1986.